CELEBRA[illegible] FRIENDSHIP
PAST, PRESENT AND FUTURE

CELEBRATING WOMEN'S FRIENDSHIP
PAST, PRESENT AND FUTURE

edited by
Ruth A. Symes
Ann Kaloski
Heloise Brown

Raw Nerve Books
York

Published by: Raw Nerve Books Limited
Centre for Women's Studies
University of York
York YO10 5DD
England

British Library Cataloguing-in-Publication Data
A catalogue record for this book is available from the British Library.

ISBN: 0-9536585-1-1

First published in 1999

Dedicated to Winnie Wong and Susan B. Anderson

Acknowledgements

We would like to thank: the contributors to this volume, who have patiently remained committed to and interested in the project despite the delays, and the participants in the Celebrating Women's Friendship conference at the University of York, who did much to encourage us that this was a subject worthy of further study. We would also like to thank all of those who helped in the organisation of the conference, including Winnie Wong and Susan B. Anderson, to whose memory this book is dedicated.

For the original idea for the conference and their work in the early stages to help bring it about, thanks to Helen Rogers, Krista Cowman and Clare Hemmings. The support of the staff at the Centre for Women's Studies, University of York, was essential and has been much appreciated: we would particularly like to thank Trev Broughton for her practical help, advice and her confidence in all three of us over the years. This book is, at least in part, intended as a celebration of the work done in and for the Centre since it was founded in 1984.

Finally, many thanks are due to Madi Gilkes for formatting the book, Hilary Doran for the cover design, and Steve Johnson and the rest of the staff at the Print Unit, University of York for printing and binding —this book would not have been possible without their help.

Permissions

For "Problems with (Girl)Friends? Contemporary women poets and tensions in female friendship" by Vicki Bertram:

Michèle Roberts, "Magnificat" from *All the Selves I Was* reprinted with kind permission of Virago Press (Little, Brown).

The author and publishers are still making every effort to contact copyright holders. At the time of going to press full details were not available. However, we wish to record our grateful acknowledgement of the following:

Jackie Kay (1993) "Got You" from *Other Lovers* (Bloodaxe Books).
Liz Lochhead (1984) "The Choosing" from *Dreaming Frankenstein* (Polygon Press).
Marilyn Hacker (1986) "Towards Autumn" from *Beautiful Barbarians: Lesbian Feminist Poetry*, ed. by L. Mohin (Onlywomen Press).
Thylias Moss (1995) "An Anointing" from *Sisterfire: Black Womanist Fiction and Poetry*, ed. by Charlotte Watson Sherman, (The Women's Press).

Contents

Ruth A. Symes, Ann Kaloski and Heloise Brown
Introduction 1

Jane Montague and Ali Andrew
Friendship, Auto/biography and the Academy 21

Juliet Betts and Shantu Watt
'Joy in the Struggle itself': a Friendship across the Racial Divide 39

Katherine Side
Making and Breaking Women's Friendships in Feminist Theory 57

Laura Potts
Sisterhood: Part of the Pretend Family? 79

Ruth A. Symes
'My Constant Correspondent and Friend': The Letters of Maria Edgeworth and Rachel Mordecai Lazarus, 1815-1838 97

Heloise Brown and Krista Cowman
Exploring Suffrage Friendships 121

Judy Giles
Maid and Mistress: Narratives of Friendship in Accounts of Domestic Service 155

Vicki Bertram
Problems with (Girl)friends? Contemporary Women Poets and Tensions in Female Friendship 181

Ann Kaloski with Francesca de Rimini and Sue Thomas
'She says she's a Woman': Feminine Friendships in Virtual Reality 215

Editorial Conclusion 237

Jackie Scott-Mandeville
The Personal is Academic: A Different Pattern 239

Bibliography 253

Index 269

Introduction

Ruth A. Symes, Ann Kaloski and Heloise Brown

Why publish a book on women's friendship?

Women's friendship has remained a relatively unexplored topic, despite both the emergence of the Women's Movement in the late 1960s and a general increased academic interest in personal relationships from the 1970s onwards. Such critical neglect is curious. Friendship so obviously intersects with the concerns of many different disciplines: sociology, anthropology, literature and history. Its very flexibility moreover makes it a topic ripe for interdisciplinary study. In her groundbreaking book, *Friendships Between Women: A Critical Review* (1992), Pat O'Connor attributes this disregard to a number of factors. Three of these are particularly relevant to our project. First, representations of friendship between women in historical, literary and sociological texts are rather thin on the ground and there are few mythic examples of the relationship. Second, there has been a tendency for sociological work to focus on institutional realities and social forms rather than private and intimate relationships (how does one deal with a relationship like friendship which, in Western society at least, is not recognised by any social, religious or legal code?). Third, any serious attempt at theorising women's friendship has been threatened by the popular habit of trivialising and derogating women's friendships by comparing them negatively with heterosexual bonds. Ironically, even the Women's Movement, with its emphasis on sisterhood, has skirted around the issue of women's friendship, concentrating instead on the more obviously political issues of women's labour and sexuality rather than on affective relationships between women. It seems that though friendship is still an experience of fundamental importance to the social and psychological well-being of most women, it continues to be regarded within feminist theory as secondary to those other social relationships—kinship ties, motherhood, heterosexual and lesbian relationships—in which women play a part. Conversely, popular culture has never validated the importance of friendship between women so keenly as within the last few years. To give a few examples: the continuing popularity of 'Forever Friends' merchandise, the development and mass marketing of friendship cards, the elevation of female bonding by girl bands such as the Spice Girls, and television programmes such as *Friends*.

Inspired perhaps by this foregrounding of friendship within popular culture, the contributors to this volume collectively demonstrate a desire to unearth friendship amongst women and to instate it as a valued object of theoretical enquiry. The range of friendships considered in this collection is broad, from the dyad arrangements of 'best friends' and lesbian couples to larger groupings: webs of letter writers, feminist organisations, colleagues within academic institutions, and the huge networks that we might encounter in cyberspace. The contributors are drawn from a variety of disciplinary backgrounds and in many cases move deftly between the disciplines. The friendships they describe range in period from the late eighteenth century to the present day, and in setting from the school playground to the seminar room. Whether commenting on friendships between women homesteaders in nineteenth-century America or on female poets' representations of friendship in late-twentieth-century Britain, the articles share a recognition of the importance of historical, political, and geographical factors in shaping the friendship relation.

This book is a celebration of a relationship in its chronological setting: the subtitle, *Past, Present and Future* indicates both the continuities detected by our contributors in their accounts of women's friendship in history, today and in the next century, *and* their sense of the changing nature of the relationship through time. The *past* is important to this volume in a number of different ways. Several chapters look back on women's friendship in other historical eras. Symes looks at epistolary friendship between women in the late-eighteenth and early-nineteenth centuries, arguing that this correspondence must be read in the light of contemporary understandings of female education and pedagogy. Brown and Cowman consider the role of female friendships within women's political movements of the nineteenth and early-twentieth centuries, and Giles takes up the story of women's friendship in the interwar period, exploring the difficulties of cross-class friendships between maids and mistresses in a period of swiftly changing economic and domestic conditions. Other writers touch more fleetingly on women's relationships in the past in order to make sense of their own contemporary understandings of friendship. Scott-Mandeville, for instance, explains how her contemporary academic interest in the romantic friendships between nineteenth-century women writers fed into and encouraged her own developing feminism and personal experiences of women's friendship. Betts and Watt consider the legacy of 1970s feminism, with its cross-currents of racism and anti-racism, for women's friendship. Whilst public political currents have affected the terms of women's friendship in all periods, personal histories have also been of enormous importance to several of the writers here. For example, when Montague and Andrew, both academics in the same department, became friends, they began to recognise the importance of their own autobiographies—their formative influences and experiences—in the construction of their friendship.

Whilst acknowledging the importance of both public and private *past* in the construction and interpretation of friendship, the greater number of articles in the collection are concerned with *present* relationships and some turn speculatively to the *future*. There seems to be agreement that friendships begun in the latter decades of the twentieth century and beyond are and will be of a particular quality. There is the suggestion, for example, that in Western society, friendship ties may be gaining in importance as marriage becomes increasingly unstable, more women join the labour force, and increased geographical mobility helps to break down older relationships such as those between members of extended families and close-knit communities. The increased number, accessibility and acceptability of female-only enclaves are in themselves creating new conditions for female friendship. Potts points out that women's spaces and feminist ideologies have asserted a more public and valid space for women's friendship and, in this vein, Scott-Mandeville describes the particular ways in which the public forum of the Women's Studies MA course at York fostered and focussed her friendships with women. Moreover, for academic friends, the evolving body of feminist theory is another changing condition of women's friendship, as Montague and Andrew demonstrate. But what does the *future* of friendship between women hold? Kaloski indicates the increasing part that computer-mediated communications will play in generating and maintaining relationships. There are also deeper, unanswered questions about the extent to which friendship signifies in our culture: for example, Potts calls for a radical mythology of friendship. Despite the proliferation of thinking about friendship within popular culture and increasingly, as in this volume, in works of feminist theory, symbolic marks of friendship are still lacking. We had great difficulty, for example, in finding a suitable logo for the 'Celebrating Women's Friendship' conference in 1995 as it became apparent that friendship could not easily be symbolised pictorially. The image we chose (created for us by the cartoonist Angela Martin) was of two women partying with raised clenched fists—or were they just holding hands? It was celebratory, but could as easily have signified sisterhood as friendship. One can only hazard a guess at what cultural symbols of friendship may emerge in coming decades in recognition of the growing interest in affective relationships.

The articles in this collection take us on an intimate, thought-provoking and sometimes contentious journey in search of the meanings and conditions of female friendship. As we explain below, the theories and methodologies deployed are wide-ranging and diverse, but there are at least some commonalities in the descriptions of how friendship is expressed. The relationships described (and in some cases enacted) in this book turn on a medley of shared experiences, from the smallest level of domestic exchange—drinking tea and bottles of wine together, making phone calls, and sharing clothes—to more general factors—common backgrounds, mutual ambitions, joint work projects, connected social lives or similar experiences of sexuality. In her description of the material help offered by Jessie P. to her housekeeper Doris Arthur, Giles reminds us that friendships between women have often been geared around economic criteria: conversely a shared intellect, or moral integrity is important to Symes' nineteenth-century women letter-writers. Of all the factors that contribute to the success of friendships between women, 'talk' appears more frequently than any other. Kaloski goes so far as to suggest that 'talk' *creates* friendships, and she offers an imaginative assessment of virtual life in which relationships are generated only through written conversations. Brown and Cowman, amongst others, show how advice and counselling have provided an important medium of exchange between women. Friendship is inevitably about reciprocity and mutual support—'loyalty', 'trust' and 'affection' are terms frequently reiterated in these articles—but Bertram reminds us in her exploration of relationships between women in contemporary poetry that female friendship is also an important means of self-validation and ego support.

Betts and Watt end their paper with an attractive definition, citing four Cs—'challenges, commitment, connectedness and commonalities'—

features which are, in their opinion, the most important in sustaining female friendships. Ultimately, however, most of our contributors eschew definitions. What binds them together is their shared fascination for and celebration of a term so freely bandied about, so commonly understood, so familiarly experienced and yet ultimately so indefinable.

FRIENDSHIP AND FEMINISM

Despite the diversity of material in the articles, a number of common threads have emerged which show how friendship can engage with familiar debates within feminism. These are: public/private; agency; theory versus practice; sameness and difference; self and other; and women's relationship to feminism.

PUBLIC/PRIVATE FRIENDSHIPS

Public and private have been seen as dichotomous concepts. As Laura Potts notes, friendship is an area conventionally seen as private, rather than something which merits public recognition. Montague and Andrew, however, argue that the notion of a public/private split is problematic: rather, a continuum exists along which events can be situated as 'more' or 'less' public or private than each other. The particular circumstances of their academic friendship have significantly shifted the meanings traditionally attached to such spatial definitions.

The question of public and private is one that is not only relevant for lived experiences, but is also a pressing problem in feminist research. Giles, Symes, and Brown and Cowman discuss how research into friendships in history is heavily, but not completely, reliant on the survival of 'private' sources. Their chapters show how researchers can make use of more public information, such as published work and records held in public-access archives, to elicit information on friendships that existed within largely private contexts. Giles' examples are quintessentially 'private' because they occur within the domestic environment, particularly as the number of servants per household diminished in the early decades of the twentieth century. Symes uniquely uses private letters exchanged between Rachel Mordecai Lazarus and Maria Edgeworth and their families, and shows how the discussions that took place in their text-based friendship were carried over into the public works of Edgeworth. Brown and Cowman consider women's role in generating public concepts of friendship in the early twentieth century, and examine how these concepts were necessarily built upon an emphasis on sameness, solidarity and support, rather than on the differences between women.

Kaloski offers insights into the shift in the public/private paradigm brought about by the new communication technologies. In the text-based virtual reality she describes, traditional notions of public and private are continually reconfigured in quite complex ways. For instance, conversations often take place between individuals who simultaneously occupy private spaces (at their home computer) and public spaces (in virtual communal rooms), but even within these busy cyberspaces it is possible to have a completely private virtual conversation with another person who is in the same virtual room. Through analysing this method of communication via keyboard and screen, rather than through voice and/or body, Kaloski advances Montague and Andrew's model of public and private as a continuum, and demonstrates the fragmentation of dualistic connotations of 'public' and 'private'.

Agency

The concept of agency is highly important in contemporary feminist theory. If feminism is fundamentally about power, agency is a tool by which feminism identifies ways in which individual women negotiate or manage structures of power. It is easy to see how friendship between women might facilitate such mobilisation. Montague and Andrew consider how their working relationship developed into a friendship which richly contributed to their personal lives and positively transformed their working environments. Their friendship informed their more public work on auto/biography, which in turn supported and strengthened their positions within their Higher Education institution. Betts and Watt show how their friendship developed and transformed their work, and became a site of resistance when their transformations were not supported by others in their workplace. Their friendship was problematised by both institutional and collective racism, and thus as the friendship influenced their employment choices and political position, it became a structural force in their lives and work. Both for Betts and Watt and for Montague and Andrew, agency shows how friendships can alter the ways in which women 'choose' to live their lives, although it is clear that Montague and Andrew strengthened their relationship to a more positive reception: it bolstered their work position and strengthened their employment opportunities. Unlike Betts and Watt, it did not force them to make changes.

One problem with studies of friendship can be the assumption that there is equality between women; another is that friendships have limited political implications. For example, Betts and Watt describe not only how the onus is on the white friend to recognise that she holds a position of power and cannot be trusted not to abuse that power, but also that the political meanings of the friendship are frequently misinterpreted by others. 'Others' in this case meant work colleagues, who, unable to recognise changes in Betts and Watts' consciousness and personal feelings, accused Betts, the white friend, of "leaning over Blackwards," attempting to be politically correct or merely maintaining a facade. Robbed of agency, their political position was both misunderstood and undermined by the refusal to engage with the implications of friendship that are political as well as personal. This said, their shared personal and professional experiences of abuses of power consolidated the trust and openness of the friendship.

This form of agency is mirrored in other chapters of this book. Jackie Scott-Mandeville's concluding chapter shows how disappointment with other areas of her life, particularly maternity and the family unit, allowed her friendships to develop and consolidated her emergent, redefined consciousness. In addition, this was re-affirmed when she went on to study in an environment where friendship meant sharing and mutual support, without carrying the conventional expectations of obligation and conformity. Likewise, the potential for friendship to affirm public goals is demonstrated by Symes who shows how, through a long process of letter writing, a correspondence that began from a fan letter became a genuine exchange of rational ideas. Rachel Mordecai, the woman who began as 'the fan', used Maria Edgeworth's ideas in the rearing of her own children, and Edgeworth *modified* her work in the light of Mordecai's comments.

THEORY VERSUS PRACTICE

British feminism has long been plagued by the incongruities between academic and grass-roots activity. Friendship, as we have argued, has been neglected by feminist theory, despite being central to feminist practice. Side and Potts attempt to rectify this by tackling the question of how friendships function, and by examining and critiquing existing explanations. Underpinning their considerations is the issue of why friendships survive, and why they fail. As Side notes, current theories of psychosexual analysis and radical feminism take an ultimately deterministic approach, while liberal ideology heads to the other extreme and individualises our successes and failures. She argues that a more realistic approach is needed, which takes account of power dynamics and recognises the existence of conflicting feelings, such as commitment and obligation, guilt and loyalty; in short, all the issues which feminist theories have considered with regard to family life, but not in relation to women's friendships. Side argues that some relationships, especially heterosexual family relations, have accrued more status and privilege than others. Feminism has, it seems, failed to successfully convey the message that other relationships can be equally/more significant, because female friendships are still not accorded the depth of study which they clearly require. Potts takes a similar view, though from a different perspective. Having tried to make feminist friendships 'work', she questions why they seem to inevitably 'fail' i.e. change and make way for other forms of relationship, such as familial ties or sexually monogamous partnerships. Drawing a thread between feminist rhetoric and reality, she asks if feminists have "too high expectations" when trying to maintain feminist communities and networks. Have we unquestioningly echoed non-feminist representations of friendship, when we idealise and over-sentimentalise the power of the webs women weave? Ultimately, she argues, the power dynamic in friendships needs to be made more explicit: can women learn to use friendship as a means of recognising belonging to one another, while still validating individual autonomy? Can the challenges of women's friendships ultimately be supportive?

In turning to theory, both Side and Potts argue that the problematics of friendship are all too frequently not to do with patriarchal oppression, but with, as Potts says, "challenging dominant patriarchal modes of relating." Such examinations highlight the importance of: recognising commitment and its limits; being able to value 'sameness' and convergence within and between women, as well as seeking out 'differences'; and learning to feel and accept the points of tension. We can see such tensions in Bertram's analysis of the discourses of friendship which rest on mother-daughter or sister-sister ties, while Scott-Mandeville's chapter offers a clear discussion of the ways in which (traditional) familial ties disguise, limit or constrict women-to-women relationships. Step out of the nuclear family unit, and suddenly whole new ways of relating (to kin as well as friends) present themselves. Such theoretical deliberations, usually applied to sexual relationships, have finally been brought to bear upon friendship. This begs the question of whether theoretical accounts of friendship may, in the future, have an effect on academic accounts of sexuality.

Sameness and difference

Early 'second wave' feminism (i.e. debates during the 1970s and early 1980s), echoing 'first wave' feminist debates (popularly conceived of as the women's movement of the 1860s to 1918) focussed on the commonalities between women. More recent feminist debates have concentrated on the differences between women, which have included 'race', ethnicity, sexuality, dis/ability, age and geographical location. Vital though such thinking is, the result has sometimes been a fetishisation of difference, without recognition of the complexities that difference inherently entails. The study of friendship offers a point at which 'sameness' and 'difference' are relevant, and indeed converge. Many of the contributors grasp this theoretically sensitive area, and question the problematics of 'difference' as well as subjecting 'sameness' to deeper scrutiny.

Symes' chapter discusses a friendship conducted across two continents, in which the main characters never met and yet shared their ties to one another with their respective families. The two writers were from very different backgrounds, but they shared an interest in educational philosophy. Brown and Cowman examine similar questions in a contrasting context—public suffrage activism in which women were thrown together by common interests and yet still developed bonds that ran "deeper than politics." These perceptions of sameness and difference are factors which affect how women's friendships function. In one sense, the contrasts between the women in Symes' chapter and those in Brown and Cowman's chapter seem to be based primarily on their social and historical circumstances. But what we are concerned with here is how women draw upon more profound structural or contextual factors in order to make sense of their female relationships.

Symes describes two women, living in similar structures of female domesticity, in Ireland and America. The driving force behind the friendship that develops between them is their shared educational and intellectual interests. Brown and Cowman take up similar questions, focussing on the concerns that emerged in Britain one century later: notably the suffrage movement. This involved large numbers of women, from working, middle and upper classes—i.e. from very different class and social structures—but the motivation for these women was their shared political interests. What happens when diverse women unite as a result of the things they perceive that they have in common? Both chapters question the frameworks which are used to determine commonalities and differences: Symes' Jewish and Christian women are bound together by the domestic sphere which they inhabit, even though this is constructed differently on their respective continents. Their recognition of sameness is focussed around their shared interest in educational philosophy, while the wider structures which contribute to make their lives similar—the enforcement of separate spheres ideology across different cultures and contexts, for example—are not addressed. Brown and Cowman's suffragettes are bonded not only by their public and private affirmations of sameness (for example, public propaganda and private mutual self-help), but by the ideologies which work to mark them as different and therefore bind them as a group more closely together. In her chapter on cyberspace communication, Kaloski approaches difference in a context which at first glance seems unrelated to these historical relationships. Yet in computer-mediated communication, 'pen friends' become 'keyboard friends' and differences between users are negotiated in an environment where it is expected that people construct fantasy characters. As Kaloski discusses in a reproduced dialogue with two of her virtual friends—Sue Thomas and Francesca de Rimini—it is not even possible to know if your virtual woman friend identifies as a woman in 'real life'.

The unity which structure can create between different women is reflected in other chapters of this book: Montague and Andrew describe how the workplace gave them the opportunity to focus their friendship, while for Betts and Watt, the common recognition of how power was used and abused in their workplace created a unity between them. They note that the workplace structure was used to create 'insiders' and 'outsiders', and their unity functioned to situate them both as 'outsiders'. Giles applies this process to class in her discussion. Her chapter draws attention to the material and economic factors which, while structuring cross-class relationships, also played a significant part in creating and maintaining mistress-servant friendships.

SELF AND OTHER

These questions of sameness and difference are directly related to issues of identity and the constant need for awareness of the boundaries between 'self' and 'other'. Whilst feminism has validated the 'self', it has simultaneously struggled with the difficulty of doing this without invalidating or alienating the 'other'. Feminist enquiry which has focussed on familial or dyadic partnership relations, such as employer/employee, has rarely taken into account the dynamics of *friendship* relations in these contexts. Yet, as the chapters by Giles and Bertram show, there is a case for examining the friendship component of familial and work relationships. They extend this debate to one of feminism's constructions of friendship: sisterhood. While sisterhood has been presented in feminist enquiry as a paradigm for women's relationships, Giles and Bertram question this construct, examining, in Bertram's case, what Helena Michie has termed the "capacious and hungry" feminism which absorbs 'others' into a generalised discourse of sisterhood (1991:67). Giles' chapter echoes these concerns, complementing the comments by employers that domestic work should be done with mistress and maid working together in a kind of socialist, sisterly harmony, with her interviews with Doris Arthurs, a domestic servant whose mistress, she told Giles, was "like a sister to me."

Questions of the boundaries between self and other show how friendship ties influence women's sense of identity. These boundaries, and the confusion which friendship can create within and between them, are problematised within both Giles' and Bertram's chapters. They highlight concerns with how other boundaries overlap with friendships: sister relationships, mothers and daughters, employers and employees. For example, the relationship between mistress and maid is one that is potentially semi-familial, because of its domestic location, yet also fundamentally economic, because of its basis in class difference. Giles illustrates how social structures create false boundaries between women in that idealised and imaginary female space, the domestic home.

One of the most troubling and important questions which these chapters raise is in part an echo of preceding chapters: the issue of sameness, of connections which are not fleeting, but instead are, as Bertram argues, "disturbingly constant." The confusion of boundaries and the quest for autonomy in the face of sameness are issues that are easy to gloss over and difficult to resolve. Friendship is inevitably about merging, to some degree: to become a friend involves an overlapping of identity, a lowering of the boundaries and an exchange between self and other. But friendship is also about the affirmation of self—the need of both parties to confirm that each is an important individual. As Bertram emphasises, the drawback of friendships can be that they hinder women from establishing and validating themselves as individuals. This is a point echoed by Side, when she points to feminism's idealisation of women-to-women relationships, particularly lesbian relationships.

Defining Women, Defining Feminism

This brings us to the theme which occupies the final chapters of this book. In very different ways, both Kaloski and Scott-Mandeville are concerned with how self-identification affects interpersonal relationships. In considering the friendships forged in the relative anonymity of cyberspace, Kaloski suggests that 'female' friendships can exist between people who may not even be women: how, then, may they be interpreted as female? Scott-Mandeville asks a similar question of feminism, by arguing that the nature of her friendships changed substantially when she began to move within networks of feminist women, both at Greenham Common and on an MA course in Women's Studies.

Do women's perceived commitments and obligations to one another change when they identify as feminist? Many of the chapters in this book, when they discuss women's friendships, are in fact focussing more specifically on *feminist* friendships, and the raised expectations which many feminists have of relationships with women who are believed to have a similar political vision. Feminist friendships create their own tensions, as well as resolving or illuminating many more. bell hooks' "bondedness of shared victimisation" may conjure up familiar images of feminists' self-representation as victims, but it also demonstrates how a shared world-view promotes relations between women founded on commonality and sameness (hooks, 1984: 45).

The issue of understanding female relationships is perhaps more central for lesbians in general, and lesbian feminists in particular, than for other women. As Bertram states, "[l]esbians obviously have a more urgent interest in delineating the varieties of woman-to-woman relationships." Scott-Mandeville illustrates this in her autobiographical account of how feminism and lesbianism transformed her personal politics: "the two desires seemed to develop alongside each other." The axis of sexuality, as both Potts and Scott-Mandeville show, alters women's all-female relationships to make friendship a central, guiding force in their lives, often replacing or transforming the functions of family. Side points to how feminism has created "competing and dichotomous ideologies of autonomy and interdependence," and the discussion by Betts and Watt is a clear example of the tensions that exist within feminism as a result of such processes of 'insiders' and 'outsiders'. What we (feminists) seem to be searching for is ways of relating that recognise the other in ourselves, without denying the 'self', the sameness, that is inherent in the recognition of the 'other'. Kaloski suggests ways in which such incongruities can be explored, while Potts notes that it can be simpler to retreat into heterosexual dyads, where the separateness is easier to find, than to struggle with the "difficult sameness" with which women have to engage within friendships.

METHODOLOGY

Methodology is, quite simply, the means used to obtain information about a particular topic. One of the motivating forces within feminism has been to challenge how different forms of knowledge come to be understood and accepted as 'true', and therefore methodology is a key issue within feminist thought. Obtaining information is not a simple procedure, but is complicated by a network of theoretical assumptions about where knowledge comes from, who has access to which knowledge, and who interprets areas of knowledge for the wider community. The relationships between 'facts', methodologies, and theories are necessarily convoluted: how a researcher seeks out material affects her findings, and this subsequently influences the theories which arise from her work, which thereby affect methodologies ... and so on. Women's friendships—a topic which, as we have seen, straddles the borders of many conventional disciplines—brings with it a host of complex and provocative methodological issues. We touch on just three of these here: finding material; reading texts; and the use of the 'personal'.

The first problem for the researcher of friendship is locating sources. Virginia Woolf's well-known lament that female friendship seems to elude novel writers (as discussed by Bertram in this volume) is echoed here by those undertaking other areas of research. Faced with a silence in many standard repositories, our contributors have been forced to root out friendship in a range of unconventional sources, from unpublished letters to emails, from newspaper reports to recollections of personal experience. Historians have found it difficult enough to unearth the experiences of women in the past, but where these experiences are wholly within the domestic environment, as friendships often are, and where they concern emotions rather than quantifiable statistics, this problem is compounded. What was clearly a very rich and complicated life-long relationship between two Preston women, Eleanor Higginson and Beth Hesmondhalgh, is reduced to a passing comment in Eleanor's obituary, secondary to her other familial and political concerns. Brown and Cowman's understanding of the friendship between these two women is the product of piecing together evidence from a number of different sources, including photographs, conversations with their relatives, suffragette propaganda, newspapers and biographies.

How, then, do we read friendships in texts? Texts are central to the work of many articles in this volume and the contributors treat us to a variety of approaches to reading them. Symes, Bertram, and Giles, for example, focus on the formal features of written texts with a view to suggesting that texts *create* as much as reflect the social relation that we call friendship. Symes considers how women's letters—with their quaint conventions and highly practical content—both register the existence and shape the contours of nineteenth-century women's friendship. For Bertram, the lyrical aspects of poetry enhance late twentieth-century friendships between women. Giles, meanwhile, makes a sensitive comparison between three texts—a novel, a social analysis, and an oral history account—which are concerned with friendships between mistresses and maids in the same historical period. She asks how the generic and discursive features of these very different modes allow for different narrative possibilities: all three texts, Giles argues, provide widely divergent evidence of the same social experience—namely cross-class friendships. In the articles mentioned above, friendship is seen as a textual construct as much as a social reality.

The method which has been seen as paradigmatic of contemporary feminist theorising is the use of one's own experience, and this is a means centrally deployed by many of the contributors to this volume, especially Montague and Andrew, Betts and Watt, Potts, Bertram, Kaloski, and Scott-Mandeville. All these writers challenge the (still common) accusation that autobiographical understandings are an 'easy' way to approach a topic. Kaloski and Scott-Mandeville offer celebratory pieces which attest to the potency of friendship in the radically altering lives of women. In contrast, Betts and Watt, and Potts write about the intricate conflicts between feminist theories of sisterhood and affection between women and their own experiences, and the challenges these bring to both conventional feminist thought and to their own lives. The vicissitudes of 'second-wave' feminism have alternatively elevated and disparaged this connection between 'theory' and 'experience', but reading these two articles suggests that there is still much work to be done if women's lives are to become an intrinsic part of theoretical understandings, and not just a supplement. Montague and Andrew pursue one common academic feminist method of integrating the 'personal' and the 'academic' by recognising how their sociological training affects their emotional relationship. But these two colleagues have taken such amalgamation further via their experimental teaching methodology. Through deploying Montague's oral life story as part of a postgraduate course on 'Managing Change,' the personal becomes a text requiring the kinds of critical assessments usually associated with theory. This is not, as Montague and Andrew demonstrate, to reduce the personal, or to 'capture' rich lives within a tight theoretical framework. Rather, Montague's story remains embodied—she was, after all, personally recounting her autobiography and the experiment suggests new ways of theorising the personal. Bertram approaches these issues through, in her case, poetry, and she demonstrates how her own affectional relationships encouraged her to search for inscriptions of women's friendship in poems. Through exposing her experiences of friendship to her readers she is able to pursue a subtle analysis of poems about friendship. The "methodology of the personal" thus becomes a vibrant and provocative way of theorising women's friendships.

This book does not attempt to offer a comprehensive account of women's friendship—we doubt whether such a project is feasible—but, rather, a series of interventions into interdisciplinary, and particularly feminist, thinking on the topic. For friendship—as experience and as theory—is not an answer, but a useful, provocative, and often joyful way of approaching women's lives.

Friendship, Auto/biography and the Academy

Jane Montague and *Ali Andrew*

Being asked to speak on friendship in the 1990s felt particularly appropriate and somehow exciting for it was in the 1990s that we began work at the college where we are now based, and it was in the 1990s that we met each other and began what we regard as a close friendship.

A review of the academic work done on friendship (O'Connor, 1992) points out that generally this is a much neglected area—associated as it is with the 'private' sphere and therefore trivialised by many academic disciplines. What has been done has tended to concentrate on the effect of friendship on women's well-being or to explore gender-differentiated patterns of friendship. There has been less attention paid to the particularities and details of women's friendships, including context-specific relationships, such as women's friendship at work. O'Connor identifies this as an area in need of research (among others): 'private'/personal relationships within the 'public' context of work.

This is probably all the more urgent in light of the increased number of women engaging in paid work. Latest figures indicate that 71 percent of women of working age in the UK are economically active (Office for National Statistics, 1997). It is likely therefore that many women will 'make' and/or 'maintain' friendships in this setting rather than in neighbourhood, community and family settings. In addition, the persistence of a highly gender-segregated labour force means that women will continue to work predominantly with women. This likelihood is further increased by taking into account the decrease in close-knit communities and extended family networks as a result of geographical mobility prevalent in Britain in the 1990s.

Women's relationships at work then are, and will continue to be, an important and very real aspect of women's lives. This has certainly been the case for us. We met at work, became friends and remain friends while continuing to work together. It is in this context that we wish to talk about the relationship between friendship, work and auto/biography as it has developed for us.

Because for us friendship and work have been linked through auto/biography in a number of ways, we want to start by saying a bit about ourselves and how we met.

The first time I met Jane was in a 'public' setting. It was the occasion of a staff development day for a course team I would later be joining. At this stage, though, I was still employed in my previous job at another college, and this was quite a nerve-wracking occasion for me, being a relative outsider among a group of people I would later know as colleagues. The meeting took place at a hotel in the Yorkshire Dales, on a glorious summer day, and driving there I felt a mixture of excitement and trepidation. As I got out of my car and walked up to a group of people who were strangers to me, except for one who had been present at my interview and whose job I was taking over, one of the first things that struck me was Jane's friendly greeting and smiling welcome. The only other thing about Jane which I have a strong memory of from that day was her volunteering to collect orders for pudding and her determination that we should have one—this was an important part of the day out! This was an indication of 'human-ness' and 'ordinariness' which did much to make me feel at ease. My general impression was of someone who behaved warmly towards me and whom I looked forward to getting to know.

I remember that day clearly. Ali walked to the front of the hotel (where we were all basking in the sun!) with the person she was to replace and I thought "Wow! what a lovely, sunny, warm and friendly person." She was not as I expected and my first impressions were that we might not have much in common: she seemed so elegant and grown-up, she was older, she was of a different ethnic background and it seemed to me she was of a different class location to myself. At this stage then I could identify only gender and occupation (including academic interests) as similarities. Some writers have suggested that these similarities are important in the process of making friends. Allen (1986 in O'Connor, 1992) for example argues that "friendships are relationships of equality in that friends are accepted as being equal within the relationship. There is no hierarchy in friendship, no differentiation." However, as O'Connor (1992) has argued, such a scenario is probably impossible. However there is evidence to suggest that similarity tends to be sought in socially and personally significant areas, typically those mentioned above: class, race, age, gender, etc. It could be suggested that the existence of differences between Ali and I would act as barriers to our becoming friends. Although I was identifying all these differences, I did secretly harbour the notion that I wanted to be 'her friend'. She oozed confidence and competence; if I became her friend perhaps I would also be identified as competent and confident. It has been suggested (Milardo, 1988; Wiseman, 1986 cited in O'Connor, 1992) that friendships play a particularly important part in reflecting and maintaining identity. Perhaps I thought there might be sufficient commonality in the academic context to achieve this.

When we next met—very briefly—I had this confirmed for me. I remember our conversations on this occasion, I remember that they were reciprocal and that there were certainly commonalities there. As we were to teach together, we felt that we needed to know more about each other's academic background and interests. To save time, Ali suggested that we should send each other our CVs. This seems highly significant now in light of our involvement and interest in autobiography, for as Miller and Morgan argue (1993: 133), "the CV can be understood as a form of autobiographical practice, centrally involved with the construction and presentation of a self in a particular occupational context." The self that was Ali that I was faced with was of course as I had thought, extremely competent and academically impressive. It did nothing for the ego at all and led me to think that she might not even want to work with me, never mind be my friend.

The CV is also of significance however on another level. It is a strange phenomenon: on the one hand it is autobiographically spotlighting the 'private' individual—in this case Ali—but on the other, it is situating her very clearly in a 'public' location. It requires examination of her work and activities and therefore does not divorce 'the auto/biographical subject' from the social contexts in which she is located (a criticism often levelled at the process of auto/biography). It was for me the first real information on Ali's history, crucial of course in accounting for her present location. The construction of auto/biography was a process which continued to have significance in both our 'private' and 'public' lives.

Apart from our one very fleeting meeting when we agreed to exchange our CVs, and a brief telephone call, our next sustained contact was on a more 'private' occasion on another beautiful summer's day, when we met at a pub halfway between Yorkshire and the Midlands, to have lunch and to discuss a course which we would be jointly teaching. Sitting outside, on a grassy bank, we did discuss the course and much else besides. We spent all afternoon talking about ourselves, our lives and our families, and we haven't stopped talking about any of these things since. This talk has been a central and significant part of our friendship, as it seems to be for many women.

For Jane and I, the accounts of ourselves and our lives, in other words the auto/biographies which we presented and continue to present to one another, provide at least some explanation of why our friendship became established so quickly and why we continue to enjoy each other's company today. Clearly, some sense of a shared past and present has been important to us; as already noted, it has long been recognised that friends tend to have similar characteristics (O'Connor, 1992). The differences between us, notably of age, marital status, ethnicity and position in family have not in our case been 'disregard criteria' (i.e. 'criteria' which cause us to disregard some people: see Gouldner and Strong, 1987) but have been relatively less important than our similarities, our 'liking criteria'. For, as Liz Stanley (1992a) notes, relationships have histories—they begin, they grow and they change—and our present biographies lie within the histories of present and past relationships.

Talk, then, and the shared construction of auto/biographies, has been important to us. As sociologists, we are unable to think about or discuss our lives without drawing on sociological concepts and frameworks, so that our talk is often social analysis, whether intended or not, focussing particularly on issues such as gender, class, ethnicity, and identity. O'Connor (1992) cites work on women's friendship (Duck et al, 1991) which shows that even conversations between friends which are perceived as mundane in content are still seen as important in creating and maintaining attachment to a person. O'Connor describes this as a closeness, an intensity, a 'we-feeling'—what Morgan has referred to as "shared understandings" and "shared knowledge structures" (Morgan, 1990, cited in O'Connor, 1992). It has also been argued (Wright, 1978, cited in O'Connor, 1992) that a key characteristic of friendship is the extent to which it provides self-affirmation, an impression of oneself as a competent, worthwhile person. For both of us this has been an important element of our friendship to date, though by no means the only one. We would therefore want to suggest that for us, friendship, and talk between friends, can be seen as significant auto/biographical events. As Liz Stanley (1994) has argued, the notion of auto/biography involves the insistence that accounts of other lives influence how we see and understand our own, and that our understanding of our own lives influences how we interpret those of others.

But auto/biography is important in our friendship in other ways too. As colleagues in an institution of higher education, involved particularly in the teaching of Sociology and Women's Studies, we are engaged both in the use of auto/biographical approaches in learning and teaching and in the critical theoretical analysis of issues around auto/biography. As a result of this, some of the content of our auto/biographical conversations has been made public to an audience of students and colleagues. Specifically, this has entailed Jane recounting some aspects of her life story in this more public context, although, as many writers have pointed out, the public/private split is a problematic one (see for example discussions in Gamarnikow et al, 1983; McDowell and Pringle, 1992). Benedicte Grima (1993), in her study of the significance of personal narratives in the lives of Paxtun women, has argued that every interaction or social interchange consists of a public act, whether it involves one or a hundred people. There is, she argues, not a public/private split, but a continuum of varying degrees of public domain, with appropriate behaviour attached to each. This continuum of publicness varies with audience size and status equality and inequality. An interaction involving total status inequality or a large audience would be closer to the 'very public' end, that between two women of similar social characteristics would be closer to the 'less public' end. The recounting of Jane's life story to a college audience therefore entailed a shift from a less public domain to a more public domain, although, importantly, for us it felt like a shift from private to public, and this feeling informs much of what we are discussing here.

The moving of Jane's life story, or aspects of it, into the more 'public', academic arena, came about on my invitation. I am coordinator for the core module of an MA entitled 'Managing Change in Community'. This differs from many courses with the word 'managing' in the title, in that it is grounded in social science and emphasises the value of a biographical approach. We utilise auto/biographical texts; incorporate students' own auto/biographies into the learning and teaching process, and require auto/biographical work for assessment. We also include sessions where visiting speakers are invited to contribute; these are referred to as 'living biographies'. The intention is that these speakers will explore some of the links between aspects of their own auto/biographies and wider social, historical and political forces. The many hours that Jane and I had spent discussing our lives had illustrated vividly for me the complex intertwinings of gender, class, and ethnicity in her own biography, and I felt that this would be of great interest and benefit to the students on the MA. Thus it was that Jane became a visiting speaker, or rather, a 'living biography' and ended up sharing some of her talk with a bigger audience than was initially intended.

Although I little guessed initially that the presentation of my auto/biography to Ali in 'private' would become—at Ali's request—a teaching and learning aid, at first of course I felt extremely excited and flattered by the request. She had listened endlessly to my life story, particularly to its more recent complexities.

It took some time for me to accept that 'my life' or at least the fragments of my life that I had shared with Ali could be of interest to students. I laughed at myself for recalling the tale that Maya Angelou has told: when discussing how the 'autobiographical mode' has brought her success and a public career, she thanks her friends who persuaded her to write down 'her life' as a result of the fascination they had experienced on hearing verbally from her stories of her childhood (McPherson, 1991). Friends then can play an important part in confirming and validating individual identity. This was certainly the case for me, new as the work and the friendship were.

When faced with the task however, that was another story. Because of the specific context, it was not just a case of going in and reciting my story. I had been asked to situate my story in wider social, historical and political contexts. I had to link 'myself' to the complex intertwinings of numerous social processes. I had, it seemed to me, to move from the 'private' to the 'public'. My stories and reciprocal discussions with Ali were to become public knowledge and property, were to be discussed, even written about by students. I could see an inverse parallel to suggestions made by Cornwell (1984, cited in Cotterill, 1992) and Cotterill (1992) that in multiple interviews with women for research purposes, 'private' accounts only came out as time went on: initial interviews only contained 'public' accounts. This was despite the fact that the same questions were asked. Cotterill suggests that this has been contingent on the development of trust. This had certainly been the case vis-à-vis my friendship with Ali; it could not possibly be vis-à-vis my relationship with the students. I was moving from private to public rather than the reverse.

I was filled with self-doubt about the success of this move. I constantly questioned my ability to do it. I doubted whether it was possible to move this 'private', 'particular' and 'unique' (for that is what all our life stories are really) account of 'my' 'self' to something that would be of 'general', 'public', even universal interest. I was not completely convinced that I could engage students or succeed in the task of connecting my own private understandings of 'my life' with more 'public' understandings and institutionalised knowledges (see Cotterill and Letherby, 1993).

As a feminist and as a Women's Studies tutor I kept thinking that this should not have been a problem. After all the 'personal is political', experience can be theorised and is valid knowledge—all feminist work is essentially concerned with experience. What seemed to be problematic for me was what I saw as the act of self-reflexivity—I couldn't quite get to the point where I saw my 'self' as a subject for intellectual inquiry which (I suppose) I was assuming I was to be. This in itself is I think sociologically interesting. I have tended to view it as a highly gendered and class-specific phenomenon: many accounts of research with/for women often include comments about how the women (usually working-class women) interviewed begin with something like "Oh I have nothing to say, my life isn't interesting". So on the one hand I think I was exhibiting facets of my original and private 'self' in the problems I was having getting started. On the other hand, I was denying aspects of my public working 'self'. To recall my working, or more particularly, my teaching role in Women's Studies, I know that the 'self', the autobiography, the 'narrative' or 'life history' is an extremely important research method for uncovering/discovering numerous hidden selves/knowledges: this has certainly been the case for subordinated groups, and therefore for women. Yet here I was unable to see my own 'self' as worthy of contributing something.

I think they were simply problems of self-worth and esteem, tied up in my gendered, racialised and class-specific location: they were, I would say, autobiographical themselves. So it was acceptable and unproblematic to talk to my friend and colleague Ali about 'my life' but to transfer it to the public and academic domain—well, that seemed to be something else ... I was extremely angry with myself in all of this, for here was I (I think) doing what the rest of society does—thinking very clearly in terms of the 'public' and the 'private' and valuing the former. It seemed that Ali was not as important as some anonymous public and academic audience, in contradiction to the view, already noted, that every social interaction is 'public' in some way.

When it came to writing there were a number of difficulties. These relate mainly to structure and content, although in the end I think they are quite difficult to separate.

The frameworks within which Ali and I discussed our lives were certainly those of gender, class and 'race'/ethnicity. McCall (1988, cited in O'Connor, 1992) argues that interaction within friendships creates socio-cultural worlds. Normative expectations are clarified, priorities affirmed and a shared culture—as we have already noted—develops. Friendships create and maintain views about the world. Our friendship definitely incorporated a 'view' of the world. We quickly established common ground in this 'view' and no explanations are now necessary vis-à-vis the dynamics and experiences of gender, race, class, etc. We were certainly agreed that the daily negotiation of a gendered self was, and would be, prominent in women's narratives and I was sure that along with other social dynamics, it would be prominent in structuring my own narrative. This then would have to be part of the 'public' account although of course there was no guarantee of a 'sympathetic' audience.

In terms of content, the deliberations were much more tortuous. One of the most important questions concerned what would go in the life story and what would not. Mary Evans (1993), for example, has argued that autobiographies are all the more revealing for what they leave out. I was not sure just how much to reveal, while simultaneously being concerned with parts of my life story that I felt were essential. However, as these were of a slightly distressing nature to me, I was preoccupied with the ethics of presenting such stories to the audience.

One of the things that struck me here was that in telling my life story to Ali, it had come slowly and as a result of getting to know her and her thoughts and feelings. There was, I felt, trust. Yet here was I to face an unknown audience: I did not know their auto/biographies, their thoughts, feelings and world view. I was unclear as to how they would react to aspects of my life history. They didn't have the same space to respond, unlike Ali did, indeed has. Unlike friendship, there would not be reciprocity and an equivalence of exchange (Allen, 1986, cited in O'Connor, 1992).

The second issue was just how much Ali did or didn't know. I was sure that I hadn't told her 'all' of my life story for when chatting as friends you do so in snippets, rather than in a block as I was to do here. So I was slightly nervous about how she would feel listening to 'more of it' for the first time while simultaneously noting that 'some of it' was missing. I am quite sure that snippets known to Ali would probably not be revealed to the public audience. She would in effect be listening to the 'same' but different story. As Stanley (1992a) has argued however, every time the biographer (and I am here tentatively suggesting that that is analogous to Ali in this situation) looks she sees something different, composed of the same elements but in a new configuration. I wondered what she would think of the version of 'me' that I would choose to present to the students. More specifically I was concerned with producing what she wanted and whether or not she would think I was a 'fraud' if I didn't include particular segments of my life story. It was this that I was particularly worried about in case it had an effect on our friendship. Ultimately however, the question of 'fraud' is probably not a viable question for, in the end, how would she know, particularly if you accept the view that all auto/biography is simply a construction? In the end I suppose you have to accept that we are "different selves in different locations" (Cohen, 1994) and that it is necessary to recognise that the "ways we tell our stories—the kind of stories we tell—are brought into being within particular power relations and are elicited by different audiences" (Middleton, 1993, cited in Mann, 1994). So in transferring the life story from 'private' to 'public', things are both added and taken away and neither setting elicits any 'truth', only a 'new' construction, a presentation.

There was however another issue to which I shall briefly refer. One of the many things I had talked to Ali about had been of a particular traumatic and highly significant life event, or epiphany as Denzin (1989) refers to it. In the request to talk about 'myself' the pertinence of this event to that/my sense of self cannot be underestimated. I have spoken elsewhere (Andrew and Montague, 1994) about the dilemmas of inclusion or exclusion of this epiphany. The point here I think is that in sharing this with a friend, our 'we-ness', shared understandings and our own socio-cultural world meant that of course it was safe to do so. In this context things did not feel so safe. There was no guarantee that the presence of Ali would be enough of a security blanket to risk it. It was, to me, crucial, yet it was placing an almost unfair responsibility on her. This really did strike me as risking our friendship, testing it to its limits. There were moments when I almost regretted the sharing of this knowledge. I so desperately wanted to 'do my best' for Ali (and of course for myself) and so my judgement here was critical: I had to assess the degree of personal distress possible and whether or not Ali would feel responsible. Cotterill (1992) has raised many of these issues in relation to research interviews that 'touch a nerve' for women respondents (particularly when they are friends of the researcher). She argues that the research relationship is inevitably affected and that "the contradiction between the researcher's position as a sociologist, a woman and a friend becomes more acute and yet seems impossible to reconcile" (596). There was certainly an element of risk to our friendship here, particularly if something did go wrong. I had no idea what we would do afterwards if it did.

The presentation on the night went well. It was warmly received and given the concerns raised above, I was extremely relieved. Ali and I were both new to our jobs and I had this horrible fear that I would 'let her down'. She is one of those people who does everything brilliantly (as a friend and a colleague) and of whom I sometimes feel in awe. I was particularly in awe of her at this time, having only known her for about six or so months. She had not had an easy passage 'taking over' the course in question and I felt sure that a negative outcome of the event would be at personal cost to her and perhaps to me—it could after all have meant an end to a friendship.

The success of the event, however, left me with little doubt that I had been competent and was therefore a valid and worthwhile friend and colleague. I was also aware that this meant Ali was as well. In our highly gendered workplace it is important to us to 'do well', 'to succeed'. I was sure that 'we' had done. Some colleagues were present and were extremely congratulatory and others who were not kept coming up to me in the next few days and offering praise. I felt then that I had contributed to our 'we-ness' and cemented and strengthened our friendship, while simultaneously helping to secure our credibility in the workplace. I felt I had performed in two roles. Performance in different roles has been cited as important in the enhancement and validation of identity in friendship (O'Connor, 1987 cited in O'Connor, 1992). O'Connor (1992) has also suggested that identity validation and status similarity inevitably change in the wake of events which imply a change of status. There was undoubtedly a change of status between us on this occasion—we were occupying very different identities, both to the audience and to our own selves. This raised issues for our friendship and did, more importantly, have the potential for a much greater and longer-term change in status between us. Ironically, it did—for me—help to equalise the relationship, even though we have focussed on issues of power and inequality that it clearly raises.

I lived with the positive feedback and praise for days. The extremely positive feedback from Ali was fantastic and what I valued most. So instead of feeling I had let her down, I felt pleased and proud. It did contribute as I had thought it would to our sense of 'we-ness'. It has of course led to interesting developments for us in other ways which are very much work-located.

Perhaps the most significant aspect of my involvement during the evening that Jane delivered her talk was that I was present in a number of different roles, and thus in a sense constituted a number of different audiences—as friend, as colleague, as tutor, as module coordinator. As Cohen (1994) points out, selfhood is a composite, and its constituents vary in public and private modes. Thus, he argues, the self is not 'replaced' by something else in the move from privacy into public social space; rather it adopts or discards elements which are/are not pertinent in more private contexts, such as intimate interaction. In the situation where Jane was presenting her autobiographical account to a group of students in my presence, an issue for us was that aspects of 'intimate interaction' were in fact transferred to the more public sphere. I was even, in a sense, part of the auto/biography, since its shape was not uninfluenced by our many conversations, interpretations and analyses. I think this is why, to my shame, my public thanks to Jane weren't as effusive as they might normally have been to a visiting speaker: our friendship got in the way of this. In displaying how clever and fascinating I thought she had been, would I have been saying how clever I was to have her as a friend?

In many ways, though, I was a different audience from the one I had been when we had our many 'private conversations'. I learned things which I hadn't known before. (Interestingly, Jane has since presented this session again, and I learned yet more things I hadn't known before. Or did I? Am I just hearing them differently now?) I also knew—or thought I knew—things which the audience did not. Not only did I know things which weren't being revealed, I also thereby had a different interpretive framework available to me for what was being revealed. I therefore felt some anxiety alongside my excitement at how good the session was. I couldn't be sure that the students were equally excited, although I felt this must be true. They might be mystified, or impatient, or critical, and this would have implications for me, partly in my roles as tutor and module coordinator, partly as Jane's friend, for I was also anxious on her behalf. I knew that she was nervous about how she would be received and I was acutely aware that I was responsible for setting up this ordeal. I knew that she had decided she wanted me there as a supporter, but that my presence, in my roles other than friend, was an additional concern for her. Cohen (1994) has noted the complexity of selves in relation to what he calls our "allegiances"; the incompatibility or even antagonistic nature of the many different groups to which we belong, for example friends and family, or different sets of friends. As he points out, we routinely juggle what he refers to as "the incompatible claims of family and work." In some circumstances 'friends and work', even, or perhaps especially, friends at work, may require similar juggling. On this occasion, I knew that what we—and particularly Jane—were attempting was much less safe than the conduct of a routine academic session (even though these too have their risks).

As Jane has already indicated, significant aspects of her auto/biography which we had discussed hinged around a particularly traumatic life event, which still gives rise to complex, sometimes painful thoughts and emotions. If Jane did decide to include these, would this be distressing for her? Could we be sure that the students and other colleagues in the audience would respond with the kind of sensitivity which one might expect from a friend? Would I be able to behave simply as a friend in this situation, or would there be competing demands on me? If, on the other hand, Jane wasn't able to include these important parts of her account, how would this make her feel? In either event, what would be the more far-reaching consequences for her, for us and for our friendship of what happened on that night?

Some of the moral and ethical issues which feminist researchers have raised when discussing research methods, and in particular the process and ethics of interviewing women, may also be relevant to the situation we are describing here; for example, the moral issues raised by an interview model which encourages friendship between women yet has the potential to exploit them in order to gain material (Finch, 1984; Cotterill, 1992). Janet Finch (1984) observes that her interviewees may need to know how to protect themselves from people like her. Although the situation we've been discussing is rather different, in that the reason for the friendship was not the gathering of material, I wonder nevertheless if Jane needs to know how to protect herself from people like me!

Indeed, as Cotterill points out, a 'friendly stranger' (which is what the feminist interviewer may be) does not exercise social control over respondents because the relationship exists for the purpose of the research and is terminated when the interviews are complete. They may even feel more comfortable talking to a 'friendly stranger' because it allows them to exercise some control over the relationship. Real friends, on the other hand, do not go away so easily. Not only have I been present when Jane delivers her accounts publicly (and we have already discussed some of the issues to which this gives rise), I am also present both before and after, and am likely to continue to be so. Furthermore, I am not only present for Jane in an ongoing way, but for the students too. This has raised significant issues about 'ownership' of accounts once these have moved into a more public arena. In my tutorials, students have occasionally asked for clarification of things which Jane has said, even using expressions like "What did she mean when she said . . . ?" Though I have been at pains to stress that I could not speak for Jane, I have found myself involved in a reconstruction of her own construction of her biography. This has undoubtedly been complicated by the fact that I felt I had 'insider knowledge' which I would not want to make use of in such a context. Indeed, on one occasion, Jane by coincidence knocked on my door and came into my room just as I was trying to answer one of these questions. This made me feel intensely uncomfortable, as if I had been 'caught with my hand in the till'. Though Jane and I later discussed this, my feelings of ambivalence about the ethics of it have not really gone away.

It has been suggested to us (participant at BSA Study Group on Autobiography Annual Conference, 1994) that one possible solution to this problem is for Jane to prepare a written version of her account, which students and I can then analyse, as we might any other text. I find this in some ways a very helpful suggestion, yet I do not think I would be able to approach this as I would 'any other text'. To me it is not, and can never be, 'any other text' and the issue of my 'insider knowledge' (though some of it may of course be assumed) stubbornly persists. I wonder, too, if this proposed solution may introduce yet more problems, albeit of a very interesting nature on a course which utilises and studies auto/biographical approaches. Joanna Bornat (1994) has noted how the performance aspects of oral accounts shade and colour narratives and that some of these are lost in written accounts. Certainly some of the pleasures for me in listening to Jane talk derive from these 'performance aspects'. Bogusia Temple (1994), however, has argued that there are both differences and similarities in oral and written accounts, with each using different tools to produce an effect. As an example, she notes that though tone and pitch may be important in oral accounts, so are layout and punctuation in written accounts. Having both available might then add to the layers of interpretation needed, and I would be coming to these layers less 'innocent' than even the general reader.

This sense of unease which I feel about using and possibly abusing 'private' knowledge and private accounts is part of a wider tension, whereby I would love Jane to continue doing these sessions, but I don't want to exploit our friendship or to treat a close friend as a 'specimen'.

Moreover, this—along with a number of other aspects of the process—has led us to think in much more general terms about our friendship 'at work' and our own individual auto/biographies and life-courses. These are issues that we are going on to explore both in our continuing writing and our research.

Alison Andrew is a Senior Lecturer in Sociology and Women's Studies within the Department of Applied Social Science and Humanities at Bradford College. She is Course Tutor for the MA 'Managing Change in Community', a key element of which is the utilization of auto/biographical approaches. She previously taught for a number of years at Nene College, Northampton and previous research includes a study of education and the working class in nineteenth-century Britain. Her current research (jointly with Jane Montague) explores aspects of the development and maintenance of women's friendship networks. She also continues to explore her interest in auto/biography and the use of auto/biographical methods in education.

Jane Montague comes from the North of Ireland but has been living in various locations throughout South and West Yorkshire for the past eleven years. She is a Lecturer in Sociology and Women's Studies within the Department of Applied Social Science and Humanities at Bradford College where she is Course Tutor for the BA (Hons) Women's Studies and Community Studies. Her current research (jointly with Alison Andrew) explores aspects of the development and maintenance of women's friendship networks and she continues to pursue her own interest in the complexities of identity, belonging and community for Irish people living in Britain.

"Joy in the struggle itself"[1]: a friendship across the racial divide

Juliet Betts and Shantu Watt

> Greetings, I am pleased
> to see that we are different.
> May we together become greater
> than the sum of both of us.
>
> Vulcan Greeting (Star Trek)

To speak or write about our friendship across the wall of racism in contemporary Britain is a daring undertaking. The friendship is the culmination of our working together, working cooperatively and collaboratively through the development of honest and open communication. It has taken us many years (nearly twenty) to nurture, work on and defend our relationship in both public and private arenas.

The existence of diverse forms of oppression in this society and the manner in which they operate, and are experienced, creates barriers to friendships which are often seen as insurmountable. In the context of racial oppression, many Black people and some white people argue that such friendships are impossible because the white person always holds the power and cannot be trusted not to abuse that power. In discussing our friendship we have found that artificial, culturally specific distinctions between the public and the private have little meaning. Our friendship did not materialise in either 'public' or 'private' spheres. We began to acknowledge the potential of friendship as a universal human concept. However, the context in which we live is ridden with the historical effects of domination and oppression. Therefore, at the heart of any such friendship has to be the need to confront the pernicious nature of racism to divide, undermine, and destroy healthy and loving relationships between people.

In reflecting on our friendship, it is clear that racism in all its pervasiveness has had to be addressed constantly in all spheres. For the Black friend (SW), the friendship itself has been questioned by some Black friends (and some white colleagues) around the issues of trust, loyalty and political allegiance. It has also been questioned on the basis that it is impossible for a white friend to be at the receiving end of racism and therefore to have any understanding of the impact of racism on Black people's lives. For the white friend (JB), it has been and is essential to work on and challenge her own racism, and to be prepared to be challenged by her Black friend. A constant vigilance about the racist processes both within and outside the friendship is vital without resorting to the "I'm all right because I have a Black friend" syndrome. In the context of this chapter, we are not seeking to comment on the dynamics of covert or overt racism within other personal relationships such as those between lovers and/or partners. For us, whatever other personal commitments have been around, our friendship has for many years been of central importance in our lives, and we have spent many hours trying to make sense of the connections between head, heart, and stomach. This process has enabled us to clarify the interwoven meanings of lived experiences and the overwhelming demand for analytical interpretation.

The quotations at the beginning of this chapter reflect two key aspects of the friendship process for us. Firstly, the Walker and Parmar (1993) quotation in the title reflects the fact that we have to struggle for our friendship, both with people and institutions outside, but also within ourselves. As with the best of any relationship, it cannot be taken for granted. And yet there is always joy as well. Often there has been laughing and crying together, privately. On so many occasions we have been able to re-energise each other in very painful situations.

The second quotation reflects a philosophy that has been central to our interactions from the start. We began with a recognition of our starting points that did not negate our different and differential positions and experiences. There has been a tendency to assume that all women share a 'common oppression'. However, we agree with bell hooks (1989) when she argues against such an undifferentiated notion of sexism. The assertion of a commonality of womanhood can further enable white women to enhance their academic and economic privileges. They can unwittingly and unconsciously continue to elude their common sense ideology (that is racist) which sustains the oppression and exploitation of Black women. In order to counteract such processes, we developed an explicit shared agenda to combat racism by exploring ways of working within a 'positive model' that demonstrates the potential for cooperative work across the racial divide. We were also seeking to demonstrate that it is possible both to be aware of and respect each other's boundaries, and to develop a common agenda. On reflection, the process of becoming friends shows an almost Taoist complementarity of the yin and yang: from seeing ourselves and being seen as opposites and separate, we continue to create an oasis of complementarity in which to sustain ourselves.

Over the years what began as a positive working relationship has become a friendship. It is important to acknowledge the similarities of class position ('middle class') and of work context (higher education, social work education) which have helped shared perspectives to be developed. There is also a shared experience of heterosexual relationships. The commonalities and differences of our life experiences as WOMEN have become more central. There are significant economic, political, and social contexts for these changes which need to be identified. In the rest of this chapter we propose to explore the development of our relationship from that of tutor/student to one of understanding as friends.

Processes and methods

We decided early on in the process of discussion and reflection for this piece that it had to be rooted in our own experiences. We did not wish to impose other people's categories on our experiences, especially since very little if anything has been written about such friendships, particularly in the European context. What will be presented here therefore is a LIVING ANALYSIS of the process of becoming friends. To adapt Alan Bennet's concept of 'Talking Heads', this process has been one of 'Talking Heads and Hearts'.

So why are we writing publicly about our friendship? We were attracted by the positive title of the University of York's conference and the idea of celebrating women's friendships. However, we were not prepared to talk in terms of a simplistic notion of 'celebrating differences'. In our experience, this concept is frequently rooted in the theoretically and politically flawed notion of 'multiculturalism' in education and related fields. Implicitly or explicitly, this framework is frequently underpinned by notions of 'tolerance' of difference that are in reality rooted in colonial relationships of dominance and subservience. Via the concealing of the power relationships of racism, white people are allowed to feel comfortable about their attitudes and behaviour because (once again) they can avoid the unpleasantness and pain of their racism.

We were aware that writing about our friendship would be another risky enterprise. But we wished to continue to demonstrate our commitment to making racism and its impact central and explicit in women's fora. As we shall discuss below, our experience of women's fora in academia INCLUDING Women's Studies does not convince us that racism is as yet on the agenda. There has been a tendency to see racism and sexism as parallel forms of oppression, and as a result Black women's experience of racism has been denied. We have been determined not to equate white and Black men's patriarchy and their culminating effects. We believe it is important to hold onto the processes of naming and renaming, and to speak out about what is happening in both the public and private spheres of women's lives. The ongoing struggle to move from rhetoric to reality involves, amongst other actions, taking risks. It involves a rejection of simplifying and sloganising, and a positive commitment to making non-competitive alliances, and to developing analyses that reflect the REAL complexities of women's lives. We have struggled to avoid the pitfalls of guilt and blame.

In concrete terms, we began the process separately by undertaking a brainstorm about our own perspectives and experiences of our friendship. It felt important in terms of the philosophy of our friendship that there should be little pressure to feel and say 'the right thing'. The results of our separate work were then shared in a series of conversations. We then took turns to prepare drafts on a word processor. The drafts were then discussed, amended and rewritten together.

Whenever we work together, the process consists of a series of conversations, mostly within a world view which has become increasingly shared. The circularity of these 'talkings' has enabled us to identify themes within the process which can then be drawn on as the basis of our collective work. This process has been an important part of the way the friendship has developed. In preparing this chapter, the conversation moved in many different directions, between the public (to be included in the chapter) and the private. We were brought face-to-face with a potent mixture of human emotions, and the complexities of the impact of different forms of oppression on us, both as individuals and as friends. We discovered many new things during the process and it has been a valuable experience for us. In particular, we shared information and feelings that we had not shared before. For example, the difference between JB's mainly linear thinking and SW's mainly rounded thinking was revealed. This enabled us to see that our work and our friendship had benefited from a synthesis of these two approaches. Overall, the process revealed similarities between our conclusions, and the sharing of many, but not all, feelings in common. The growth continues.

Although we have deliberately not referred to academic theory, we have been influenced by theoretical ideas. We have explored them in some detail in previous publications (Watt and Cook (now Betts), 1989; Cook and Clarke, 1989; Watt and Cook, 1991a; Watt and Cook, 1991b; Cook and Watt, 1992). We have also chosen not to enter the divisive world of defining terms in the field of oppression such as class, racism, sexism, heterosexism, although again some of our previous publications include working definitions of some of these terms.

Contexts

There are many contextual influences that impact upon all friendships. In our case, we have identified three main sources of influence which interweave and overlap. Firstly, there is an overall and emerging economic and political context deriving from a society undergoing massive economic, political, and social change from the late 1970s until now. This context includes an increasingly hostile environment for any effort to contest oppression/inequality in society. Secondly, there has been a more specific context about issues of racism and anti-racism. Thirdly, there has been a women's issues/Women's Studies context.

Within our historical backgrounds, the economic, political, and social context had a clear influence not only on our lives, but also on our friendship. In the late 1970s and early 1980s, little progress had been made within white British society and its institutions to promote anti-oppressive practice, but some struggles were gathering momentum. Although there has to be scepticism about the power of the law to bring about greater equality, a glimmer of hope of more changes to come was offered by the Equal Pay Act (1970), the Sex Discrimination Act (1975), and the (Third) Race Relations Act (1976). In the higher education/social work context in which we 'lived', moves were afoot to introduce anti-oppressive (particularly anti-racist) practice and theory into the curriculum. At that time the need for state welfare provision was not widely questioned and unemployment had not become the chronic feature that it is today. As professional workers, we believed it was possible for education, particularly community education, to be a vehicle for promoting racial and other forms of social justice. It was a context in which it seemed possible and necessary to struggle for equality and justice in the organisational sphere. For example, much of our early work centred on arguing for and developing policies and procedures on equal opportunities in recruitment and selection, and the curriculum.

Since the early 1980s there have been major upheavals and changes nationally and internationally. The gap between rich and poor, both within and between nations, has widened. Britain is no exception to these trends. In current right-wing/New Right political thought and practice, inequalities in society are frequently seen as justifiable in terms of rewarding the 'enterprising' and penalising the 'unenterprising and lazy'. The resistance to anti-oppressive practice has become more vocal and politically acceptable. It has become widely accepted that education is no longer about social justice, but about meeting the needs of the economy. As a result of the tensions and dilemmas that these societal changes engendered, our exchanges became more intense. We became increasingly aware of the growing pressures on us as individuals to take sides and to engage in a wide range of different struggles. We continued to work together to challenge racist practices in organisations, including white women's organisations. SW made a conscious decision to channel most of her energies into working on Black empowerment with Black self-help groups and voluntary organisations. JB continued to challenge the racism and sexism of white education and training organisations. By the end of the 1980s, it was becoming more difficult to sustain an optimism that organisations could, or would, embrace anti-oppressive practice.

In the 1990s, reformulating the classic feminist phrase, our political struggles have very definitely become personal. The failure of the white organisations in which we were employed to change has meant that, in the end, our own personal survival and integrity were on the line. We have continued (separately and together) to struggle for organisational change, but have also had to make difficult employment 'choices'.

The second context is that of work organisations. The following words from Audre Lorde contextualise our experience of the academy:

> The master's tools will never dismantle the master's house (Lorde, 1984: 173).

Our cumulative experiences confirmed the insidious nature of the way power can be used and abused in work organisations. The web of power and control in such organisations, in our experience, is complex, subtle, and, above all, secret. What is at issue is not the overt level of professional competence and practice. It is about the deeper processes which exclude those activists who behave in a principled and consistent manner on issues of equity and justice. A fundamental organisational dynamic that we have identified over many years is the process of creating insiders and outsiders. Many organisations have their own politics of engagement with employees at certain determined levels. In bringing our dual experiences together, we have searched, talked, and re-searched into these experiences in order a) to make sense of the experience, b) to understand and identify the impact of particular experiences, c) to find a way forward and a safety net for continuing our careers and our personal dignity, and d) to understand the insider/outsider process in relation to our positions as a Black and a white woman.

The fundamental dynamic of organisational power maintenance is a well-documented one. However, in the academy there is a level of contradiction at work in terms of a public liberal ethos of academic enquiry, academic freedom, and the supposed sponsorship of new ideas and originality. Since members of the academic establishment generally think of themselves as an enlightened élite, to challenge their sexism and racism is seen as a considerable affront. This applies not only to the majority of white men, but frequently to white women as well. Many white women, whether feminist or not, are outraged at the idea that they could be racist (this is discussed in greater detail below in our discussion of the Women's Studies context). In our experience, there is often an assumption that because one has some knowledge and understanding of one form of oppression, that by definition, one is 'sorted' on other forms of oppression. To teach about oppression as an academic subject is NOT the same as having uprooted the internalised chains of oppression that are part of everyday living and manifest themselves in many different ways. At one point, we decided to apply for a job share at a university department with a strong reputation for feminist and anti-racist thinking and practice. We were disappointed that our initial approach was not received positively as a job share between a Black and a white woman.

From SW's experience, it was no longer about 'issues' of racism and sexism: this was the reality of living, maintaining strength, retaining dignity, and knowing that what is reasonable, acceptable, and sensible to her is not necessarily within the organisational dictionary. It was difficult to continue with a level of energy and commitment in an environment where the 'club' rules were not explicit but known only to the select insiders. In some instances it meant remaining the silent minority whilst the 'right on' colleagues continued discussions of issues of racism as experienced by students. It might be argued that their intentions were honourable, but the manner in which these debates were conducted put SW outside the circle physically, socially, and emotionally.[2]

JB on the other hand may have been perceived as an insider in some contexts, but her continual stance against racism as well as sexism quickly resulted in an outsider position in the organisation. There were many incidents of being ridiculed, ignored and excluded, denied seniority and insulted, for example, the accusation from a woman colleague of "leaning over Blackwards" when arguing an anti-racist position.

When we began to talk about our experiences at work, we found that these incidents were not isolated, individual events. There was a clear pattern, and we began to piece together a jigsaw, which eventually became a picture of the manner in which organisations create and sustain insiders and outsiders. We undertook to utilise such examples at conferences and through our writing in order to communicate to others the ways in which organisations divide and rule. We began to realise that there could not be a division, in our conversations or our lives, between public and private. The pressures placed on us were experienced as "assaults on self" (Freeman and Cook, 1992: 2). Through a series of encounters, we began the process of naming our experiences and their impact on us. The relief involved in naming gave us a renewed strength. We decided that the way forward was not to remain silent. Although we have been true to that decision, we are aware that there have been and still are pressures to silence us. A recent joint labelling of us as 'too subversive' by a woman academic represented to us both our success in breaking the silence, and our 'thorn in the side' status both politically and organisationally.

The third context in which much of the joint work has taken place has been in the women's issues/Women's Studies arena. Our agenda for conferences and papers, as well as different forms of organisational work, was to make sure that the complexity of different forms of oppression was recognised and acted upon within women's fora. Specifically, we felt able to make a strong case for putting racism onto the agenda of white women's organisations. We found that, on many occasions, the interpersonal agendas and the collusive networks took over the platforms. This left little time for moving into any real actions. As a result of working together, we felt we could make some statements about the difficulties and the opportunities that such collaborations could offer.

Why has it been so difficult and painful?

Women's Studies has certainly blossomed in Britain over the last ten to fifteen years and this is to be welcomed. Walk into any academic bookshop and there is a large section devoted to Women's Studies (even in some mainstream ones too). Look closely at the books in this section. Books by and for Black British women are few and far between. Search for a section on racism and you may find a few books usually subsumed under general sociology.

This pattern has enormous implications. It reflects the fact that the study and the impact of racism has still not reached 'take off' point in the academy, although it has had a small niche within some universities for much longer than Women's Studies. Courses on racism are still few and far between, with the exception of social work courses. Over recent years, professional social work bodies have required the inclusion of evidence of work on oppression, racism, discrimination, and practice implications. Sadly, since 1995, a combination of outside political pressure with a lack of social commitment within the caring professions has led to a diminished emphasis on anti-oppressive theory and practice. Academics with a commitment to anti-racism are rare and publishers have been less interested in supporting books on racism compared with books on Women's Studies. As a result, courses which do offer this subject matter are often starved of experienced staff and lack a solid literature base. The process becomes circular.

There are many reasons for the neglect of racism in the academy, not least the operation of racism itself. We have both been involved in proposing, writing, and trying to run new courses on institutional and individual racism, and have had first-hand experience of the hostility, trivialisation, and marginalisation that this engenders. There is an endemic lack of potential allies not only because of the struggles for the very few Black academics, but also because of the unwillingness of most white academics to stand up and be counted. There is usually an enormous gulf between the rhetoric of 'commitment' and 'challenge', and the reality of taking risks and experiencing the cost.

In the case of promoting a Women's Studies agenda, there are usually at least a small number of like-minded women to start the ball rolling. This cannot be guaranteed when the issue is racism—often it is necessary to stand alone against not only colleagues but the academic power structures and organisations themselves. Individuals in such situations have to make hard choices about how important promotion and career are, or how to survive, and sometimes whether survival is possible.

When we were invited to write our first chapter, we felt we were making an important contribution in a number of ways. Firstly, to the subject matter of the book which was on women and poverty in Britain—a pioneering book at the time. Our chapter was on Black women and poverty (Cook and Watt, 1992). The chapter was hard because of the limited sources available specifically related to Black women and poverty, but we were committed to ensuring that the topic was included in such a book. Even though we were aware that in some ways it may have been a 'token' chapter, we were making a statement about the centrality of the issues relating to Black women's poverty.

Subsequently, we have been invited to write other chapters and have offered articles and conference sessions on similar issues. In terms of our publications it has to be said that in many ways we have continued to provide token pieces on racism for books with overwhelmingly white feminist perspectives. We are aware that there is often a 'hunt' for Black women to contribute to the proliferation of Women's Studies publications, because the networks with Black women are still not in place. Black women are aware of these agendas *vis-à-vis* being used to give credibility to white women's publications and are making informed choices as a result. There is a growing body of work by Black women and, in spite of the negative context, their work is already making an impact on various so-called established theoretical perspectives. However, in Women's Studies, there are still many examples of lip service being paid to the impact and dynamics of racism and there is an unspoken resistance to moving beyond some understanding of racism to a position of real personal commitment.

In line with our other emerging strategies to put racism on the agenda for ACTION in as many contexts as possible, we took the same approach in Women's Studies. We were hopeful that this would not only be a responsive environment, but might actually offer us support, encouragement, and nourishment for battles being fought elsewhere. We also looked forward to sharing the challenge of theorising racism and sexism and relating this to practice with other women. Sadly this was not the case.

Our experience of Women's Studies conferences was that they operated very much on traditional academic lines, e.g. plenaries with 'important' speakers, papers read in groups with very little opportunity for discussion, a prioritising of theory rather than practice to theory, a sense of scrambling for position, publications, and other rewards of 'the system'. The level of knowledge and understanding of racism was pitifully low. Although our sessions were well-received by the relatively small number of participants, our questions and challenges on racism in other sessions were definitely unwelcome. On some occasions, it was as though we had broken ranks with our 'sisters' (predominately white) by speaking about the unspoken, the taboo of racism. We were often left speechless and alienated. It is impossible to quantify the enormous impact of the feelings generated by the intentional or unintentional racism of many of the women at these events. We were also aware that to enter into any discussion regarding their behaviour was to be greeted with outrage: "So, are you calling ME a racist?" At times our response has been one of exasperation, and, of course, perceived as that by those who seem to recognise that there is a gap between what is said and what is practised. Many people have told us that for them, it is somehow 'easier' to deal with sexism than to deal with racism. But in our experience, racism and sexism are inextricably entwined. This combination produces extremely strong emotions and reactions both for those who experience it, and for those who contribute to its maintenance and perpetuation.

We gradually withdrew from this environment with our dignity intact. On these occasions, we would remind ourselves of the words from the struggles and survival of women, past and present, that we admire.

There has been a tendency from both white and Black feminists to be over-prescriptive about various women's public and private life styles. Within the academic and social work spheres, this was translated into norms of acceptability which were allowed to dictate practices which again created insiders and outsiders. One of the deciding factors for questioning our efforts to 'model' collaborative work was our experience at a European women's conference. Early on in the conference proceedings, the issue of racism was ignored within the discussions about the constitution for a new Women's Studies organisation in Europe, a Europe in which racism is frighteningly pervasive. Once again, it fell to a handful of women to spend most of the conference trying unsuccessfully to ensure that racism was included. We decided not to misuse our energies and eventually left the conference as soon as we could. During this conference, SW wrote the following poem (Watt and Cook, 1991b: 19):

Yet again I witness
The resistances
Are these what I think
And understand them to be?
Around the North and South Divide
Or about geographical boundaries
We vote within a so called
Democratic framework
The bases of this democracy
Have already excluded some
Women by definition-
From general to specific EXclusion
Resistance to specific INclusion
A list of oppressions
Becomes unattainable, unthinkable
A mockery? Through EXclusion
Why do white women
In majority always seem
Not to comprehend
They have a problem
It is not only in Britain
That racism exists...

(Shantu Watt)

We have outlined our experiences within Women's Studies in the hope that positive developments will take place. There is still an urgent need for Women's Studies seriously and consistently to avoid tokenism and to become a real and inclusive 'sisterhood' movement.

Conclusion

Within the process of our efforts to make connections, we have discussed the many contradictions and controversies of our living experiences. We sought not to generalise that all Black women's experiences are those of victims, or that all white women's experiences result from being in positions of power. How could we find a device which moved us on from the inadequacies of this stereotyping deeply imprinted by the colonial past and exposed the amoeba-like qualities of racism? In spite of the ways in which power and ideology undermine connections between people, we began to identify some common threads of meanings and experiences as women. Individually, we were also with women from various backgrounds where these questions were addressed differently, and alliances made on a variety of platforms. Shared personal and professional experiences of the abuse of power by a number of individuals consolidated the trust and openness of the friendship.

In our more lighthearted moments, we identified four 'C's in our friendship: challenges, commitment, connectedness and commonalities.

When we began to talk about our life experiences, we identified some commonalities even within the differences. In order to retain this connectedness as a flexible thread between us, we recognise the need to remain mindful of our friendship. When we were asked to address a conference on 'Greening Communication', we thought of a question to be asked about friendships: "Who do we grow with?" Our friendship has facilitated our growth, both together and separately. Obviously, we continue our commitment to the friendship by maintaining a conscious effort to share the responsibility for not allowing outside influences to polarise us. We are aware of the over/misuse of the word challenge. Nonetheless, any friendship has to face up to both internal and external challenges in order to continue.

In concluding this chapter, three thoughts remain. Hopefully, in due course, such a chapter about women's friendship across the racial divide will no longer be necessary. There is an onus on women to consider moving beyond some of the divisive manifestations that skin boundaries create and maintain. And finally, we choose to leave open and undefined women's friendships.

Notes

1. From Walker and Parmar (1993), 37.

2. For a current discussion of Black/white women's relationships in academia, see Sonia Thompson (1997). For further reading related to this chapter, see Bedi (1993), Henfrey (1994), hooks (1991), Morgan (1988), Morrison (1993), Shiva (1989), Tan (1993).

N.B. J. Cook is now J. Betts.

Juliet Betts has recently taken early retirement after thirty years in academic life. During that time, she has researched and published widely. She can recommend liberation from "The Academy."

Shantu Watt is an independent consultant, researcher and trainer in the management of organizational, professional and personal change. She was a senior lecturer in applied social studies at Warwick and

Bradford Universities, and has published widely. She has worked as a consultant to both public and private sector bodies on diversity in staff recruitment, selection and retention; and has also undertaken organisational reviews.

Making and Breaking Women's Friendships in Feminist Theory

Katherine Side

There is a large body of feminist scholarship that addresses women and family relations.[1] There is, however, a smaller and more uneven body of feminist scholarship that addresses women and non-familial relations, particularly friendships. Existing scholarly works that consider the topic of women's non-familial relations, and in particular women's friendships with women, have tended to emerge from specific academic disciplines and their influence has been confined mainly to those disciplines.[2] Despite assertions about the importance of women's friendships with women and some academic interest in them, feminist scholarship has been slow to integrate scholarly work on this topic across the disciplines. The result of this has been twofold: interest in women's friendships with women has been largely overshadowed by scholarly inquiry into women's family relations, and theorising women's friendships with women has occurred at a generally sluggish pace.[3]

In this chapter I critically examine some attempts in contemporary feminist scholarship to theorise women's relations with women.[4] I evaluate them for the insight they offer toward the project of theorising women's friendships, specifically the formation, maintenance, and demise of these relations. I consider some of the reasons why current models and theories are, as yet, inadequate for fully understanding women's friendships. Finally, I suggest reasons why women's friendships should remain an area of interest for feminist theory and feminist scholarship.

In her landmark article "The Female World of Love and Ritual", historian Carroll Smith-Rosenberg makes an important distinction in the theoretical approaches used to explain the nature and origin of women's relationships with women. She distinguishes individual psychosexual approaches, characterised by associations with individual psychic and sexual development, from cultural and social approaches, characterised by the interconnectedness of social and cultural factors (1975: 2). While this remains a useful distinction for outlining theoretical approaches to women's friendships, the influences of Western, second-wave feminism of the late 1960s and early 1970s has contributed an important third perspective, that of radical feminism, characterised by a belief in patriarchy as the origin of women's oppression. Psychosexual, socio-cultural and radical feminist perspectives are the lens through which I will view ideas in feminist thought about the formation, maintenance, and demise of women's friendships. My treatment of these three approaches is not intended to survey each perspective in its entirety. Rather, it is to provide illustrations of how each perspective has been used in feminist thought to account for women's relations with women, and specifically their friendships.

Conceptualising Women's Friendships With Women

Fischer notes the term 'friend' is used ambiguously in theoretical and empirical analyses (1982: 287). One of the foremost difficulties in considering women's friendships is the lack of a common understanding or definition. This challenge, however, should be considered no more consequential than the lack of a common definition and understanding around family, a limitation that has not deterred attempts to theorise family relations. In fact, feminist contestations of a common understanding or definition of family have instigated a proliferation of research on the topic.

In feminist scholarship there is a rich source of historical material that traces and examines historical friendships, romantic friendships and Boston marriages between women as far back as the Renaissance (Smith-Rosenberg, 1975; Faderman, 1981; Donoghue, 1993).[5] Largely these works define women's friendships as historically-specific relationships and do not suggest a continuous link with the structure and nature of contemporary women's friendships. There is also a large and rapidly expanding body of literature concerned with documenting and recording particular friendship histories as they are understood and experienced between two women (Thompson, 1987; Souhami, 1991; Raitt, 1993; Freeman, 1995).[6] And there is a body of feminist literature, derived primarily from the disciplines of psychology, social psychology, and sociology, that examines the contingency of women's friendships as defined through specific signifiers such as marital status (Oliker, 1989; O'Connor, 1992), age (Bleiszner and Adams, 1992), and culture (Abu-Lughod, 1985; Uhl, 1991).

While these considerations of women's friendships may appear hopelessly disparate in the project of theorising these relations, their definitive commonality, a recognition and consideration of the importance of women's friendships in women's lives, is the starting point from which I begin understanding the formation, maintenance, and demise of women's friendships in feminist thought.

Making Friends: Feminist Thoughts and Theories On The Formation Of Women's Friendships

A psychosexual approach to feminist thought considers women's relational capacity to be a crucial component of individual psychic and sexual development, and believes that Freudian psychoanalysis can be useful for understanding women's relationships. Nancy Chodorow's *The Reproduction of Mothering* is among the most recognised feminist models of the psychosexual approach. In her examination of how mothering is reproduced in women, Chodorow uses object-relations theory to both rely on and challenge the Freudian notion that women's individual psychic development occurs through processes of separation from the mother or women. On the one hand, she retains the centrality of development through a primary relationship with the mother or women. On the other hand, she challenges it by arguing that for girls and women, individual development occurs through processes of attachment, contrary to Freudian ideas that individual psychic and sexual development occurs through separation:

> As a result of being parented by a woman, and growing up heterosexual, women have different and more complex relational needs in which an exclusive relationship to a man is not enough ... This is because women situate themselves psychologically as a part of a relational triangle in which their father and men are emotionally secondary or, at most, equal to their mother or women (Chodorow, 1978: 199).

According to Chodorow, mothering not only reproduces mothers, but it reproduces heterosexual women whose identity is defined through, and who have a psychological need for, other women. Jessica Benjamin, in *The Bonds of Love*, concurs with Chodorow's thesis. She further develops this premise that women's identity is formed through processes of attachment and locates women's psychological need for attachment more specifically in the concept of recognition (1988: 12).

Other feminist thinkers have engaged further with this theme of women's psychological need for connectedness. Carol Gilligan's *In A Different Voice* argues that moral reasoning in girls and women can be characterised by connectedness as opposed to separateness. Gilligan states that:

> male and female voices typically speak of the importance of different truths, the former of the role of separation as it defines and empowers the self, the latter of the ongoing processes of attachment that creates and sustains the human community (1982: 156).

Women's psychological need for connectedness has also been extended to their differential 'ways of knowing'. Mary Belenky *et al.*, in *Women's Way of Knowing*, argues that women's differential relational capacities explain how women acquire knowledge (1986; Coates, 1996: 306).[7] Linguist Deborah Tannen (1990) also argues for women's need for connectedness and intimacy in conversational speech.

The overall ability of psychosexual models of women's relations to shed light on the formation of women's friendships is hindered, first and foremost, by an incomplete understanding of psychic and sexual structures and processes. An increasing distrust of Chodorow's and Benjamin's heterosexist assumptions and of the sharp gender dichotomies implicit in these explanations is discernible in feminist thought. Chodorow's presumption that women grow up heterosexual, for instance, is contrasted in feminist theory by Adrienne Rich's lesbian continuum. In a move that raised more than a few feminist eyebrows, Rich positioned all women, whether self-defined as lesbian or not, along this continuum. The positioning of women's relational capacities, through their moral reasoning and knowledge and language production, as oppositional to men's, has been critiqued for its implicit gender polarisation and entry into overly simplistic equality/difference debates.[8] The reliance of psychosexual approaches on the work of Freud and Freudian ideas, for explanations of women's individual development, has been treated with considerable suspicion by radical feminists. Psychosexual approaches to the formation of women's friendships can be set apart from radical feminist approaches by their willingness to engage with Freudian thought. Despite this significant difference, both approaches end up on the side of difference in equality/difference debates and both psychosexual and radical feminist approaches share a fundamental belief in the necessity of women's relational capacity to form individual attachments with other women. For psychosexual feminist theorists, these attachments are a precursor to full individual psychic and sexual development. For radical feminist theorists, they derive directly from, and serve as indicators of, women's essential psychic and sexual difference and distance from men.[9]

Radical feminist theorising assumes, in its most simplistic form, the innate ability of women to connect with other women against their oppression under patriarchy. Perhaps because of this assumption, radical feminist theorising has been consistently attentive to the particular relationship of women's friendship. Adrienne Rich's "Compulsory Heterosexuality and Lesbian Existence", a paragon of the radical feminist approach, provides a context and validity for the consideration of women's friendships by stating that "the original deep adult bonding is that of women for women" (1980: 647).[10] The innate ability of women to befriend other women is also presumed by Janice Raymond in *A Passion For Friends* (1986) and Mary Hunt in *Fierce Tenderness* (1994), both intentional models of women's friendships that derive from this perspective. Raymond contests that a valuing of women's friendships with women is a return to an "original state" for women (1986: 59). Her model of friendships between women pivots on her vision of Gyn/affection, women-to-women attraction, influence, and movement, presented in opposition to hetero-reality, defined as relationships determined by men (1986: 5). In Hunt's model of women's friendship relations, the act of valuing women's friendship relations is reportedly "an act of justice" (1994: 21).

It remains unclear how all of these radical feminist theoretical models of women's friendships actually translate into friendships between and among women. Furthermore, it is unclear how these models challenge the legacy of patriarchy, the origin of women's oppression according to radical feminists. Entry into equality/difference debates by radical feminists comes down unequivocally on the side of difference.[11] Radical feminist approaches to the topic of women's friendships are plagued further by an idealisation of lesbian relationships. They venerate the formation of friendships among lesbians as higher forms of friendship than are possible among heterosexual women. Raymond and Hunt's theories, in particular, have difficulty explaining the importance of women's friendships to heterosexual women. And despite their concentration on lesbian friendships, Raymond and Hunt follow Rich's example in portraying lesbian relationships in ways that fail to acknowledge the possibility of inequities within them and occlude the place of sex and sexuality.[12] Furthermore, Raymond and Hunts' models derive from what Humm has characterised as the "poetic and metaphorical mode of post 1970s" radical feminist writing. This "poetic and metaphorical" mode often leads Raymond and Hunt into confusing language and ideas (1989: 232).[13]

The accusations of essentialism that are sometimes levelled against radical feminist approaches are at odds with a social and cultural approach to the topic. Social and cultural explanations for the formation of women's friendships have received less prominence in this literature, perhaps because they have tended to consider women's historical, as opposed to contemporary, friendships. Smith-Rosenberg suggests the formation of women's romantic friendships in nineteenth-century America reflected a variety of social and cultural circumstances, including a rigid gender role differentiation that allowed for the development of homosocial friendship and extended kin networks, social conventions that actively discouraged criticisms of women by other women, and severe restrictions on intimacy between women and men (1975: 9). She openly refutes William Taylor and Christopher Lasch's hypothesis that women's friendships were an outcome of the breakdown of the colonial family in the mid-nineteenth century (1975: 1). Smith-Rosenberg's contention that women's romantic friendships were as common to the eighteenth century as they were to the nineteenth century is supported by numerous examples in Lillian Faderman's *Surpassing the Love of Men* (1981). Sheila Jeffreys suggests that during this same approximate time period, in Britain, the social factors that precipitated women's friendship relations were primarily demographic.[14] She notes an imbalance in the population resulting in significantly more women than men. This imbalance, along with improved educational opportunities for women and their entry into white-collar professions, accounted for large numbers of unmarried women, and thus facilitated patterns for women's friendship relations (1985: 96).

Social and cultural explanations are contextually specific. They are also geographically specific. Consider Jeffrey's demographics. Unlike Britain at the end of the nineteenth century, Australia had a surplus of men, not women. Also, in Britain and Australia, as elsewhere, the movement of women into higher education and white collar professions was open then, as it is now, to only some women.

Staying Friends: Thoughts and Theories On The Maintenance Of Women's Friendships

There are far fewer considerations in feminist thought of the maintenance of women's friendship relations than there are of their formation and demise. In fact, only recently have the normative guidelines that maintain family relations even been considered (Finch, 1989; Finch and Mason, 1993), and this despite the fact that family relations are bolstered directly and indirectly through state policies and are often enforced in laws. Psychosexual approaches to women's friendships attempt to explain not only why women act in particular ways with other women, but why they might continue to do so. They assume that gendered identity formation hinges on early relational experiences with women, particularly the mother-daughter relationship. Chodorow's thesis, that women seek to recreate this relationship through their relations with women, might loosely be read as an explanation for the continuation of these relationships, as might Benjamin's thesis that the recognition of the self and other is a necessary constituent of individual development. Gilligan, Belenkey and Tannen's work also hinges on the importance of women's relational capacities and the on-going development of women's morality and capacity for knowledge and communication.

It is reasonable to assume that there is less of an impetus for radical feminist theorists to explain the maintenance of women's friendships, as friendships signify women's unique ability to form connections and attachments with other women. But even radical feminist theorists have recognised the value of social conditioning and social conditions in the maintenance of women's friendships. Rich suggests that the social institutionalisation of compulsory heterosexuality makes lesbian possibilities, including women's friendships, difficult. Raymond's account of women's friendships considers the importance of particular social institutions, such as the convents of Beguines nuns in the thirteenth century, the Chinese marriage registers of the rural Kwangtung region in the late-nineteenth and early-twentieth centuries, and present day religious convents, in maintaining friendships. And while she contends that these institutions have been historically supportive, they must be considered in relation to their larger context. The Beguine movement existed within the exclusively male-governed papacy, as do present day religious convents. Chinese marriage registers existed within the highly regarded institution of heterosexual marriage.[15]

Presumably in social and cultural explanations, the conditions that facilitate the formation of women's friendships maintain them by remaining in stasis. For example, women's close friendships with other women are possible as long as strict gender role differentiation is the norm, as long as women's homosocial networks are acceptable and criticisms of other women are actively discouraged. But these conditions are inadequate in explaining why changes might occur.

Breaking Friendships: Thoughts and Theories On The Demise of Women's Friendships

For psychosexual theorists, the demise of these relations can be explained by inchoate development, resulting in fragile attachments. The highly individualistic character of this explanation ultimately places the burden of responsibility on individual women and less so on the social and material conditions that shape their lives.[16] It also assumes that while women are directly accountable for their individual development, they do not play an active role in determining the social and material conditions of their lives.

Ironically, radical feminist theorists explain demise in women's friendships by side-stepping their unfailing conviction in an essential nature for women. Radical feminist theories of women's friendships often look instead to social and cultural explanations to explain the demise of women's friendships. The most prevalent explanation is homophobia, termed "compulsory heterosexuality" by Rich and "hetero-reality" by Raymond. Assuming her more recognisable radical feminist stance, Jeffreys makes the unsubstantiated claim that women's friendship relations have been historically undermined because of a distinct possibility that a strong female network could bond against men (1985: 103). Jeffreys also situates blame for the demise in women's historical, romantic friendships with women reformers, in particular Stella Browne and Marie Stopes. She condemns Browne and Stopes for having "promoted an idea of heterosexual love which fitted with sexological prescriptions" and for having "expressed anxieties about lesbianism" (Jeffreys, 1985: 115). Radical feminist theorists are to be credited with bringing to the forefront the reality that some relationships, in particular, heterosexual familial relations, accrue more status and privilege than others. And they are also to be credited with exposing homophobia as a contributing factor in the demise of women's friendships. Consider this specific Canadian example, of which there are, no doubt, many more:

> In a small village in Quebec in the 1880s a teacher named Elizabeth Hebert was persecuted because of her intimate friendship with an older woman in the community; she lost her position as a result, but was 'exonerated' in the hearing that the Quebec Department of Public Instruction held at her request (Prentice *et al.*, 1988: 151).

The contradiction in the simultaneous assertion of an essential basis in the formation of women's friendships, and the omission of it in explaining their demise, is a glaring inconsistency in radical feminist theories.

It seems rational to surmise that changes over time in cultural and social conditions explain the demise of these relations in socio-cultural approaches. While this hypothesis perhaps holds validity, considerations of the demise of women's friendships with women are no doubt more complex. Feminist theorists, particularly those from a socio-cultural perspective, give extensive consideration to the role that late-nineteenth-century and early-twentieth-century sexologists played in the demise of friendships between and among women. In particular, they consider the influence of Sigmund Freud, Richard von Krafft-Ebing and Havelock Ellis to be key determinants in the demise of women's romantic friendships. In the context of middle-class, heterosexual society, these sexologists viewed women's sexuality as entirely dependent on men's sexuality (Segal, 1994: 76) and viewed women's intense ties with other women as a prelude to assumed full heterosexual maturity. Social and cultural explanations for the demise in women's romantic friendships hold these sexologists accountable for arousing a cloud of suspicion over women's friendships with women.

However, the influence of the nineteenth-century sexologists should not be considered straightforward. Their influence may in fact have been confined to professional circles and may not have been widespread until after the demise of women's romantic friendships had already begun.[17] In considering the demise of women's historical and romantic friendships and the relative neglect of these relationships, not enough attention has yet been paid to factors outside of the influence of sexologists. More extensive consideration needs to be given to the effects of other intimate relations on women's friendships, including the hegemonic paradigm of the heterosexual family.

In a context where romantic love between members of the opposite sex was institutionalised and legal marriage and reproduction were their most desirable outcomes, the possibilities of a fluidity of relations between family and friends needs more thorough consideration. Further to this, Nancy Fraser and Linda Gordon suggest that the liberal individualism that prevails in Western states of the nineteenth and twentieth century shapes not only economic models and relations of commerce, but it also shapes social relations (1992: 52-53). In a framework of liberal individualism, social relations, including friendships, become matters of individual 'choice' and as such, are presumed to be exempted from customary obligations, responsibilities and entitlement. Thinking along these lines renders the practices of friendship invisible. In addition to the influence of the sexologists, the exclusivity of the nuclear family and liberal individualistic thought, competing and dichotomous ideologies of autonomy and interdependence in feminist thought might also be considered. It may be the case that feminist theories, in asserting women's capacity to be autonomous and independent, simultaneously bolster women's reluctance to reveal their dependencies on others, including women friends (Hamilton, 1990: 87). The overall structure of friendships themselves might also be considered to be a direct factor in the demise of women's friendships. Iris Marion Young suggests communities—in this instance communities of friends—have the potential to be not only inclusive environments, but also exclusive environments that instigate a kind of social closure (1990: 312).[18]

Some Limitations of Feminist Theories and Models of Women's Friendships

As yet, current models and theories are inadequate in fully understanding women's friendships. Reciprocity, mutuality, trust, and understanding are all repeatedly cited in feminist scholarship as key components of women's friendships (Raymond, 1986; Hunt, 1994). There is however, a false sense of assurance in claiming the universal presence of such characteristics when meanings of reciprocity, mutuality, trust, and understanding are varied, complex, and socially and culturally contingent.

All three approaches, some to a greater extent than others, hold up women's friendships as relations *par excellence* of equality and insinuate a political potential for these relations. Assertions of women's friendships as relationships characterised by equality are problematic. Models that assert equality in friendships fail to recognise that structural differences may serve to privilege some women in friendships with more power than others, and that power in friendships does not always look like power (Phillips, 1991: 134). One of feminism's monumental contributions has been the recognition that everything is enshrouded in a power dynamic and an ensuing politic. Friendships, while they may be reciprocal, are not necessarily symmetrical. How these relations acquire a political potential is also unclear. While Raymond, in *A Passion for Friends*, envisions friendships that "invest women with personal and socioeconomic power" (1986: 9), O'Connor notes that women's friendships are typically seen as having relatively little access to power (1992: 35). By and large, these models of women's friendships do not reconcile their inexplicable public potential with the often private nature of these relationships. Finally, these models are further limited by the fact that the processes by which women's friendships are to reach their political potential are not made explicit. Suggestions that women's friendships serve as a model for all other personal and intimate relations are vague (Hite, 1994). It is not clear which aspects of women's friendships are expected to translate to other forms of relationships and how this might be achieved.

Examinations of these relations are methodologically complex and difficult, and future considerations of women's friendships with women must engage not only with questions about the content of these relationships, but also with questions about methodological approaches. The most complete theoretical considerations of the formation, maintenance, and demise of women's friendships will likely emerge from some combination of perspectives, from the discernment of theoretical models with the richness of ethnographic details and from a variety of methodological approaches that consider the wider social, cultural, economic, and geographic contexts in which women's friendships with women exist.[19] The range of variations in, understandings of, and conduct in women's friendships must consider the significance of factors such as sexual preference, marital status, life stage, class, age, culture, race, ethnic background, immigration history and experiences, presence and ages of children, geographic region, and/or educational level, to women's friendships and the social construction of these factors, as similarities and differences among women.

THE IMPORTANCE OF THEORIES OF WOMEN'S FRIENDSHIPS WITH WOMEN FOR FEMINIST THOUGHT

Despite a rather slow integration of existent bodies of work that consider women's friendships there are a number of reasons why women's friendships with other women should prevail as a topic of inquiry and importance in feminist theory. First, there are claims that we are currently undergoing a period of alterations to, and modifications of, personal relationships including friendships. These are not merely alarmist cries from the traditionalists that feminists have become accustomed to rebutting. Rather they signify a recognition of change by those without an explicitly overt, traditionalist agenda.

Anthony Giddens, in *The Transformation of Intimacy*, contends that a transformation of intimacy is indicated by a move away from traditionally conceptualised relationships, like family, and toward relationships which are, at their very essence, voluntary. He refers to these emerging relationships as "pure relationships":

> a social relationship entered into for its own sake, for what can be derived by each person from a sustained association with another, and which is continued only in so far as it is thought by both parties to deliver enough satisfaction to stay in it (1992: 58).

Shere Hite suggests in her report on contemporary families that the current period is one in which understandings of family, love and friendship are being questioned, negotiated, and redefined (1994: 371).

If such a transformation is indeed underway, the role of women's friendships with women merits closer scrutiny.

The central contradiction of such a democratisation of relationships is that as voluntary as these relationships appear, they are often based on commitment and thus entail some sense of obligation. In addition, both Giddens and Hite risk romanticising the ability of individuals to determine the conditions of their associations. Not all individuals have the power necessary to untangle themselves from undesirable relationships. Nor do all individuals have the power to establish and maintain satisfactory relationships. While the maintenance and intensity of relations may be freely chosen by some, others, due to a host of factors such as poverty and history, cannot choose physical and/or emotional distance.

The problem with the notion of a move from family to the pure relationship is that on the one hand, it ignores the ways in which family relations are privileged over friendships, and on the other hand, it assumes the psychic structures built around family relations can be easily broken down and replaced by relationships of free association and affect—relationships that lack similar kinds of institutional support and reinforcement. Giddens and Hite also romanticise the existence of equality and open channels of communication between and among relations, in particular among friends. Nevertheless their proposals hold an appeal for feminist scholarship because they authenticate the plurality of relationships that have long been attested to, and demonstrated in, feminist scholarship. They also invite serious consideration of relationships beyond the already heavily researched nuclear family and add support to the view that a clearer, more precise understanding of the complexities of women's friendships with women enhances an understanding of these relations as constituent components of the broader concepts of kin and community.

Second, women's friendship relations should remain a topic of inquiry for feminist thought because traditionalist forces, including neoliberal governments, have already involved friendship relations in social policy decisions, particularly around care-giving. This is the case in Canada and Great Britain, as psychological, emotional and material well-being increasingly becomes the responsibility of the individual and not the state.[20] General scholarly neglect of the experiences of women's contemporary friendships has resulted in relatively little available information about the capacities and resilience of friendships in the face of such demands. More explicit attention to the material conditions of friendship relations would ensure that social policies are solidly based in actual experiences of friendships, rather than in lofty, ideological expectations often driven by market forces.[21] If there is a trend toward a democratisation of relationships and if, as research suggests, familial relations do not necessarily constitute bases of support and access to material resources (Finch, 1989: 7) such as child care and employment, then understandings of friendships, and in particular women's friendships, have wide-reaching implications for the role of personal relationships in social policies.

Lastly, as work in feminist thought on the topic of women's friendships clearly demonstrates, both in their historical and contemporary contexts, women's friendships with women remain important relationships in the lives of women. For this reason alone, women's friendships deserve full, theoretical consideration.

Notes

1. For some feminist examinations of women and family relations, see Barrett and McIntosh (1982); Eichler (1983); Anderson *et al.* (1988); Finch (1989); Finch and Mason (1993).

2. In history, see Smith-Rosenberg (1975) and Donoghue (1993). In sociology, see Rubin (1985) and Oliker (1989). In philosophy, see Raymond (1986) and Friedman (1993). In literature, see Faderman (1981). In psychology, see Fehr (1996) and Blieszner and Adams (1992). In liberation theology, see Hunt (1994). O'Connor's (1992) *Friendships Between Women* attempts to bring some of these works together. Her primary emphasis is on consideration of women's friendships from the disciplines of psychology, social psychology and sociology.

3. See Side (1997).

4. While there is a body of scholarship that considers women's cross-sex friendships, I do not consider it here.

5. The term Boston marriage was popularised in New England to describe the relationship between two women who lived together. Women in Boston marriages tended to enjoy a degree of financial independence, either through inheritance or as an pioneer in the professions, that gave them the option of residing with another woman instead of being financially dependent on a man. Boston marriages were assumed to be asexual, the name conveying their puritanical nature (Rothblum and Brehony, 1993).

6. These texts, specifically concerned with documenting particular dyadic friendships, are not considered here.

7. Further to positing how women differentially acquire knowledge, Belenky *et al.* (1986) suggest that the failure of present systems of education to acknowledge women's 'ways of knowing' leaves women disadvantaged.

8. For examples of these critiques, see Broughton (1983) and Benhabib (1987).

9. On the issue of essentialism in feminist theory, see *Differences: A Journal of Feminist Cultural Studies* 1, no. 2 (1989). This issue is devoted to the theme "The Essential Difference: Another Look at Essentialism".

10. Rich's continuum of women's relationships with women answers Smith-Rosenberg's indirect call for one in "The Female World of Love and Ritual". Smith-Rosenberg states, "I would further suggest that rather than seeing a gulf between the normal and the abnormal we view sexual and emotional impulses a part of a continuum or spectrum of gradations strongly affected by cultural norms and arrangements, a continuum influenced in part by observed and thus learned behaviour" (1975: 28).

11. Prentice *et al.* rightly point out that this emphasis on women's 'difference' has served as a major intellectual justification of study and research focussing on women (1988: 359).

12. These have been criticisms of Rich's lesbian continuum (see Thompson, 1981). Thompson also criticises Rich's "Compulsory Heterosexuality" for its monolithic portrayal of the social world and for its assumed connection between lesbianism and feminism.

13. Unclear language and meaning have more often been associated with the radical feminist writer Mary Daly. On the topic of women's friendships, Daly says women's friendships are important for "[w]eaving a context in which women can realise our self-transforming, metapatterning in Being" (1984: 374). Both Raymond and Daly rely extensively on Daly's work but neither offers clarification of its meanings. For example, Hunt's key concept of 'justice' is explained only as "a fundamental relational goal that stems from communities of accountability where change takes place" (1994: 21).

14. While Jeffreys is more commonly associated with a radical feminist perspective, the explanations she offers in *The Spinster and Her Enemies* (1985) for the formation of women's friendships, are primarily social explanations.

15. It is an interesting point to note that Daly, Raymond and Hunt share an involvement in women's religious communities and all of them credit this environment for informing their radical feminist insights into women's friendships.

16. There is a tendency in some psychosexual literature to blame mothers for their mothering. Rosenzweig suggests that blaming mothers is not new to the twentieth century, but is a continuation of the nineteenth-century

trend "emphasising the importance of moral motherhood" (1993: 2). For examples of this trend in contemporary feminist scholarship, see Friday (1977) and Arcana (1979).

17. I am in debt to Lesley A. Hall for this comment during a discussion of these ideas at the Celebrating Women's Friendship conference, April 1995, at the University of York, York, UK.

18. For additional consideration of the relationship, and the lack of one, between community and feminism, see Elshtain (1982) and Zagarell (1988).

19. I would suggest that some of the most insightful work to date can be found in ethnographic accounts of women's friendships. Ethnographic accounts of women's friendships make evident the processes of women's friendships and situate these relations contextually. They account for variables such as individual personalities and make explicit women's agency. Stack's work, *All Our Kin*, is as yet unparalleled in this regard (1975). By tracing patterns of reciprocity and cooperation, and the daily exchange of goods and services, Stack demonstrates the ways that friendship relations in an urban Black community generate instrumental relations of economic survival. Her analysis cannot be read separately from the systemic racism and the conditions of extreme poverty that exist for her subjects. In this regard, her work is important for situating women's friendships in the context of the circumstances and relationships around them and for noting the ways that cooperation between family and friends contradict and mutually reinforce one another.

20. In both of these examples one could argue that ideologies of motherhood have been used to justify women's role in community care. In Great Britain, the Invalid Care Allowance compensates individuals for lost wages due to full-time care-giving responsibilities. Friends, as well as family members of an invalid, are eligible for this compensation, although it is a paltry amount (Groves and Finch, 1983). For Canadian examples, particularly from the province of Ontario, see Side (1996).

21. The impetus is not concern with adequate care and expanding the parameters of community, but instead is economic and political. Changes are concerned with the politics of reducing wealth distribution by

delimiting the state's role in the care of individuals. They are also, as I have suggested, inextricably linked to ideological assumptions about women as nurturers and 'natural' care givers. See Side (1999).

Katherine Side is an assistant professor in the Department of Women's Studies at Mount Saint Vincent University, in Halifax, Nova Scotia, Canada. She has completed a MA in Women's Studies (University of Kent at Canterbury) and a PhD in Women's Studies (York University, Canada). Her dissertation was titled *In the Shadow of the Family: Women's Friendships with Women*.

Sisterhood: Part of the Pretend Family?[1]

Laura Potts

"Boon companion . . . a compassionate blessing" (Mary Daly, 1988).

A note on the writing of this:

What I write here started as a spoken and more interactive narrative; in transposing it to this traditional and bounded academic context, I have tried to keep the text open to all sorts of possible paths of thinking and experiences. Just as when we speak with others, or when we allow the mind to wander around a subject, many tangentially related associations arise, so I have tried to keep a liveliness in this writing and to follow the variety of relevant strands, and, I hope, to leave space for the reader to enjoy her own routes and reflections too. As Irigaray has said in *When Our Lips Speak Together*, "Why only one song, one discourse, one text at a time?" (Irigaray, 1980). The truths about women's close friendships are more likely to be revealed by this "complexity of versions" (Stanley, 1992a). So this is a personal, a subjective, and, inevitably a partial—in both senses of the word—account; a non-unified vision, with no pretensions to be definitive or even complete. It is both passionate and polemical, for friendships with other women matter centrally to me, both personally and politically. In particular, it is concerned with trying to MAKE SENSE for myself of the history of my friendships and of their current reality, and to investigate whether there is a/any shared sense of friendship between feminists, and between lesbian-feminists in particular.

"Elemental Feminist Philosophy: a form of being/thinking that is rooted in Metapatriarchal consciousness; reason rooted in instinct, intuition, passion ... the philosophy of Wonderlusters returning to the Original Questions of childhood" (Daly, 1988).

I start from three losses. Three experiences, occurring in the same year, prompted my thinking, driving a need to understand what had happened and how I felt. The death of a best friend, a 'sister', revealed doubts about there being any feminist consensus on the role of friendships between women and how they stand in relation to kin and kinship. Her life had been a vivid realisation of her belief in the primacy of friendship, a sure and joyful commitment despite the difficulties always inherent in living against the dominant norms. Secondly, the loss of a best friend to a heterosexual partnership and new-motherhood, with an emerging emphasis on ties of kin and blood, and the re-instatement of her parents as central in her relationships, made me wonder whether biology is the supreme determinant of our most significant connections after all. Certainly this new patterning seemed to bring her a calmer satisfaction than the years of 'woman-centred' living. And then the disappearance of another best friend, an ex-lover, to immersion in a new relationship, raised questions about why a number of women are now retreating from the multiplicity of webs of friendship into coupled-hood, into intimate dyads. These are familiar tales: many women tell of similar experiences. Are my concerns shared concerns?

Meanwhile ... I also want to identify the positive features of friendship, not to construct what my friend Polly was concerned would become a *Guardian*-esque lament for a vanished, golden communitarian idyll. The losses are swallowed, gripe and grind in the belly, gradually are soothed; other friendships, newly savoured or established favourites, sustain and please, are consistent nourishment.

Making sense might start from clarity about terms, from identifying what Weedon calls "moments of signification" (Weedon, 1996). What is friendship, anyway? What are its meanings? What is it to be sisters—but not blood-sisters? What are the features and functions of sisterhood?

> Construct your own pictures and stories in the silences falling in the socio-psychological theories of friendship and kinship.

Much of the mainstream research on friendship (notably the work of Duck, 1988 and 1991; Jerome, 1984) lays emphasis on the individual, affective, relational states by which friendship may be recognised. The necessity of locating relationships in social structures is acknowledged by Allan (1989), and this work yields a useful focus for a consideration of the role friendships have in the context of women's lives, which O'Connor (1992) develops. Friendship, then, is contextually framed by the meanings which inhere in our lives; it both reflects and informs the social conventions within the culture to which we belong.

The variety and pluralism of the location of friendship in women's lived experience tend, inevitably, to be subsumed by the dominant societal norms, precluding any authentic sense of women's friendships. Thus there are few reference points for a reliable mapping of the reality of relationships between women other than those framed by discourses of love-and-romance, sex-and-passion, wife-and-mother heterosexuality, and partnerships determined by these forms. Insofar, however, as all relationships are characterised by social organisation (Allan, 1989), and by the ideologies informing those modes of organisation, other perspectives must necessarily be possible. The anthropologist Brain (1977), for instance, tells different stories; of societies where the best friend is the chief mourner, where friends are central and permanent to social structures and are established as such by ritual; and where the sanctions against the betrayal of a friend are more powerful than against the betrayal of kin.

In trying to make sense of my own stories, and those of women I relate to most closely, feminism has, over the years, usefully provided ways of understanding and interpreting experience, providing an alternative set of meanings and establishing a political re-vision of values and beliefs. So I looked to the ideologies and discourses within feminism(s) to reveal an understanding of women's different lives and experiences, our friendships, which is obscured in the psycho-social canon. Allan (1989) identified the notion of 'personal space', a co-efficient of material and social space, which has a determining impact on the making, maintaining, and breaking of friendships. Feminism as theory and activism, is, however, about pushing back the boundaries of personal space, and about challenging the contextual constraints on our lives, both individually and collectively. Feminism is about wanting it to be different; having a different version of what that personal space might be like, and so expanding the potential for friendships beyond the established boundaries. And so, as Benhabib and Cornwell (1987) state, while feminists, like communitarians, acknowledge "the situatedness of the disembedded self in a network of relations and narratives", the "renegotiation of our psychosexual identities" is regarded as essential. Evidently, that process cannot be solely an individualistic and private undertaking; it must involve the refiguring of our psychosexual identities in relation to each other, and demands, therefore, shifts in what are accepted as social and cultural norms. Allan (1989: 104) states authoritatively that these are the agreed rules for friendship: there is little expectation "that friends will disrupt their own domestic organisation: family comes before friends; and friends are not expected to travel long distances to care" ... and so on. "Friendship is recognised by all as secondary and having no established claim over resources" he states (105)—but it just isn't like that for many feminists! Somehow that 'all' doesn't include feminist lived experience.

O'Connor (1992) emphasises the identification of a related set of rules and norms for roles within friendships between women, and the conformity to these that is demanded: the reciprocation of intimacy and confidences, and an actively mutual loyalty and trust are required, while competitiveness is outlawed. The extent of any articulated consensus on such 'rules' is often, I would judge, pretty minimal; each of us could probably make her own list of expectations of required behaviour between friends. And while an often cited distinction between friendship and kinship is said to be the voluntary nature of friendship (Duck, 1991; Allan, 1989), the distress and resentment provoked when these implicit rules/norms/expectations are broken or defied, and, indeed their very existence, have to cast doubt on the validity of such a distinction anyway. (While the very fact that we can speak of 'the breakdown of the family'—let's celebrate it!—implies its status is not that of a given, 'natural' order, but as voluntarily constructed as any other social relationship.) Raymond recognises that "as any cultural tradition cannot be assimilated by a simple and unilinear idea of civilisation, neither can the culture of female friendship be absorbed by more catholic ideas of friendship in general. The culture of female friendship has a distinctive purpose, passion and politics" (Raymond, 1986: 38).

Friendship is also conventionally characterised by the lack of any institutionalised forms or functions of the sort that identify kinship and partnership/marriage—and not just in straight society either.

> Two friends of mine, a lesbian couple (their definition), held a party to celebrate ten years of their relationship, as partners, lovers—a public event for 'family and friends' with elements of ceremony and ritual, and so in many ways not dissimilar from such social markers in the straight world.
>
> Where are the parties to celebrate our friendships? Perhaps lurking behind the socially acceptable fronts of birthdays or re-unions, but seldom explicitly manifested.

There are no established conventions for losing a friend, as there are for the break-up of a partnership, and, according to Orbach and Eichenbaum (1994) neither is there much language which readily accounts for or explains (makes sense of) what is experienced. Convention is wary of the bonds of non-romantic, non-sexual love, with, perhaps, the exception of the classical Greek and Judaeo-Christian tradition, and even then, when loyalty is prized, it is only as a male attribute. Mary Daly's *Wickedary* again: "brotherhood: transitory and shallow substitute for friendship; condition dependent upon emergencies, violence, and the existence of The Enemy; male merging in the communal 'ecstasy' of self-loss; bonding of those who are mal-functioning/ male-functioning as cells in a military organism: necrophiliac comradeship" (Daly, 1988). O'Connor (1992) has demonstrated how in industrialised western societies friendship is essentially regarded as private, and the characteristic rituals of gift exchange are personal and private too:

> I think of the detail and content of my friendships: sharing pots of tea or bottles of wine, ideas, meals, phone calls, hugs, comfort; lending books, ears, crayons, shoulders ...

But feminist ideologies have asserted a more public and valid space for women's friendships and perhaps, as Flax (1987) claims contentiously, even made them possible in a newly legitimated sense.

> From my late teens to my 'discovery' of feminism, I was one-of-the-lads; my old friends were lost to boyfriends so I took a desexualised route into the male world too, discussing Marxism to a background of esoteric modern bands, and relying on a self-punishing Christianity as a repository of emotion. My re-connection to women came through feminist activism and through lesbian-feminist thinking and living. Coming home.

The primacy in social structuring which feminism grants friendships between women is one way, among many, of challenging the dominant patriarchal modes of relating and the centrality of family; importantly, too, it poses a direct challenge to the dichotomous separation of what is conventionally regarded as public and what should be kept private. Raymond claims that "female friendship can give back the right of primogeniture to women by establishing a firstness among our Selves" (Raymond, 1986: 39). This is her vision of Gyn/affection, and certainly within the personal sphere a reordering of our relationships is possible, and brings a different sense of relation to self too; friendships between feminists may be both personal and collective consciousness-raising. But within the public sphere, the persisting dominant values and social structures refuse to yield.

After Carol died I became anxious: had there been any broader consensus on what friendship meant within feminism? Was I making inappropriate and inaccurate assumptions about other women's ideas for living? And while that insecurity was greatly eased by the sense of a net-work, a sisterhood of those of us who were her friends, other reactions provoked a strong sense of being on the outside of what were in any way acceptable social norms. Back at work after Carol's death, a colleague asked where I'd been that she hadn't seen me for a while. "I told her why I'd been away from work—that one of my best friends had died very suddenly and I'd taken time out to help organise her funeral ... 'How awful!' she replied, 'Did she have any family?' I was suddenly furious, wanted to yell 'Yes! Me! Us!' but talked instead of her specially loved daughter and new grandson, how dear they were" (Potts, 1993: 35).

The friendship was suddenly public in a different context, and had different meanings ascribed to it; my meanings, and the meanings we had shared, seemed suddenly insecure. The meaning was reaffirmed by being part of a larger network of Carol's friends with something of a shared vision of the primacy of friendship—but not every woman is that fortunate. At the 'Celebrating Women's Friendship' conference at York University (April 1995), when I first presented this work, a woman came and told me afterwards how much it had meant to her to have the death of her best friend some long years ago at last recognised; she had never had her grief validated in any way before. O'Connor (1992) speaks of friendship "weaving a world of meaning and value"; the loss of a particular friendship, and that shared world-sense, can mean a corresponding loss of meaning and value, a precarious inner state.

What, then, of the other losses? There is a tone of dis-affection and disillusionment in the movement of women away from a complex multiplicity of friendships, or from location of other women at the centre of their lives, and into conventional dyads and blood-defined relationships. It is often said—yelled—friend to friend, between women, that we have had 'too high expectations', the implicit assumption being that to choose a different 'reality', to modify our needs, hopes or expectations would be more acceptable, more mature and well-balanced. It is, as O'Connor (1992: 182) claims, usually "commitment and the realistic limits of it" which mark the 'point of tension' in women's friendships. Raymond, however, states that the falling away from other women's friendship is the result of not having a realistic picture of 'Gyn/affection', of being too sentimental in our idealism of friendship: hence the feelings of betrayal, and of the dis-affection which, she claims, "produces a nihilistic attitude toward feminism and female friendship" (Raymond, 1986: 198). But what shapes and informs these expectations? Other features of friendship identified in the socio-psychological literature may help to shed light on this.

Friendship is said to involve similarity and identification with other(s), the sharing of beliefs, attitudes and values, "to cement a world view, to support the sharing of meaning structures" (Allan, 1989: 61). 'Sisterhood', in the feminist sense, has implied this too. In a discrete and compounding sense, shared feminism may be a common identifying feature, a shared identity, creating its own particular tensions within Sisterhood and between friends.

What, anyway, is this 'we' of whom I speak here? of whom others write and speak? what assumptions do we all make, and on what

> grounds? This is ill-defined in any of the literature I have read for this work. Academically, it is often an authority to hide behind, and an assumption of consensus. Socially, in common usage, it makes a statement about the inclusive/exclusive status of speakers and hearers. In the English language(s) this is implied rather than explicit in reference. Living in the Philippines briefly, I tried to learn Waray-Waray, the language of the island where I was based; one of its delights and complications for me was that there are numerous different words for 'we' which make clear who is being included by the pronoun. Is it possible to redeem ourselves (we: those of you who might agree with me on this) from the ambiguity of we-ness, particularly in the context of our personal relationships?—such as one partner's use of 'we' which invisibly and inappropriately subsumes the other. Family says this is us, we are we, we are a discrete homogeneous entity, we are not them, out there.

The challenge is, as Haraway says, "to craft a poetic/political unity without relying on a logic of appropriation, incorporation and taxonomic identification" (Haraway, 1990: 198). It seems to be this implicitly necessary invisibility of the self, the differentiated self, which makes some women reluctant to be part of a 'Sisterhood'. Nonetheless it remains true that 'real' or 'true' friends are marked by symbolic kinship terms: "she's like a real sister to me" (Allan, 1989: 115). Perhaps this affective component is as implicated in feminism's adoption of the term 'Sisterhood' as the historical antecedents from socialist, communitarian and civil rights movements, and may provide some answer to Anne Ackeroyd's open question at the 'Celebrating Women's Friendship' conference: why has the term 'sisterhood' been claimed by feminists anyway? And this lived reality of women's friendships which stakes out what is recognisably familial territory—of connection, shared identity, jealousies and rivalries, love and loyalty—belies the rather dismissive label O'Connor (1992) applies to close bonds—"fictive kin", with its prefiguring of Tory spleen in the 1980s against the 'pretend' families of lesbians and gay men—and against the patriarchal social models which dominate.

hooks writes of a suppressive model of Sisterhood which excludes other non-identified women, based in racism, classism, and sexism, a "bondedness of shared victimisation" and the obscuring of difference (hooks, 1984: 45). Lorde writes of the "pretence to a homogeneity of experience covered by the word sisterhood which does not in fact exist" (Lorde, 1984). Orbach and Eichenbaum (1994) write of the suppression of individual identities within women's relationships, of the loss of the self. In political terms, then, there is a failure to recognise difference; in psychological terms there is a failure to recognise the 'differentiated self'. As Young has written, in the context of her ideas about the communitarian ideal, "the desire for unity in discourse generates borders, dichotomies and exclusions" (Young, 1990: 301); the desire for mutual identification in social relations generates exclusions in a similar way. And while, as O'Connor claims, "the process of creating, maintaining and terminating friendships is about making individual identity within a social and cultural reality" (O'Connor, 1992: 177), it seems often to be the case that a mutual or a shared identity is also being constructed. And if a dimension of that social reality is feminism, with its own ethos of shared identity and commonality, then it is perhaps not surprising that confusion about the locus of individual identity may be felt. The social reality shapes the friendship(s) and the friendship(s) shape the social reality.

Just as in a political context feminism has to struggle to accommodate difference, so in friendships it is often hard to allow the other to be different or to change. This generates the resentment, the "envy and competition" in the title of Orbach and Eichenbaum's book.

> I remember my confused fury when my best friend Edith chose the same nightdress as me from Marks and Spencer. I was probably around thirteen, so she would have been eleven years old. I wanted her to be the same as me; in fact one of the defining emphases of our friendship was how we had to like the same and do the same—and as the older and more powerful, I exerted a lot of pressure to control for these characteristics.
>
> to like
> to be liked
> my friends must be like
> I must be like them
>
> But this time I also wanted to have (be) something unique and different. Probably I would have been equally confused and furious if she had, alternatively, chosen a different nightdress from mine!
>
> As my friend Elspeth Owen (1993) points out in her work about her relationship with her blood-sister, *Between Me and My Sister*, the word 'between' has two quite distinct and utterly opposed meanings: an expression both of what is shared and what divides. Is the title of Orbach and Eichenbaum's book on women's friendships, *Between Women*, consciously chosen to reflect this irony?

Both Flax and Orbach offer explanations from psychoanalytical theory for these tensions and difficulties in women's close relationships, citing "the character of mother-daughter relationships" (Flax, 1987) in particular. From the recognition of gender-sameness with the mother, the daughter comes to experience the tension between the urge to stay merged and the urge to separate; thus the sense of self and of self-identity is both given and threatened in relationships with other women. "Women seek support, love and acceptance from one another. At the same time they anticipate restriction and rejection" (Orbach and Eichenbaum, 1994: 128). While the theory is predicated on assumptions which imply a universality of experience, and confirm a heterosexual norm which pertains ideologically but not necessarily, there are pertinent insights to be gleaned from this thinking, which contribute to the making-sense of our friendships.

Flax (1987) claims that "our sense of self is bound up with other women in an intensity and depth simply not present in relations with men." The two unreconciled desires in women's relations with women are for nurturance and autonomy; she identifies these 'psychic roots' as source of women's expectations of the 'women's liberation movement'/feminist relations, and of the "anxiety, (the) competition, and (the) unmet needs" which arise. So perhaps retreats into exclusive we-ness (us not them) can be explained, in part, as falling away from the precarious balancing of the need for nurturance and the need for autonomy; a tilt towards having the former fulfilled if at the expense of the latter (which may perhaps be sought in work, or other aspects of life). Dominant lesbian culture certainly sanctions, and socially legitimises dyadic, coupled relations, a public and a private merging of selves: the 'fusion theme' which Krieger discusses (Krieger, 1982). Heterosexual dyads, and the ideological culture which sustains them, support a duality of different worlds, on an emotional/psychological level, and so perhaps are seen to offer relief from the precarious balancing act for women (ex?-lesbians) weary of trying to assert their autonomy—a vanishing into sameness. Similarly, Orbach and Eichenbaum (1994: 152) claim it "is possible to see the re-assertion of the priority of the couple relationship as a retreat from the difficulties encountered in women's relationships"—another kind of vanishing which "appears to provide the women with the sense of differentiation and separateness that she seeks" (153). A lean in either direction, a re-positioning, ideologically necessitates a withdrawal from the difficulties of sustaining complex close friendship with other women.

Different discourses, however, yield different and equally convincing arguments. Coward (1992) suggests that women's exhaustion with struggles of feminism helps explain the shift towards compromise, complicity and collusion with 'the enemy' which she has noted. Certainly it is hard to find, create and to live new ways of emotional bonding

> not bondage
> the making of bonds which do not bind

to permit changes in personal relationships and changes in social organisation. Weariness with trying to realise those basic premises of feminism is well documented then, but there is little that offers guidance on how to acquire better balancing acts.

The 1990s are very much a time of individual solutions. The need to assert a differentiated self is a dominant value—a post-modern notion of multiplicity overlaid with prevailing taints of liberal humanism! Conversely, there is little validation of difference or diversity in the public sphere; individualism does not necessarily only flourish within a context of the celebration of difference, as Douglas states (in Beattie,

1993). Crucially, then, must the development of individuated selves mean a fragmentation into individualism? Must the recognition of difference invoke an infinite dis-location of differentiation? As Haraway says "in the consciousness of our failures we risk lapsing into boundless difference and giving up on the confusing task of making partial, real connection" (Haraway, 1990: 202). In the context of relations with other women, then, we risk losing the potential for the delights and joys and discoveries of friendships by moving into other, more exclusive sites of prime relational focus. The challenge is to find ways of being connected while remaining distinctive, discrete individuals, to be together and yet to be separate. hooks (1984) says we need to acknowledge that we are divided in order to build solidarity; Orbach and Eichenbaum (1994) urge the necessity of forming "separated attachments". It is, I believe, this recognition of difference within unity which tempers the tendency to fascism which Young (1990) sees in the assertions of communality, and the blind gloss of homogeneity which Lorde (1984) identifies. Haraway urges "recognition of another response through coalition—affinity, not identity", and of being "committed to building a political form that actually manages to hold together witches, engineers, elders, perverts, Christians, mothers and Leninists long enough to disarm the state" (Haraway, 1990: 197).

Eventually, as Milner says "one must find and face the 'other' in oneself, rather than in other people" (Milner, 1986: 210); so too, I think, we have to face the sameness in ourselves, rather than in another. This demands a letting go of the pervasive fiction of fusion, of two-in-oneness, that determines a norm of couple relations. Perhaps this can usefully be informed by returning to the family, pretend or otherwise. For good family relations recognise kinship, a belonging, while also legitimating the individuals; and this, then, is my enduring picture of sisterhood, of sisterly relations between women and of the many good friendships I enjoy. Hawkes, writing of Woolf's *Three Guineas* tells us how "Women had taught [Woolf] to believe in herself, to say 'I am I ... ' . Her connections to literary sisters and to her women friends thus gave her the basis for her developed aesthetic and political beliefs. Her psychological need to discover 'Who am I' was answered by these women. And then she turned her answer—the reciprocal relation between the self and the other to be found in women's sympathy—into a political stand. If women can say 'I am I', they can also say 'We are we'" (Hawkes, 1987: 57).

Raymond (1986) recommends "thoughtful passion" in friendships, in order to ensure that the friend does not lose her Self in attachment to the other woman. Way back in 1978, Daly claimed that it is "the ability to self-center that generated and re-inforced women's ability to spark, that is, how to bond with other women" (Daly, 1978). That spark is not extinguished, is kindled into glorious flames by many women; as Yorke writes, "we still have a political need to sustain and celebrate the woman-to-woman bond as between one subject and another subject, rather than conceding anything to the subject-object model typical of heterosexual patriarchy" (Yorke, 1994: 72). It is politically important, as she says, and invokes the "necessity of making this commitment to mutuality and equality—and creating a political and cultural context where such a relation may have a chance of being realised"; the shaping of our worlds in the image of our selves. While she identifies the role of desire in poetics as the ideal language for this task, I think our lived tales and pictures of women's friendship could as well serve this purpose, a re-visioning of social relations in the celebration of networks and connections and the primacy of women's lives together. A different story needs to be told, otherwise there is only the choice of a loneliness or a partnership with one other (just like only being allowed to have one best friend at a time at school).

Milner also writes of the "psychological necessity" to find our "own pantheon of vital images, a mythology of one's own, not the reach-me-down mass-produced mythology of Hollywood, of newspapers, which are the propaganda of dictators" (Milner, 1986: 232). This, she claims, can be set against the lust for security and submission, the getting lost in another. According to Jung, whom she quotes, the mythological image has the capacity to reconcile idea with feeling: thus the lusty passions of Daly's *Wickedary* may both entertain and inspire in the re-forming of thought and vision. So, perhaps the emphasis of this work needs to shift now, to find other paths through tale-telling and song-singing, and awareness of the Crone: the "Great Hag of History who has Dis-covered depths of Courage, Strength and Wisdom in her Self" (Daly, 1988). I need a mythology of how to live differently—just as there *are* women whose lives inspire me and from whom I learn.

Note

1. With thanks to Pat Spallone, who inspired and encouraged me, and helped shape this.

Laura Potts enjoys her women friends' company for good talking and walking, plotting and dreaming, eating and hanging out, at home and away, as well as more solitary preoccupations with writing, gardening, yoga and botanising. A dabbler in work terms too, she is currently Senior Tutor for Women's Studies at the College of Ripon and York, and has edited and co-written *Ideologies of Breast Cancer: Feminist Perspectives* (Macmillan, 1999) with a group of newly-met friends, after long years of activism and teaching around women's health issues.

"My Constant Correspondent and Friend": The Letters of Maria Edgeworth and Rachel Mordecai Lazarus, 1815-1838

Ruth A. Symes

> Ever since the year 1814 [sic] she has been my constant correspondent and friend I may truly say. I am surrounded by proofs of her kindness, proofs of her continually thinking of everything that could gratify my tastes or give pleasure to my feelings and my heart. My father thought her the most sensible and amiable of all my American friends (Edgeworthstown, 10 August 1838: 315) (Macdonald, 1977).[1]

Such was the tribute paid by the Irish educationalist and novelist Maria Edgeworth (1768-1849) on the untimely death in 1838 of a woman she had never met, her correspondent and friend of twenty-three years, the Jewish American, Rachel Mordecai Lazarus (1788-1838). The correspondence, which had begun somewhat inauspiciously with what might be termed a 'fan letter' sent by Mordecai (then a schoolteacher from Warrenton, North Carolina) to Edgeworth in 1815, had developed by the time of Mordecai's death into a rich exchange of intimacies which was evidently of great significance to both women.[2] The relationship between Mordecai and Edgeworth, developed over dozens of lengthy letters, documents the specific workings of a friendship between women of widely divergent backgrounds in the early nineteenth century. For the historian, the friendship is important for what it reveals of the factors which connected as well as those which divided the two women. I argue that a certain unifying ideal of middle-class womanhood was central to each woman's self-portrayal and hence to the survival of the friendship. How and why that ideal presented itself are questions which can help us understand the situation of women and the particular dynamics of female friendship in an earlier century. Secondly, the correspondence between Edgeworth and Mordecai, written at the height of a period of furious public debate on educational issues, focussed largely on pedagogical themes acted out in the private domestic arena. The letters illustrate the potential for female friendship to transform both the educational lives and the writing of women in this period, and also bears witness to the importance of female friendship in shaping early nineteenth-century educational discourse itself.

In the early months of the correspondence, the development of a friendship between Mordecai and Edgeworth seemed at best unlikely, and at worst riven with irreconcilable incompatibilities. Mordecai was Edgeworth's junior by twenty years. They were separated by continent, culture, and by race—Mordecai was of educated Jewish descent (a member of the only Israelite family in her area) whilst Maria Edgeworth, with her English and Irish upbringing, belonged firmly to the middling country gentry, and though remembered for her rational rather than her religious outlook, was firmly Christian. The later lives of both women continued to attest to their differences. Mordecai married, became stepmother to seven children and had four of her own, whilst Edgeworth remained single. Finally, whilst Mordecai led an obscure life and never wrote for publication, Edgeworth was a literary figure lionised in her own lifetime. Such differences in status were reflected in the style and content of the correspondence: Mordecai wrote her letters, for the most part punctually, replying with measured deference to each point raised by Edgeworth. Edgeworth, on the other hand, answered confidently and breathlessly, sometimes neglecting to respond to specific questions, and often repeating herself (Colvin, 1977: xviii).[3]

Despite early hiccups, Mordecai and Edgeworth were soon corresponding at length several times a year. It is easy to understand why Mordecai valued Edgeworth's friendship. By her own admission she was intellectually stifled by the society of North Carolina: "You inquire what kind of people our neighbours are. Very pious, charitable, kind and good, but with one or two exceptions, indifferently educated, and little improved either by reading or conversation. I esteem many but assimilate with few, and when intelligent and improving society is occasionally within our reach, we enjoy the luxury with additional zest" (Wilmington, 13 April 1828: 163). One might ask why Edgeworth, on the other hand, was so motivated to maintain her friendship with Mordecai when, as a well-known writer, she had more than enough correspondents. Christina Colvin notes that two thousand letters survive from Edgeworth to her family alone and she also wrote on and off for vast stretches of her life to many other famous literary names, for example, to the English writer Elizabeth Inchbald (1753-1821) and the Scottish writer Elizabeth Hamilton 1758-1815). Edgeworth herself commented to one of her correspondents that she "would not be at the trouble of corresponding with any, except those whom I really consider as friends" (to Etienne Dumont, 7 August 1813) (Colvin, 1977: xxviii). What then was the source of her commitment to a relationship with an obscure young American? The answer lies in the tones of the letters themselves. Alongside the potent sense of difference, there is concomitantly a real sense of intellectual affinity, of shared integrity, mutual admiration and a desire to learn each from the other. In the letters, both women seek actively to conform to a well-known contemporary stereotype of rational middle-class womanhood that rises above religious and national affiliation. This stereotype had dominated educational writing by, about, and for women in Britain, and by proxy in America, from the 1780s onwards. Edgeworth herself had helped to promulgate the idea in her writings for children. Her pleasure in the correspondence with Mordecai lay quite simply in her recognition that they shared, or aspired to share, certain qualities of 'heart and mind' which, to some extent, nullified the specific conditions of their respective backgrounds.

From the beginning of the correspondence, it was apparent that where culture might put asunder, conformity to the model of enlightened and reasonable womanhood would ultimately triumph. In her first letter to Edgeworth, Mordecai praised the older woman's educational books effusively, but criticised Edgeworth for making the Jewish character—a coachmaker (also coincidentally called Mordecai)—in her recent novel, *The Absentee* (1812), the villain of the piece:

> Relying on the good sense and candour of Miss Edgeworth I would ask, how it can be that she, who on all other subjects shows such justice and liberality, should on one alone appear biased by prejudice: should even instil that prejudice into the minds of youth! Can my allusion be mistaken? It is to the species of character which wherever a Jew is introduced is invariably attached to him. Can it be believed that this race of men are by nature mean, avaricious, and unprincipled? In those parts of the world where these people are oppressed and made continually the subject of scorn and derision, they may in many instances deserve censure; but in this happy country, where religious distinctions are scarcely known, where character and talents are all sufficient to attain advancement, we find the Jews to form a respectable part of

> the community. The penetration of Miss Edgeworth has already conjectured that it is a Jewess who addresses her (Warrenton, North Carolina, 7 August 1815: 6).

Edgeworth, suitably abashed, responded in the same measured and rational tone, promising "to make all the atonement and reparation in [her] power" and declaring that Mordecai's own letter was "the very best evidence that could have been offered of the truth of all you urge in favour of those of your own religious persuasion." In her subsequent novel, *Harrington* (1817), Edgeworth allowed the hero, despite his prejudice, to fall in love with a Jewess, Berenice Montenero.[4] This early débâcle—which turned on the differences between the two women, and was resolved through a confirmation of their mutual adherence to the same intellectual ideal—was crucial to the ongoing success of the friendship. It established from the beginning an assurance of honesty and a degree of openness that was to be essential to the ongoing correspondence.

With time, social similarities between the two women became more apparent. Both were the eldest daughters of large extended families. Both had lost their mothers as children, both were close to fathers who were passionately interested in education, both showed a keen interest in schools run by other family members, and both surrounded themselves with children whose education occupied them at a practical level. Whilst Edgeworth and Mordecai might have lacked a common culture, they shared a common discourse—an interest in contemporary educational philosophy and the practicalities of teaching which had been captivating women of their class on both sides of the Atlantic for a generation.[5]

The correspondence charts a friendship that became more rounded as the years progressed. From early formalities concentrating mainly on Edgeworth's works, the content broadened to include a wide variety of family detail, personal opinion, records of births, deaths, marriages and illnesses as well as perceptive commentary on some of the more pressing contemporary political issues in both the American and European contexts: Irish independence; the slave trade; the condition of the American Indians; the rebellions in Europe and the accession of Queen Victoria. However, it is in the theory and practice of education that the letters between Mordecai and Edgeworth chiefly abound. Edgeworth had, of course, shared her father Richard Lovell Edgeworth's enthusiasm for the practicalities of education. With him, she had experimented with various teaching methods and kept detailed records of the achievements of her numerous younger brothers and sisters. In 1798, she co-wrote *Practical Education*—a textbook which combined actual lessons with the theory of teaching. From the 1790s, her stories for children including *The Parents' Assistant* (1795 onwards) and *Early Lessons* (1801 onwards) were published in series. These works met with immediate success in Europe and were soon published in America, where they had been warmly received by Rachel Mordecai and her family some time before the correspondence with Edgeworth began.

The letters witness a remarkable exchange of pedagogical ideas developed over several decades. Mordecai was to express a constant debt of gratitude to Edgeworth, seeing in her a mentor to emulate:

> It is almost superfluous to say that *I* have never written a line for publication, but in making notes on education for my own guidance, and on the plan suggested to me by your inestimable work on the subject, how often have I wished that your better

> judgement could assure me I was pursuing the right course. To your precepts it is true I had ready access, and gladly have I resorted to them, pleased when they occasionally confirmed my opinions and practice (Wilmington, 16 September 1821: 28-29).

The increasingly personal contact with Edgeworth appeared to Mordecai, above anything else, as an opportunity to expand her pedagogical repertoire. As she commented in 1823, "America does not yet abound with authors of either sex, nor do I believe that there are ten ladies in the US who have ventured to write any book for publication. This does not probably so much arise from incapacity as from incidental circumstances. It is only within a few years that female education has been deemed an object of importance, and even now it is but imperfectly conducted" (Wilmington, 20 December 1823: 45). In Edgeworth, Mordecai had found a tutor who presented the intellectual sophistication of the Old World in a form palatable and useful to the New.

Edgeworth, on the other hand, took all the greater pleasure in selecting for Mordecai the better educational works by women writers from the masses flooding the British presses. In carefully directed parcels the latest works for children (Edgeworth's own and those of other similarly enlightened women writers) were shipped regularly across the Atlantic. Mordecai, delighted by each volume received, was impressed by the "sound sense, fervent piety, and strong argumentative powers," of writers such as Mrs Barbauld (127), but always reserved her strongest commendation for the writings of her friend:

> Ere I lay aside the pen, I must once more indulge myself in expressing my sense of obligation towards the authors of *Practical Education*, and of the other various works for which the world is

> indebted to the same enviable co-partnership. They have been useful to me, both in the regulation of my own mind, and in forming those of others (Warrenton, 3 March 1821: 20).

On her marriage in 1821 to Jacob Lazarus, Mordecai found herself surrounded by step-children, "docile, affectionate, and reasonable; accustomed to obey, and desirous of improvement." She commented that it was a pleasure "to guide, to direct, and to contribute by every means in my power, at once to their present and future happiness" (Wilmington, 16 September 1821: 27). It was a joy that multiplied with the birth of her own children, "the period has now arrived when I may hope to look forward with increased delight and interest to the effect of these invaluable lessons. I am a mother, and for my sweet promising boy now in his 6th month, I already begin to experience a mother's hopes, her fears and her solicitude! Already are his dispositions and little habits to be formed and cultivated; and deeply sensible as I am, of the importance of training them rightly, it is not surprising that I should be watchful and diffident in undertaking a task so interesting" (Wilmington, 29 July 1822: 30). Such sentiments with their focus on the aptitude of the very young, of course accorded exactly with ideas espoused by the Edgeworths in their educational writings.

Maria Edgeworth's stories for children, in particular, suited Mordecai's practical commonsense approach to teaching. In *Harry and Lucy*, for example, sections are devoted to such matters as "How to Make a Bed and Why," "How Cream and Milk are Made," "Bee Stings" and "Making Bricks". The books are based on real conversations which Edgeworth had had with her own younger brothers and sisters, and were supposed to be read in short snatches. They were presented as textbooks with parents being asked to introduce their pupils to the terms and objects described by the books, before reading them. Pupils were encouraged to study the dialogues and learn them by heart. Edgeworth soon realised the value of Mordecai's appreciation and began to ask for criticism of her works. Mordecai duly responded with respect but honesty, recording the observations of her family and friends on Edgeworth's books but always obeying, as she put it "the scrutinising jealousy of friendship":

> You request me to mention any little remark I may hear on the different parts of *Frank* and *Rosamund*. Both are favourites that deservedly stand unrivalled with our young people but I heard one observe that she thought Godfrey was allowed to be too *provoking* and too little considerate of the wishes of Rosamund, for a boy so well and so wisely educated. The affair of the Palanquin, I believe, occasioned this remark. The incident of Frank saving the life of his mother and fainting from excess of emotion was objected to as being "like a novel" and making him too much of a hero, and they thought the project of making an orrery too high a flight for so youthful a genius. All were enraptured with the contents of the traveller's box which they declared they could almost *see* in the description, and a young sister of mine asked if we did not think Miss Edgeworth the Walter Scott of children? And the *Miss Edgeworth* of grown up people might have been the reply. You see, my dear Madam how readily I comply with your invitation to "write freely" and yet I own in addressing you, I always practice a degree of restraint because I fear to displease by simply expressing the sentiments with which such wit and talents, united with so much wisdom, with all the gentle virtues and with a yet more rare simplicity of character inspire me (Wilmington, 20 December 1823: 46-47).

Perhaps the best commendation of Edgeworth's works came from

Mordecai's children themselves as they grew up: "Our youngest daughter, nine years of age, has been reading some of the second part of *Harry and Lucy*, which I found perfectly adapted to her comprehension. She was much pleased to find on a reperusal that she could in almost every instance anticipate Lucy's replies" (20 December 1823: 47). Mordecai's role as educator of her children and step-children was aided enormously by both her public and her private relationship with Edgeworth. Edgeworth, on the other hand, through Mordecai's detailed private accounts, was able to witness her own lessons in action and learnt to make adjustments as and where necessary. It was a dynamic which aptly suited her practical nature and bent for experimentation. By the early 1820s, then, the friendship had moved beyond an exchange of pleasantries and was becoming something more akin to a working partnership in which ideas about education were formulated and sounded out.

In the hands of two lively, intelligent women, the instructional possibilities of letter-writing became infinitely varied. The friends exchanged shoots, roots and seeds with plentiful advice on the best ways of stimulating growth in different climates. They progressed to sending examples of local entomology: silkworms, a caterpillar's nest, beetles and even a spider. To complete the transatlantic extravaganza of flora and fauna, Mordecai even sent a live mocking bird to Ireland in 1828. Unfortunately the bird died on the voyage. Those objects which survived were greeted with delight by the children of the Mordecai and Edgeworth families. The exchanges grew bolder. Whilst Edgeworth made sure that Mordecai received each new volume of her work as it came out, Mordecai stitched a lace mantle (the object of great admiration) for Edgeworth. Later Edgeworth was to grace Mordecai with a number of engraved rings. In addition each sent the other pictures of their respective dwellings drawn by younger members of the family and portraits of their relations. In a letter towards the end of the correspondence, Edgeworth even sent a sample of Irish earth encased in an old tin pipe. The delight in receiving objects with such associations was something that Mordecai and Edgeworth shared. As Mordecai commented in 1830, "there is something very agreeable in looking on an object and thinking it has once been beheld by one who loves us or whom we love" (Wilmington, 24 January 1830: 197).

There was more to this exchange of objects than simple pleasure, however. Both Edgeworth and Mordecai were passionately interested in educational theory and particularly in the importance of objects to classroom experience. In *Practical Education*, Maria and her father had commented thus on the teaching of natural history:

> To those who acquire habits of observation everything that is to be seen or heard becomes a source of amusement. Natural history interests children at an early age; but their curiosity and activity is too often repressed and restrained by the ignorance of their tutors. The most inquisitive genius grows tired of repeating, "Pray look at this? What is it? What can the use of this be?" when the constant answer is, "Oh! Its nothing worth looking at, throw it away, it will dirty the house." Those who have attended to the ways of children and parents well know, that there are many little inconveniences attending their amusements, which the sublime eye of the theorist of education overlooks, which, nevertheless are essential to practical success (Edgeworth and Edgeworth, 1974, first published 1798, 1: 28-29).

Observation and hands-on experience of real natural objects were the starting points for much of the Edgeworths' teaching. Their ideas had been enlarged upon by the Swiss philosopher Pestalozzi who had argued similarly for the use of objects in the classroom, suggesting that they might act as a prompt for students and teachers on a whole range of subjects (Pestalozzi, 1801, 1803). Thus, the rice bird's wings carefully wrapped in pasteboard and sent from Rachel Mordecai's son to Maria Edgeworth's youngest brother, Pakenham, were not simply objects of cultural curiosity but would almost certainly have been put to use in the schoolroom to introduce a lesson on the different climatic characteristics of the American states and their animal life, or to demonstrate the engineering principles of flight.

Over the course of the correspondence, Mordecai moved from being Edgeworth's pupil to acting as her self-appointed deputy—putting into practice the ideas that Edgeworth had so carefully outlined for mother-educators in her educational writings. But in an occasional reversal of roles, Edgeworth also learnt much from Mordecai. In the light of Mordecai's comments on their success or failure with her own children, Edgeworth corrected those of her stories that were republished in the years of the correspondence. Edgeworth had created in Mordecai the ideal Edgeworth reader, a rational female pedagogue committed to the exploration of practical educational ideas. Mordecai's input to Edgeworth's developing educational oeuvre on the other hand was the perfect complement to this process, illustrating exactly the economical and reciprocal transfer of educational knowledge between women, which Edgeworth was so keen to foster.

The transformative effect of the friendship is most easily tabulated in educational terms, but Mordecai and Edgeworth also shared a delight in the peculiarity of their friendship, a passion which at times amounts almost to an attempt at theorising the very nature of female friendship itself. Mordecai, for her part, was appreciative of—indeed thrilled by—the contact with the great minds of Edgeworth and her family:

> what term can I find so expressive of my feelings when assured of being thus highly appreciated by persons whose judgment I respect, whose opinion I value, and whose sincerity gives sterling worth to every expression of regard or commendation (Wilmington, 1 January 1835: 263).

Reading Edgeworth increasingly became a part of Mordecai's family life—a fact which occasioned some ingenious commentary on the peculiarity of friendship with a published writer: "I have been almost daily enjoying a delightful and never tiring intercourse with your mind, opinions, and sentiments, through the medium of these admirable works which in various editions enrich my shelves. My children are so happy with Frank or Harry and Lucy as companions, they realise so much, and make so many enquiries about Miss Edgeworth that I seem to be passing half my time in your society. Thus you are brought much nearer to me than I possibly can be to you" (Wilmington, 1 January 1837: 280).

At times, Mordecai became charmingly eccentric in her adoration. So strong was her approbation of Edgeworth's writing that she named her eldest son Marx Edgeworth in honour of her famous friend. In 1826, she recorded gleefully that "he does not exactly understand how a lady so very far off can be named his name, and can know that he is here, and want him to send her feathers of a rice bird" (Wilmington, 20 July 1826: 104). At times, moreover, she fantasised about the resemblances between her own children and the child characters in Edgeworth's stories:

> I sometimes think how happy I should be to show you my children; maternal partiality does not mislead me so far as to make me imagine my son a second little Frank or Harry. Yet his good

> sense and candour frequently remind me of both. (Wilmington, 13 April 1828: 64).

If Mordecai was inclined to fantasise about the role of herself and her family in Edgeworth's writing, Edgeworth, was struck, on occasion, by the larger philosophical resonances of the friendship. For her it was a link between the Old World and the New, between traditions and cultures which might mutually benefit each other. When the English writer Harriet Martineau made a trip to America in 1834, Edgeworth hoped that the published account of her travels would forge connections rather than antagonise the Americans:

> Miss Martineau has gone out to America now and I hope she will give us the result of her observations in a form that shall not be invidious or tend to set nations at variance instead of making them good friends, and emulous, not envious, of each other, giving each other the advantages of their respective differences in character and manners resulting from their different *ages* in society and positions in the world (Edgeworthstown, 18 September 1834: 258).

This deliberately double-edged comment is, of course, a lightly-concealed educational maxim on the nature of successful friendship in general and more specifically on the continuing satisfaction gained from Edgeworth's correspondence with Mordecai itself. Extraordinarily, by the later years of the correspondence, Edgeworth's sentiment for Mordecai was such that she began, rhetorically at least, to blur the boundaries between friendship and familial ties: "You see, I treat you as if you were one of the family and tell you all our little arrangements" (Edgeworthstown, 10 January 1830: 94). This increasing intimacy was, of course, created in part by the fact that each woman read the letters of the other aloud to members of her respective family.

The readership of Edgeworth's and Mordecai's letters was usually multiple, a fact which must always underwrite our conception of individual friendships between women in the early nineteenth century. Encouraged by a visit to Edgeworthstown by Mordecai's brother, Edgeworth figuratively opened the doors of the domestic environment to Mordecai's ever-interested gaze:

> I am quite pleased and touched by your being so constantly awake to whatever interests me. You seem to be always up to whatever I am doing and to know where I am and all my domestic concerns as well as if you were near me and one of ourselves (Undated but letterbook records 1 August 1831: 208).

Mordecai responded to Edgeworth's invitations with imagination, at one point laughingly suggesting that she fly by magic carpet into the Edgeworth family circle. The degree to which Mordecai had, by the mid 1830s, become important to many members of the Edgeworth family and vice-versa is confirmed by the fact that the two families continued to write to each other long after the deaths of the principal correspondents.[6]

The friendship between Mordecai and Edgeworth is in many ways typical of women's epistolary correspondence in the late eighteenth and early nineteenth centuries (Favret, 1993).[7] Letters, both private and public from this period, record the emergence of new kinds of intimate relationships between women. Female friendships are characteristically sentimental, indicative perhaps of the desire amongst the middle classes to ape the manners of those above them in the social hierarchy and illustrative too (by the sheer volume of those letters which survive) of the increasing amounts of leisure time afforded to the wives of the bourgeoisie. At the same time, what touches the reader about such correspondence is its strikingly practical nature, the inscribed need amongst women of a certain social status to acquire standards and know-how on a whole range of new domestic subjects, including and most particularly, education.

Intricate webs of friendship might be traced between many of the key female figures of the late eighteenth and early nineteenth century. Amicable correspondence blossomed, for instance, between Hester Mulso (later Chapone) and Elizabeth Carter, between Fanny Burney and Madame de Stael (1766-1817), and between Anna Barbauld and Mary Wollstonecraft who met in the rooms of their mutual publisher, Joseph Johnson, in St Paul's Churchyard London in the 1790s. Epistolary friendship was undoubtedly a thriving social pastime among women, but it was also an important literary device, informing the plot of eighteenth-century novels, and acting as an important structuring principle of narrative. In her discussion of relationships between women in novels of the period, Janet Todd has commented that "female friendship was a fascinating and inspiring theme in the eighteenth century. It was an historical phenomenon, fed by and feeding into fiction, expressing itself sometimes in companionable lives but most often in letters" (1980: 359). Epistolary narrative was a form favoured by women writers, and the genre reached the height of its popularity between 1780 and 1800.

Novels were not the only genre to foreground female friendship; educational advice works also used friendship as a structuring device. The late eighteenth century had witnessed an enormous surge of interest in the learning capabilities of young children and in the appropriate methods of educating the daughters of the middle class in particular. Whilst male philosophers wrote lengthy and authoritative educational treatises on the subject, published letters on educational themes by female writers provided an informal and less erudite, yet nevertheless significant, counterdiscourse. In *Plans for Education* (1792) and *The School for Widows* (1791), for example, Clara Reeve played out various educational ideas in letters "between Mrs Darnford and her friends," likewise Elizabeth Hamilton used correspondence in *Letters on the Elementary Principles of Education* (1801) and in *Letters to the Daughter of a Nobleman* (1806) written to a former pupil. Other educational advice works and novels, many of them written by those in and around the Edgeworth circle, are similarly either addressed to friends or laid out as correspondences between friends. Given the lack of public educational provision for women in this period, such material was invaluable to the aspiring middle-class mother anxious to maintain or to improve her daughter's social status through an education at home. Letters between female friends—whether real correspondences or fictional exchanges in novels or prescriptive works—had become, by the end of the eighteenth century, rich repositories of private female opinion on a subject of the greatest public interest.

In an era when educational letters between women were commonly published in novel form or as educational advice works, Edgeworth and Mordecai could hardly be unaware of the public resonances of their own writing. For Maria Edgeworth, fictional correspondence had long been of interest as a narrative technique in educational works and her letters to Mordecai therefore in some senses enact, develop and even contradict earlier ideas about the importance and workings of female friendship by correspondence. For Mordecai, on the other hand, corresponding with Edgeworth allowed for the playing out of a private fantasy: an opportunity to enter as a subject into the educational discourse that she so much venerated.

Long before Maria Edgeworth's correspondence with Rachel Mordecai began—in fact from the earliest part of her career—she had acknowledged the powerful narrative and educational structure provided by women's friendship by letter. In 1782, under her father's supervision, she had translated the highly successfully educational tract, *Adelaide and Theodore,* from the French of Madame de Genlis.[8] This book, which was laced with educational theory and practical pedagogical information, consisted of a fictional exchange of letters between a virtuous lady who had retired to the country to educate her children and her sophisticated friend in the capital. The book turned on the contrasting lives of the two female correspondents. In her earliest original work on education, *Letters for Literary Ladies* (written 1787 and published in 1795) Edgeworth began her own exploration of epistolary friendship. The first of the book's three sections consists of letters between a gentleman and his friend on the importance of female education. The piece is a mock-up of what Edgeworth perceived to be masculine modes of expression and argument; the language is erudite and scattered with literary allusions, and the tone is heavily rhetorical. Though one might agree with the comments of the first gentleman, the density of the argument is offputting. By deliberate contrast in the second piece, Edgeworth picks up a mock epistolary exchange between two female friends based on the same topic. In "Letters of Julia and Caroline", we are treated to a livelier and more dramatic narrative sequence of letters which vividly illustrate the dilemmas of female education.

Unlike Edgeworth and Mordecai, Julia and Caroline are from similar social backgrounds, indeed their very similarity at the beginning of the correspondence is the point of the piece. Linked by their middle-class status, education and general expectations of life, the women seem—on the surface at least—to be ideal companions. But Caroline is crucially distinguished from Julia by her superior mental virtues. Whilst Caroline is the embodiment of 'reason,' Julia is 'imagination' and it is this difference in temperament which leads to disaster. The contrast between the two women is typical of that encoded in other epistolary advice works in the period. Julia's flighty reading habits in girlhood are seen as co-incident with her misguided choice of a husband, and to the later collapse of her marriage, morals and health. Her life becomes a re-enactment of the kinds of romantic novels that she reads, and her moral laxness is implied by her own loose, fanciful, epistolary style. By contrast, Caroline's philosophical reading and sensible education, her espousal of reason rather than imagination, lead to a model marital life of domestic bliss—a life heralded in the sober prescriptive tones of her letters.

Despite Caroline's warnings and advice, Julia leaves her husband and elopes to France. The friendship, ever weakened by the clash of mentalities, founders. As Caroline attests, such a friendship cannot be allowed to compromise Caroline's other (more important) female roles: "your past confidence I will never betray; but I must renounce all future intercourse with you. I am a sister, a wife, a mother; all these connexions forbid me longer to be your friend. In misfortune, in sickness, or in poverty, I never would have forsaken you; but infamy, I cannot share. I would have gone, I went, to the brink of the precipice to save you; with all my force I held you back, but in vain ... Companion of my earliest years! Friend of my youth! My beloved Julia!" (Edgeworth, 1993, first published 1795: 58). Perhaps it is the passion recorded in this tale of friendship lost that has led critics to suggest that it is an autobiographical piece registering Edgeworth's disillusionment with her own childhood friend Fanny Robinson, who, on marrying Charles Hoare, embarked upon a fashionable life in London much to Edgeworth's consternation (Butler,1997, first published 1975).[9]

Edgeworth's success in *Letters for Literary Ladies* depends on her reader's recognition of the staple traits of the epistolary genre; shared social codes, contrasts and comparisons, and a tight connection between the different moral and intellectual powers of the correspondents. She educates her readers through the rigorous control of these techniques, exploiting the pedagogical potential of a genre already familiar to them. Like many other educational writers of her era, Edgeworth saw that the letter was well-adapted to the dissemination of educational theories. The published letter allowed women writers to negotiate the tricky boundaries between private experience and public utility. Moreover, as *Letters for Literary Ladies* shows, the epistolary form—and especially letters between friends—allowed for the expression of contrasts: the differences, for example, between age and youth, between old-fashioned views and progressive ones, between the moral and the immoral, between town dwellers and country dwellers and between the merely accomplished and the truly virtuous. The convention of letter-writing thus allowed published advice writers to put forward several different points of view at once. In "Letters of Julia and Caroline", Edgeworth herself was freed from the exigency of explaining the educational problem. Instead she let the correspondents speak for themselves, leaving the final moral judgement to the reader—a tactic which she believed would, in itself, educate the reader.

Fictional correspondence, such as that imagined by Edgeworth, could, of course, employ a number of devices to captivate and educate the reader: carefully balanced oppositions, telescoping of time, and rapid reversals of fortune leading to appropriate retribution, for example. Edgeworth's actual correspondences with Mordecai and others, by contrast, were limited by the real problems of letter writing: the need for propriety, actual gaps in time, and the inevitable banality of much of everyday life. In her correspondence with Mordecai, Edgeworth was no longer the educational mistro setting up and resolving fictional dilemmas, but a participant in a mutual exchange of educational information. The dynamic of a successful friendship between competent writers of similar intellectual, and by implication, similar moral status freed Edgeworth to focus on the practical aspects of education in ways that her fictional correspondents could not.

As far as Mordecai's writing was concerned, the friendship with Edgeworth seems to have acted as a stimulus to literary endeavour. Despite her protestations that she had never written anything for print, she frequently displayed the talents of the educational writer, egged on, it would seem, by her delight at finding herself and her family the objects of Edgeworth's pedagogical eye. In letters she recounted conversations she had had with her own children in a manner very reminiscent of Edgeworth's own children's books:

> We are all delighted to hear of a continuation of the *Parent's Assistant*—even my little Edgeworth when I told him exclaimed with a countenance full of animation, "Do Mother, tell Miss Edgeworth that I am *very* much obliged to her!" "I will my dear, but why!" "Oh Mother, because I know you will read some of the stories to me, so that I can understand them, and if Miss Edgeworth had not written the book, and then sent it to you, you could not do that you know." He loves to read *The Cherry Orchard*, *The Orphans*, and some other 'easy' ones for himself, and he dwells upon any little circumstance related as *true*; indeed he appears uncommonly interested in historical facts, and his wee books of history are among his chief favourites. I find the wooden cubes

> recommended in *Practical Education* an admirable auxiliary in the first steps of Arithmetick; he had always been inquisitive about numbers, and almost insensibly learnt the multiplication table, before he knew a single figure, and with the aid of his dear cubes has learned in a few weeks to add and enumerate with ease. I must tell you all this, because it gives me pleasure, and I owe it all to you (Wilmington, 24 June 1827: 133).

Mordecai's accounts of the educational activities of her children borrow the tone, the language and the layout of practical educational manuals published in Britain in the period. They are also infused with the detail of American life, tempered by the need for particular kinds of tolerance in a new and uncertain world. Mordecai's letters to Edgeworth are one of the most concrete examples we have of the transfer and the transformation of educational genres from the British to the American educational scene in the early decades of the nineteenth century.

In their correspondence, Maria Edgeworth and Rachel Mordecai were tapping into a discourse on female education (and education by females) which was already well-established by 1815. Their considerable social differences were overcome by their decision to write as models of the kind of rational femininity that permeated many published educational texts of the age. As such they are useful examples of the ways in which women have in certain periods and to certain ends deliberately presented a uniform identity in pursuit of common goals. This conformity might be seen to be tightly connected with their desire to maintain a successful friendship relation. Beyond this, Edgeworth and Mordecai each used the correspondence as a means of enhancing her own domestic, educational and even authorial identity. Finally, if we place the correspondence in its correct context amongst the many hundreds of similar exchanges, both fictional and real, between women in the early nineteenth-century period, it becomes apparent that such friendships were not merely participating in a debate on education, but in fact helped to shape the very contours of that debate. Friendships between women helped to reinflect the educational issues that had tormented the great philosophers of the late eighteenth century, infused them with an endearing mixture of affection and practicality, and brought them into the heart of the Victorian family and hence to the centre of public consciousness.

Notes

1. The correspondence was edited and published by Edgar E. Macdonald (1977). Where no other reference is cited, page numbers refer to this work. Henceforth Rachel will be referred to by her maiden name, Mordecai.

2. Edgeworth cites the date 1814. In fact the correspondence began in 1815. Such a mistake is typical of Edgeworth's relaxed attitude to the correspondence, see the discussion of this later in this chapter.

3. Christina Colvin comments on the inaccuracies of Edgeworth's letters to her own family in *Maria Edgeworth: Letters from England, 1813-1844* (1977: xxviii).

4. In startling tribute to Mordecai, Edgeworth chose to put words lifted directly from her original indignant letter into the mouth of Berenice's father.

5. For more on the emergence of this practical educational discourse and women's role in promulgating it, please see my DPhil. thesis, *Educating Women: The Preceptress and her Pen, 1780-1820* (University of York, 1995).

6. After Mordecai's death, her sister Ellen continued the correspondence with Edgeworth. When Edgeworth herself died, Ellen continued to write to her stepmother, and to her sisters until her own death in 1884. At this point, Mordecai's half sister, Ellen, continued the correspondence with

the Edgeworth ladies, particularly Maria's half sisters, Lucy and Harriet, and later Maria's niece, Harriet Jessie Edgeworth, until her death in 1906. A niece, Augusta Mordecai, and great niece, Rosina Mordecai continued the correspondence until 1942 with Harriet Edgeworth Butler, Maria's younger half sister. All in all the correspondence begun by Rachel Mordecai lasted a total of 127 years (Macdonald, 1977).

7. Favret (1993) looks particularly at the epistolary writings of Helen Maria Williams, Mary Wollstonecraft, Jane Austen and Mary Shelley. She considers the importance of the role of the Post Office in the late eighteenth century alongside a more literary evaluation of epistolary discourse.

8. Edgeworth's translation was in fact never published.

9. For more on the life and writings of Maria Edgeworth see Butler (1997, first published 1975) and Claire Connolly's Introduction to Maria Edgeworth's *Letters for Literary Ladies* (1993).

Ruth A. Symes is a teacher and freelance writer and was formerly a Lecturer at the Norwegian Study Centre at the University of York where she taught nineteenth-century Women's History and Literature. Her DPhil, *Educating Women: the Preceptress and her Pen, 1780-1820*, explored connections between women writers and educational discourse. She is co-editor, with Dr Trev Broughton, of *The Governess: An Anthology* (Sutton Press, 1997).

Exploring Suffrage Friendships

Heloise Brown and Krista Cowman

In this chapter, we discuss friendship as a means of understanding women's networks within the political context of the suffragette movement. The first section, 'Networks of Women', written mainly by Krista Cowman, argues that suffragette mobilisation developed from the context of male-dominated political groups, particularly the Independent Labour Party (ILP), but that the suffragettes also redefined ILP conceptions of comradeship, and introduced their own notions of friendship. The second section, 'Defining Friendship', written mainly by Heloise Brown, continues this discussion of the nature of friendship- and comradeship-type links and argues that the existence of these ties between suffragettes was a crucial factor in the success of the movement's mobilisation of a relatively large number of women over a ten-year period.

So how did the suffrage movement draw in women, and establish a discourse of friendship? Between 1904 and 1914, hundreds of thousands of women came into contact with the Women's Social and Political Union (WSPU). For many, their first taste of the political message of the militant suffrage campaign came at one of the Union's public meetings or national demonstrations. At these carefully stage-managed events, they would have heard repeatedly the words of Dame Ethel Smyth's suffrage anthem the 'March of the Women', with its catchy refrain that invoked the close comradeship of the Union:

Firm in reliance, laugh a defiance
(Laugh in hope for sure is the end)
March, march, many as one
Shoulder to shoulder and friend to friend.
(Smyth and Hamilton, 1911.)

This was popular at many suffrage gatherings following its composition in 1911 (Richardson, 1953: 191). Within suffrage politics, friendship was promoted as a key issue. Your fellow suffragettes were not just co-workers, but friends; the implication was that friendship brought a new dimension to public politics. In line with this, friendship has formed the focus of much recent work on suffrage, sometimes implicitly through research which has focussed on 'networks' of women, and often explicitly via the medium of collective biography. Publications such as Les Garner's biography of Dora Marsden, Liz Stanley and Ann Morley's *Life and Death of Emily Wilding Davison*, and Sandra Stanley Holton's *Suffrage Days* have tried to reintroduce or recover the context within which suffragettes lived and worked by focussing upon, among other things, their relationships to their colleagues (Garner, 1990; Stanley with Morley, 1988; Holton, 1996).

Little, however, has been done which looks at what constituted 'friendship' within the WSPU, or how friendship related to the notion of comradeship: discussions of suffragette networks have not examined the complexities of the relationships that were ultimately tied to, and took place within, political campaigns. In practice, the study of friendship is often hard to apply to the sources available: here, we unpick some of the factors that could be argued to have constituted friendship for suffragettes.

Networks of Women

The first point we wish to stress is the fact that the WSPU as an organisation grew from the Independent Labour Party. Most historians of the WSPU use hindsight to dismiss this as 'incidental', or as an historical error which was soon rectified by the WSPU leadership. Indeed, Les Garner has gone so far as to state that "the most important [of the WSPU's] political and feminist ideas ... was [its] move away from its socialist and labour background" implying that socialism represented nothing more than a starting point against which the Union's slide to the right could be measured (Garner, 1984: 44; see also Garner, 1992). Such a reading is tempting, especially for those engaged in the type of research which necessitates an explanation for Christabel Pankhurst's later defection to the ranks of the Conservative Party, albeit some twenty years later. However, if we empty our minds of such facts and step back into the world of socialist politics at the beginning of the twentieth century, a markedly different picture emerges. Rather than veering off immediately, we discover a WSPU which begins at the heart of the ILP, remains there for some time, and retains some ties until its eventual demise in 1914. This means that the original cast of the WSPU were well-versed in the language and tactics of radical socialist politics. Central to these was a strong understanding of the importance of comradeship, the unity of socialism which could transcend barriers of nationality, and possibly even of class.[1]

Readers of the weekly socialist paper *The Clarion,* which covered socialist activities throughout Britain by the ILP and many smaller non-aligned socialist societies, were first made aware of the existence of the WSPU in the week of its formation through a letter from Rachel Scott, herself an active socialist and the WSPU's first secretary. Her socialist contextualisation of the Union was continued the following week by Julia Dawson, *The Clarion*'s women's page editor, who alerted her readership to the fact that "some women members of the ILP have formed a committee for the promotion of women's suffrage" in November 1903.[2] The ILP women who dominated the initial years of the WSPU drew on both the theoretical and the physical elements of their socialist heritage as they moved into suffrage campaigning. Hannah Mitchell, one of the WSPU's first organisers, recalled how early suffrage activists often found that their street meetings laid them open to verbal and physical abuse, but that through their political connections they could depend upon "the local ILP to form a sort of bodyguard. They did not all approve of us, but as Socialists they had some experience of the hooligan, and came to see the women got a fair hearing" (H. Mitchell, 1977: 128).

In 1906, a difference of opinion occurred between the two organisations which has since been presented as an irreconcilable split (Garner, 1984: 45; Liddington and Norris, 1978: chapter 9; Rosen, 1974: 76-7, 84-5). The WSPU sent some speakers to the Cockermouth by-election. The local ILP was glad to provide food and accommodation for the women's delegation, which included ILP members Christabel Pankhurst and Mary Gawthorpe, assuming that they had come to aid the socialist candidate. However, Christabel chose Cockermouth to launch her famous policy of political independence for the WSPU. The women stayed with ILP members, but used their campaign to promote no cause other than their own. Understandably, bitterness ensued. Jill Liddington and Jill Norris, in their study of Lancashire suffrage *One Hand Tied Behind Us,* have dismissed these events as "arrant disloyalty" by the WSPU, claiming that Christabel's actions and policy "lost the support of most working class women" (Liddington and Norris, 1978: 207). Women such as Annie Kenney are portrayed as 'token' working-class activists from this point, their involvement explained away as following from their blind devotion to Christabel (D. Mitchell, 1977: 92). Yet more recently, local studies have questioned the adherence to this non-party policy at the grass roots of the WSPU. They demonstrate that whilst officially the WSPU forbade its membership to undertake public activity for any political party until such times as the vote was won, this command was often ignored by socialist suffragettes (Cowman, 1997: 171- 92). For a significant number, the socialism which led them into suffrage was not something which they were willing to lightly forgo. Socialist women located their fight for the vote as part of their broader political concerns regarding a transformation of society, and had little time for a suffrage comprised of single-issue politics. Liz Stanley and Ann Morley's collective biography of Emily Wilding Davison and her friends reveals a group of women in London who retained strong links with the ILP until 1914, although the work is vague as to how these were demonstrated, or how formal they remained (1988). Better documented is the case of Mrs Alice Morrissey, founder of the Liverpool WSPU and secretary of the Liverpool ILP Federal Council, who died unexpectedly in November 1912. Her obituaries reveal much about how joint activity was possible. Alice Morrissey was always a militant. She served two terms of imprisonment as a suffragette, in 1906 and 1909, both after the alleged split with the ILP. She was for a short time in 1911 a WSPU organiser, and spoke at hundreds of meetings for the cause. Yet her obituaries in the socialist press reveal another side to her activity. She had represented the ILP at the local Trades Council and Labour Party for a year in 1909, at the height of the suffrage agitation. In by-elections in Liverpool she worked hard for socialist candidates despite the Union's official ruling against this, with seemingly no negative effect on her suffrage credentials. *The Labour Leader* noted that only a few weeks before her death she had been involved in a tour of Kent with her husband breaking new ground for the ILP (5 December 1912). Her life provides just one example. Similar joint concerns can be found in the work of Merseyside WSPU organiser Helen Jollie. Between 1912 and 1914 she spoke at local ILP meetings on suffrage. This was not a one-way exchange. She used ILP chairman John Edwards to open the Union's new premises, and organised suffrage meetings with speakers on the theme of socialism. Her socialist credentials were affirmed when she appeared in court in 1913, having broken the windows of the Union's own office as a protest against their being sealed for a royal visit to the city. "Respectability has never been the claim of any reformer" she declared as she was led to the cells (*Liverpool Forward*, 7 March 1913).

These are interesting stories, but how do they help us in an exploration of suffrage friendship? What we find most significant in a perspective which recognises a continuity of links between the WSPU and socialism is the effect that such links had on WSPU organisation. Much of the militancy of the Union was lifted from a broader socialist tradition: heckling at public meetings, holding 'monster' public demonstrations, stone-throwing and martyrdom all came from this route (Cowman, 1997; see also Fletcher, 1996). Hannah Mitchell was clear that the first instance of suffrage militancy when Christabel Pankhurst and Annie Kenney heckled Sir Edward Grey in the Free Trade Hall in Manchester in October 1905 was rooted in local socialism. Attending the women's release celebrations, she recalled a large crowd including:

> a large contingent of the Manchester ILP. This latter branch had arranged a meeting ... for the same evening ... Keir Hardie came to voice his protest. Leonard Hall, a well-known propagandist in the ILP who had himself been imprisoned for his share in the agitation for free speech in Boggart Hole Clough some years before was in

the chair (H. Mitchell, 1977: 131).

Such links are fairly obvious, and to be expected. After all, it is natural that a body of women who received a common political education within the socialist movement would apply the lessons they had learned in their new political campaign, and sometimes bring personal friends with them. More interesting, once one accepts that a large proportion of the tactics of the militant suffrage movement came from socialist campaigns, is what was altered or omitted by the WSPU. We now wish to focus on one concept which altered significantly in its voyage from socialist to suffrage politics: the issue of comradeship, and its metamorphosis into a more feminised friendship.

As a generation of labour historians have observed, whilst the socialism of the ILP lacked the revolutionary fervour of its continental associates within the Second International, it was distinguished by a unique synthesis of politics and religion (Yeo, 1977: 5-56; Pelling, 1965: chapter 7; Gordon, 1991: 261-6). Unlike much continental socialism which developed around the workplace, British socialist culture flourished in a myriad of religious and quasi-religious secular shrines. Labour Churches, Socialist Sunday Schools, radical chapels and people's halls all fused the language of Christianity and Socialism. Hence a particular form of comradeship became a key factor within British socialism. This comradeship stressed the importance of a universal brotherhood where all were equal through Christ. Christian socialism fused Utopian, Revolutionary and Christian ideology to declare that Christ's kingdom would only come about on earth when His disciples realised it.[3] Therefore it was the duty of all Christians to realise the Kingdom by striving for a transformation of society. This idea is reflected, and was reinforced, through the variety of songs and hymns which featured regularly at British socialist gatherings. These gatherings featured many popular European socialist anthems, including the ever popular *Internationale*. Their rhetoric of class struggle imported from the Continent contrasts starkly with the language of popular British socialist songs such as this example by Edward Carpenter:

> England Arise! The long long night is over
> Faint in the East behold the dawn appear
> Out of your evil dream of toil and sorrow
> Arise O England for the day is here
> From your fields and hills
> Hark! The answer swells
> Arise O England for the day is here
> (This version from Bush and Swingler, 1935.)

Carpenter's echo of popular Victorian hymns with their plagal cadences and promise of bright mornings to follow emphasises much of what was unique within the British case.

The synthesis of comradeship and brotherhood was intended to be ungendered. However, the language of fraternity reflected a reality which all too frequently excluded women. Another popular song was William Morris' 'March of the Workers'. With no irony intended it identified Britain's socialists: "We are men and we battle for the world of men" (Morris, various editions). Whilst they may have been encouraged not to, socialist women often had no choice but to take these lines literally. The ILP admitted women into membership, it is true, but provided them with no separate organising space such as was available on the continent.[4] And whilst some of the most popular and effective ILP speakers were women, such as Katharine Conway, Caroline Martyn, Enid Stacey and Isabella Ford, the party had virtually no female representation at executive level. How women were to fit into the "battle for the world of men" remained a mystery.[5] Indeed, it was possibly the attitudes underpinning such rhetoric which acted as midwife to the WSPU in its first incarnation as a 'ginger group' within the ILP (Holton, 1996: 108).

As its embodiment was frequently exclusively male it is not surprising that 'comradeship' did not figure too prominently within the vocabulary of the WSPU. However, what appears to replace it is a stress on the extent and importance of female friendship between suffragettes. Hannah Mitchell's memories of the WSPU were not all fond, but she recalled with pride "the many notable women who honoured me by their friendship" (1977: 135). Annie Barnes, active in the East London Federation with Sylvia Pankhurst, developed a friendship with her organiser which transcended political differences (Harding and Gibbs, 1980: 5,18). The suffrage friendships of Mary Gawthorpe and Dora Marsden, and the friendship network surrounding Emily Wilding Davison have been the focus of close historical attention (Garner, 1990; Stanley with Morley, 1988; also Holton, 1996). Can we argue that there is any real difference between these friendships and the ideal of socialist comradeship? It is true that one often derived from the other. Indeed, in the 'March of the Women' quoted above, fellow suffragettes identify each other as both 'friend' and 'comrade' in subsequent verses. However, the two are often invoked in slightly different contexts. Comradeship is often located within descriptions which emphasise the thrill of militancy. Indeed, the 'March of the Women' identifies 'comrades' as women who have shared in the suffrage battle. Similar language is utilised by both the WSPU's newspaper *The Suffragette* and its first, by then ex-official organ *Votes for Women,* in reporting the funeral of Emily Wilding Davison. Her action, the culmination of a high-profile militant career, was frequently applauded in terms somewhat inappropriate for a feminist. Without a trace of irony, a banner behind her coffin proclaimed the words so often used for those fallen in battle: "greater love hath no man than this, that he lay down his life for his friends" (Stanley with Morley, 1988: 108). "Comrades" attended her coffin on its journey from London to Morpeth (1988: 108). This division between comradeship and friendship is unconsciously acknowledged by Stanley and Morley's research on Emily Wilding Davison which refers to individuals such as Mary Leigh as Emily's "close *friend*" and WSPU "*comrade*" (1988: 105, 111, emphasis added).

By contrast, suffrage friendship appears to consist of something deeper than comradeship. Indeed, it could be argued that friendship was the bond that remained when the thrill of militant-based comradeship wore thin. Discussing the plight of several WSPU members who were being force-fed in prison in 1910, Mary Gawthorpe, the Lancashire organiser, wept openly, exclaiming "these are women quite unknown—nobody cares about them except their friends" (Lytton, 1914: 235). Her definition of friends extended to the wider WSPU membership, not necessarily personal acquaintance with individual women. Often this difference between friendship and comradeship can be further identified through the emotional outpourings which so frequently accompanied the former. Take, for example, these extracts from the correspondence between Dora Marsden and Mary Gawthorpe. Dora appears to have attracted ebullient sentiments from many of her fellow suffragettes. Emmeline Pethick Lawrence had hailed her as the "sweetest, gentlest and bravest" following her first arrest (Garner, 1990: 22). However by 1911 she was firmly off Mrs Pethick Lawrence's Christmas card list, having abandoned her position as paid organiser of Southport WSPU, amid longstanding disagreements over autonomy which had come to a head over the issue of a bazaar she wished to organise. Her resignation led her through a variety of twists to found the feminist paper *The Freewoman*, which Mary briefly co-edited. The letters which flew between Dora and Mary at this time show some of the differences between comradeship and friendship which produced a warmth which remained after their shared political interest had gone. Despite her own resignation, Mary retained a certain amount of loyalty to the WSPU, and was worried by Dora's refusal to guarantee that the paper would not attack the Union. Differences became irreconcilable, and the joint project floundered, but the friendship remained. "Mark one thing" Dora wrote to Mary at the height of their disagreement, "[a]mong all acquaintances, friends and the like which you will ever make, you will find none ever who will be as faithfully your admirer and firm champion when you are absent as I have been." Mary responded in similar vein "Bless you, dearest Dora ... all this (argument) is between your soul and my soul and ... I say it in no name but that of love" (Garner, 1990: 59).

From this example, the most accessible of many which could have been selected, it is clear that there is a distinct line drawn between comradeship, which is purely political, and frequently superficial, and friendship, which forges deeper ties. We would wish to push this further and argue that whilst the frequently fraternal notion of political comradeship permeated the socialist movement on paper, it made very little difference to the lives of the majority of socialists. Friendship, on the other hand, actually delivered. Obviously this is a contentious point. There were many cases where comradeship came through, notably during strikes and times of struggle. However, as the later parliamentary experience of the British Labour Party has revealed, whilst it was fine to claim that there was 'no weal save commonweal', the marked material differences between middle- and working-class socialists remained for the most part intact. Outside of the exceptional circumstances of strikes, comradeship remained prolific on paper and difficult to pin down in practice. Within suffrage branches, however, the metamorphosis of comradeship into friendship created strong networks and webs of friendship. These underpinned branches and were vital to their day-to-day functioning. They could also cut through divisions of class, religion or party politics, uniting women on the basis of their gender alone.

One of the best examples of this we are aware of can be found in the experience of the Birkenhead suffragette Dr Alice Ker, who was imprisoned following her participation in mass window-smashing in London in March 1912. Dr Ker was one of the many suffragettes who came into the WSPU through friendship rather than through politics. At the time of her first contact with the Union, she was a widowed General Practitioner involved in a variety of radical causes from theosophy through to anti-vivisection, and situated her suffrage activity within the non-militant Liverpool Suffrage Society. This altered when she met Lady Constance Lytton of the WSPU. A friendship developed between the two women, who stayed at each others' houses on occasion. Following Alice's conversion to militancy, Constance sent her a short postcard in which she exclaimed "I am so happy that you have at last become one of us ... we are not all wicked, you know" (Constance Lytton to Alice Ker, 1909, Autograph Letter Collection, Fawcett Library).

Alice's friendship with 'Lady Conny', as she called her, was not the only important suffrage friendship in her life. From the moment that she joined the WSPU she was surrounded by a network of fellow suffragettes, with whom she shared a deep level of political activism mingled with social activities. Several times a week she crossed the River Mersey from her home in Birkenhead to the WSPU offices in

Liverpool for political business, and the pleasures of friendship, both of which she recorded in her diary. It is often difficult to discern where one stopped and the other began, as this extract demonstrates:

> Saturday 29 March 1914: Got up about 8. Went over to Liverpool and called at Office to get papers. Lunched with Margaret at Reeces where Mrs Imlach [another WSPU activist] joined us and [we] went to [the] Picture House to see Sylvia Pankhurst leading East End women to Westminster Abbey. Hurried home for tea. Dorrie Callendar [also in the WSPU] and two guests came back between 11 and 12 ... (Dr Alice Ker, diary 1914, private collection).

This shows the truly hectic pace of suffrage activism. (This was a 'free' day, but in the week Dr Ker was still seeing a number of patients.) What is also interesting is the way that she chooses to distinguish between Dorrie Callendar and her anonymous 'guests'. WSPU members appear to have had the right to each others' households here, and appear almost as family members, certainly not as formal 'guests'.

Following her imprisonment, Alice Ker's main concern was for the welfare of her two young daughters, who were forced to fend for themselves. Both the Ker girls supported the cause, and Margaret, a student at Liverpool University, was active in the WSPU herself, as well as in the local Fabian Society. Their suffrage beliefs, and the way in which WSPU members had become almost part of their household, enabled their mother to use the Union as a means of keeping an eye on her girls. To Margaret, she wrote "I wonder if you are seeing any of the Renshaw Street people?" [the local WSPU office address]. "Do go to any big meetings that they have (and little ones for that matter) and help all you can .... You might go and see Patricia [Woodlock, a leading local activist] when you have time. I told you that before." On another occasion, she told the girls to ask Mrs Abraham (another Birkenhead suffragette) or Lady Conny for anything they needed. The girls too used the Union to help their mother. After about six weeks in gaol, Alice wrote to Margaret "I had a visitor yesterday ... Miss Wright came in response to your request to Clement's Inn. It was awfully good of her, and shows how well HQ looks after us all" (Dr Alice Ker to Margaret and Mary Ker, 7 March 1912, Autograph Letter Collection, Fawcett Library; same to same, 5 March 1912; same to Margaret Ker, 16 March 1912).

Although HQ did respond to a request from Margaret Ker, the majority of support that Alice received came not through the official WSPU channels, but from her friends in the movement. Lady Conny was a frequent visitor, bringing food and warm clothing. Another visitor was Ada Flatman, an ex-Liverpool WSPU organiser who was by this time based in Cheltenham, who stopped off in Holloway with a gift of fruit for Alice during a visit to London. Again it was not just the prisoner who benefited from these close connections. Both Margaret and Mary were closely guarded and guided by the local WSPU branch during their mother's time away, as the letters show. Away from the glamour of militancy, Dr Ker found that her inability to run her household during her time in gaol caused her great anxiety. A major problem arose over the gas bill which remained unpaid. The prisoner had no access to money, and her daughters could not use her account. Dr Ker wrote to the borough treasurer requesting more time under the circumstances but was refused. Desperate, she fell back on suffrage friends. Margaret was instructed to mention the matter to Miss Hoy, a WSPU friend from Birkenhead who was also active in the Church League for Women's Suffrage. The borough treasurer was "a great pillar" of Christ Church, where Miss Hoy also had connections. Miss Hoy presumably cast public doubt over the extent of the gentleman's

Christian convictions under the circumstances, with the subsequent outcome that the bill was deferred until after Alice's release. Here we see suffrage friendship delivering the goods in a very basic, practical way. The pattern continued. When Alice was finally sentenced after serving two months on remand, the girls were sustained by Elsie Howey who spent the weekend with them and then wrote to reassure their mother (Dr Alice Ker to Margaret Ker, 3 May 1912). Elsie Howey was not a local suffragette, but had forged strong connections with the area during the first half of 1910 when she came to help with the General Election campaign, was arrested and imprisoned locally, and remained in the region conducting a post-prison propaganda tour. Alice frequently acknowledged the importance of such friendships. "I am so glad that Margaret has you near her just now when I am so completely shut away from her," she wrote to another sympathetic friend. "Please use her as you would a little younger sister, and advise her as you would your own sister in the absence of your mother" (Dr Alice Ker to Miss Henderson, 15 March 1912).

Aside from revealing the complexity of the web of friendship which underpinned a WSPU branch, these letters document its importance to a political struggle. Admittedly it is possible that Dr Ker could have served her sentence without practical help from her suffrage friends. However, it is equally likely that anxiety about the welfare of her daughters could have prevented her from undertaking the type of militant actions that guaranteed imprisonment, were she not assured that their welfare would be considered by the Union. The WSPU was aware of this, and attempted to organise around it. One of Dr Ker's branch associates was thanked for "active service"—a common euphemism for militancy— when she looked after the child of another member attending a demonstration (*Votes for Women*, 26 June 1909). The autobiographies of suffragettes teem with similar accounts.

Suffragette friendship repeatedly proved itself able to deliver in practical ways. Taking the children of the movement into your home and feeding them; cooking an evening meal for the 'man' of a suffrage prisoner; looking after hunger strikers following their release; acknowledging the political work of a branch member with a very personal gift of jewellery or similar; all of these are occasions when suffrage friendship delivered what comradeship promised.

So it would appear that for many suffragettes, friendship represented something more than comradeship. The former appears to have required a deeper relationship. Comradeship, by contrast, could remain at a more superficial level of duty to one's co-workers. Furthermore, friendship appears to have developed much more easily within feminist politics than within the socialist arena, despite the prominence of rhetoric regarding comradeship found within the latter.

Defining Friendship

From the arguments above, it is clear that strong attachments existed between women in the suffrage movement and that these relationships contributed to the strength of their political ideals. But what exactly was the nature of these attachments? In the above section, we have argued for a difference between comradeship and friendship; here, we reiterate this point and suggest that other ties—namely shared experiences and beliefs, and concepts of selflessness and self-sacrifice which interlinked with the polite rhetoric of deferential eulogies—were also important in the suffrage movement. In the discussion which follows regarding friendship, comradeship, common bonds and self-sacrifice, the differences between these relationships are drawn out, though hopefully without presenting them as mutually exclusive. The aim is to show how 'friendly feelings' were exchanged between women as a means of aiding the suffrage campaign *and* using the campaign to make friends who were significant in the women's personal lives.[6] It is important to problematise how friendship would have related to other feelings: was it inspired by shared experiences, by 'fandom', by selflessness, or did it develop separately from these ties?

Studies which look at networks of women within the suffrage movement often use the term 'webs of friendship' repeatedly, as if there is nothing to be said about women's friendships beyond establishing that 'webs' existed. There is much to be gained from studying the relationships between suffragists, but a clearer picture is required to show what these relationships involved and how far they extended. Awareness is needed of the nature of the attachments that existed, in order to understand how friendship functioned, and how less 'personal' relationships might have provided women with friendship-type support networks. In distinguishing between relationships that were based on personal affection, political affiliation, and the fusion of personal/political that feminism has engendered, we hope to promote an understanding of women's friendships that makes them more open to feminist analysis. A number of factors stand out as being particularly relevant in considering the relationships operating within the WSPU: these are shared experiences and beliefs, comradeship, selflessness and self-sacrifice, and friendship.

The first of these four, shared experiences and beliefs, was important because the WSPU was for most of its existence a controversial organisation, due to its use of militant action as a campaign strategy. Militancy covered a wide range of activities: attempting to enter the Houses of Parliament, throwing stones, hunger striking, locking men into political meetings from which women had been excluded, and more violent attacks such as arson and bombing campaigns. But the reactions to these strategies were often extremely negative, not only from anti-suffragists, but also from other pro-women's suffrage groups who espoused more 'womanly' behaviour. Suffragettes were often threatened if they protested in public, and on numerous occasions there were reports of violent physical and sexual assaults committed against them by male members of the public, and the police. Yet publicly admitting to having experienced sexual assault risked strengthening the anti-suffrage case, as critics could present such attacks as the inevitable result of women trying to enter the 'male' domain of politics. Thus, the fact of violence against women had the potential to fuel the campaign against women's entry into public life. Consequently, suffragettes faced protest situations knowing that while they might be subjected to violent assault, they would be unable to publicly campaign or protest against it. It is therefore difficult to discern how far the loyalties and attachments between suffragettes were based on shared fears and shared experiences of violence, and how far they were based on friendship relationships that placed the women's characters and personalities as central, rather than their political views or shared experiences of oppression. The need to protect one another forged bonds which could lead to friendships, but these bonds existed between the women regardless of whether or not they were extended onto a more personal level. As Holton has argued, the fact of militancy forged "intense personal loyalties" among suffragettes: the support networks that they established were independent of the central leadership, creating a "courage [that] arose out of comradeship and solidarity among the ... [mass of women] who made up a real force in the movement" (1996: 242-3).

So why did so many women join the WSPU, and what were the factors that bound them together? The WSPU was the original militant suffrage Union, giving it a measure of authenticity. Many women were inspired to join the movement on hearing of Christabel Pankhurst and Annie Kenney's first imprisonment in 1905, and thus the Pankhursts became identified as the originators of militancy. They inspired a measure of loyalty from the WSPU membership: following splits with the women who formed the Women's Freedom League, and with their WSPU partners, the Pethick Lawrences, only the most dissenting members actually left the WSPU to move to new, rival organisations. Furthermore, membership of the WSPU was by signing a pledge card, so unless they were paid organisers women could not be expelled from the organisation. This factor was important because it gave the vast majority of members freedom at grass roots level. Stanley and Morley note how one 'freelance' militant suffragette, Mary Leigh, refused to leave the WSPU despite the leadership's growing dislike for her, simply because she saw it as "*her* Union," the strength and influence of which she had helped to build by virtue of her own militant action (Dora Marsden in the *Freewoman,* 22 August 1913: 263-4 in Stanley with Morley, 1988: 119 [emphasis in original]). Finally, the WSPU commitment to getting votes for women in any form made it a radical, single purpose society, which superficially unified its members and ensured that the campaign never lost momentum. Every setback was met with a reiterated demand or an intensified protest. Therefore, the considerable external pressure which WSPU members faced on a regular basis meant that common bonds within the organisation were easily and readily forged: a sense of sisterhood that was based on shared perceptions was instinctively produced by the experience of WSPU membership. Indeed, the process of being an active WSPU member forged a sense of sameness with fellow members, and exacerbated the conceptualisation of difference that 'non-members' came to represent as the campaign progressed. The next question to consider is how this form of sisterhood (if that is what it can be called) differs from the second category of relationship, comradeship.

The origins of comradeship within the WSPU have been described above, including how a 'comrade', as a fellow militant member of an organisation, could be someone with whom a level of solidarity was felt. But as we have argued, suffragette comradeship could also work in very superficial ways. A typical example of how the language of comradeship was used to obscure the nature of personal ties lies in the messages of sympathy sent after Emily Wilding Davison's death. Both Christabel Pankhurst, whose attitude to Davison was at best ambivalent, and Sylvia Pankhurst, who was more sympathetic, drew upon established labour discourses. They wrote "with the love and admiration of a comrade," and "to honour my dear comrade" respectively (Sleight, 1988: 99).

Despite this, it can be argued that comradeship also 'delivered' for some women. Rhetoric could be transformed into very real practical assistance, which furthered the progress of the movement as a whole because it did not discriminate against 'unknown' women. For example, during their time on the WSPU committee, the Pethick Lawrences, as wealthy upper-class members of the WSPU, would undertake to bail any suffragette out of prison. This was a service in much demand in the early days of the movement, when it was common practice for magistrates to give suffragettes a choice between paying a fine and going to prison. Imprisonment conferred greater 'honour' on the suffragette from the perspective of the WSPU, and also gained her more publicity. In an attempt to starve the suffragettes of publicity, therefore, magistrates would offer them a fine which could be paid at any point during their sentence to gain them instant release.

The Pethick Lawrences undertook to pay the fines of any suffragette wishing to get out of prison, so that women would not be deterred from taking part in public demonstrations.

One example of such a woman is Mrs Rose Towler. Mrs Towler was a Preston suffragette who attended a 1908 deputation to the Houses of Parliament, and as a result was arrested and sentenced to six weeks' imprisonment in Holloway Gaol. Before leaving Preston for the London deputation, Mrs Towler had spent a week baking enough food to keep her husband and four sons going for a fortnight: so after spending a fortnight in prison, she requested to be bailed out so that she could go home and provide for her family again. The Pethick Lawrences—a couple with whom Mrs Towler had no connections other than through the WSPU, and who there is no evidence to suggest that she even met—duly bailed her out (*Votes For Women*, 1908: 82-83; Hesketh, 1992, first published 1966: 52-54). This type of unconditional support was a substantial factor in what made the suffragette movement work, particularly in its early stages: the knowledge that women without financial means could still command the support of wealthy members of society gave every member of the movement a degree of strength, whatever her own class or financial situation. It also forged an unprecedented sense of unity. This cross-class economic support differs from the relations based on shared experiences that are discussed above. Common bonds may have helped to forge an imagined sense of identity and belonging, but comradeship ensured a (limited) equality of status whereby all women members could request access to the resources of a small number of wealthy members. This suffragette comradeship offered something less conditional and less emotionally demanding than the attachments of friendship.

Our third consideration in examining the factors influencing friendship among suffragettes is the existence of support networks that were based on selflessness and sacrifice. The idea of offering oneself in place of another—laying down your life for your friends—placed the individual and her commitment to the WSPU membership as a central factor, and offered her the opportunity to go as far as she wished in support of the cause. Mary Corbett has argued that WSPU members "redefined selflessness as a positive political value" (1992: 150). By such a redefinition of the self and one's 'comrades', making a sacrifice in order to protect another woman from attack, for example, was a primary element in the suffragette sense of collective female solidarity.[7] Yet this solidarity differed from comradeship in that such devotion of the self to others led to eulogies *to* particular women, rather than an emphasis on comradeship *between* women.

Eulogies to the 'leadership' were a common feature of suffragette propaganda. Stanley and Morley have suggested that Christabel and Emmeline Pankhurst in particular seemed to be "admired and ... almost adulated" by many suffragettes, as the guiding hands of the WSPU (1988: 176).[8] However, this admiration should not be seen as being entirely uncritical: many secondary works, including Stanley and Morley's *Life and Death of Emily Wilding Davison* (1988), have shown that some WSPU members were nothing less than open critics from within. In the face of much evidence to the contrary, the WSPU has often been constructed by historians as an autocratic organisation due to the authoritarian approach of Emmeline and Christabel Pankhurst, and their confidence in their own abilities as leaders. However, a closer examination of the Women's Social and Political Union at both local and national levels indicates that to a large extent this was little more than political rhetoric (Vicinus, 1985: 252; Rosen, 1974: 243; Raeburn, 1973: 40; Stanley with Morley, 1988: 86). The autocratic nature of the WSPU is an assertion which many historians have accepted without question, while other Pankhurst representations of their own power and influence have been subjected to greater scrutiny.

It has also been assumed that the personal admiration that was evident in the movement meant that many suffragettes placed political aims low on their list of priorities. To take an extreme example, David Mitchell, describing the all-female head offices of the suffragettes, has argued that this “WSPU convent” fostered “the hothouse crushes common in such institutions” (D. Mitchell, 1977: 92; and for a critique of Mitchell, see Sarah, 1983). His evidence for such widespread ‘infatuation’ with famous WSPU women is the eulogising about leader members that was common. However he fails to locate this language in the context of Edwardian feminism and the discourses that were in common use during this period. It is more likely that the common bonds forged between suffragettes, combined with the dedication to selflessness and sacrifice, gave rise to these forms of language and behaviour. Mitchell’s reasoning is also extended to militant action: he argues that women, supposedly captivated by the rhetoric of the Pankhursts, would commit militant acts *en masse* out of devotion to their heroines. There is very little substantive evidence for this, and this chapter will show that a fuller discussion of mutual admiration and respect as factors in the meanings of and motivations for militancy demonstrates that ‘heroine worship’ is far too simple an explanation. The example given in the following section returns to the issue of selflessness as a motivation for militancy, and gives one instance of how it worked in practice.

Finally, there is the issue of friendship itself: the term ‘friend’ can be used to mean a person with whom affection and concern is shared, or it can also mean a supporter, a ‘friend’ to a cause or movement. But what do these different definitions offer us? The distinctions between friendship, comradeship, shared experiences and selflessness are hard to delineate because the language of friendship as employed within a political context is very limited, and there are no clear discourses with which to compare it. The comparatively overused imagery of comradeship may have been one way in which to forge a cohesive movement, but this language did not directly affect suffragettes' attitudes to and relationships with one another: rather, other factors were present which made it common for members (or 'comrades') to become friends. In a political organisation, personal relationships which offered mutual support, the validation of ideas, ideals and motives, self-affirmation and confidence, and opportunities to reflect and maintain identity, were invaluable not least because they strengthened the individuals who made up the whole.

The historical study of friendship as an interpersonal relationship is in many ways more problematic than the other types of relationship discussed above. Methodological problems abound in the process of trying to discover what a 'friendship' may have consisted of, or may have meant to the women involved. Women's primary relationships are nearly always assumed to be familial; sources detailing personal feelings for other people rarely survive or become available to the researcher; sources may skew the evidence, as close, day-to-day friendships are less likely to be documented than those which are carried out over a distance and are perhaps less intense; and indeed, the subtleties of friendships themselves are rarely committed to paper at all. Faced with a lack of sources which detail the nature of friendships, the subjectivities of those involved, or how the relationship fluctuated over time, it is perhaps easiest for the researcher to rely on quantitative evidence. Women who kept in touch after the suffrage campaign ended, or who accepted their friends into their lives in more formal ways, can imply the existence of an enduring relationship, the everyday importance of which outlived the fight for the vote. In the next section, the distinctions needful in studying friendships are shown in a case study of the Preston branch of the Women's Social and Political Union. The examples drawn upon give practical illustrations of the ways in which the concepts referred to above—friendship, comradeship, selflessness and shared experiences or beliefs—functioned in practice throughout the suffrage campaign.

Preston WSPU

As a branch, Preston WSPU was small, averaging around one hundred members who were both working and middle class, single and married women. Three members in particular were highly active militants: Edith Rigby, Eleanor Higginson and Beth Hesmondhalgh. All three had been active within the local Labour movement, but Edith Rigby persuaded both Eleanor and Beth to become involved in the WSPU. Beth Hesmondhalgh was recruited at an ILP meeting, while Eleanor Higginson was called upon in her home by Mrs Rigby, the two of them then being previously known to one another by reputation alone (Hesketh, 1992, first published 1966: 34-35). Although Mrs Rigby orchestrated the initial meetings, the friendships between all three were to last for decades.

During her spell as WSPU secretary of the Preston branch, Eleanor Higginson relied upon the co-operation of other members so that she could attend a London deputation in May 1914. She later said that of those suffragettes who "wouldn't" go to prison, one volunteered to look after Eleanor's son while she was in prison, one took her daughter, and another woman came to her house to look after her husband! (Raeburn, 1973: 229). Although this type of material support could have taken place within friendship relationships, it also demonstrates a unique level of solidarity and co-operation between suffragettes *as* suffragettes, whereby each woman contributed what help she could. Their shared belief system, perhaps combined with comradely sentiments, meant that women could rely on mutual support to enable one another to participate in suffrage protests. This support could come equally from strangers and from friends.

There is also evidence of Edith Rigby offering counselling and support to an anonymous suffragette who was experiencing a domestic crisis. Edith Rigby's niece, Phoebe Hesketh, wrote a biography of her aunt in which she described how Edith:

> conducted a sort of help-and-advice bureau [in her home] as she sat cross-legged on a Persian mat, smoking endless Turkish cigarettes.
>
> One evening a certain member stayed on after the others had gone home—to seek advice on serious 'husband-trouble'. Mrs Rigby was exceedingly helpful and sympathetic and, what was most unusual in one so reticent, confided that she herself had suffered the same sort of difficulty—though on different grounds (Hesketh, 1992, first published 1966: 35).

Evidence from the local press in 1910 confirms that a woman who had been a militant suffragette was prosecuting her husband for assault. The exchange which Hesketh describes between these two women, particularly regarding an issue so emotionally charged, clearly implies a close personal relationship that was initiated through a more structured framework as common members of an organisation.

Hesketh goes on:

> [A]unt Edith was able to offer sound advice to others on marital and various problems. By such means the Preston Women's Social and Political Union grew into a fellowship united by deeper bonds than those of politics. Its members were to become my aunt's friends and allies; she counted herself fortunate in having met them (1992, first published 1966: 35-36).

Such friendships lasted long after the campaign for the vote had ended. Eleanor Higginson and Beth Hesmondhalgh lived together in the 1950s and 1960s after the deaths of their husbands—Beth is described in Eleanor's obituary as a "life-long friend"—and both women visited Edith Rigby in the days before her death in 1950. Eleanor Higginson's third child was named after Edith Rigby, who was also appointed as the child's godmother. Eleanor Higginson was still corresponding with another WSPU committee member, Mrs Scholes, in 1939; and with another active militant suffragette, Nancy Reeder—who also corresponded independently with Mrs Higginson's children—in the 1930s to 1950s (Hesketh, 1992, first published 1966: 185; 1969, private collection of Mrs Eleanor Redshaw).

Here, quantitative evidence can be used as an indication of a friendship relationship, rather than more personal information. But even if there are no surviving sources suggesting the nature of their feelings for each other, these small details can imply that this group of women formed close, lasting bonds that existed outside of their relations to one another in the context of the campaign for the vote. The suffrage campaign created a new political context in which public and private distinctions were no longer useful: women could support the cause by supporting their own friends. We might ask whether it is the emotional attachments between women that matter above everything else, or the political nature of the cause which they are supporting? Being a friend to a cause or movement places the aims of the movement as central, rather than the women involved, although in the case of suffragettes (as for many feminists today) this is confused and often contradictory because women's emancipation was a primary aim of the movement. To show how the different forms of relationship developed and functioned, what follows is an example of Edith Rigby's militant activity which shows how the bonds between suffragettes affected the nature of their personal campaigns.

Edith Rigby was the Preston branch's honorary secretary from 1907 to 1913, and was a highly politically active middle-class woman. She had joined the WSPU within a year of its inception, as well as being active within the Women's Trades and Labour Council, the Liverpool Women's Suffrage Society and the Independent Labour Party (*Votes For Women*, 8 October 1908: 20; Hesketh, 1992, first published 1966: 34, 141; A.J.R., 1913: 343). By March 1913 she had been convicted of six criminal offences as a suffragette, ranging from obstruction to bottle throwing and window breaking, and had been imprisoned four times in six years. Her personal campaign for the vote gained momentum in July 1913, when she turned to increasingly violent methods of protest. On Saturday 5 July, Edith Rigby placed a bomb in Liverpool Cotton Exchange (it failed to detonate) and on Tuesday 8 July, she burned down the exotic holiday home of Sir William Lever, a locally-based entrepreneur.

She gave herself up to the police on 9 July, and made it clear in court that her actions had been motivated by the Cat and Mouse Act—a policy by which imprisoned hunger striking suffragettes would be set free when physically debilitated, and then brought back to prison when fit to complete their sentences. Although Edith Rigby had no personal connection with the Pankhursts, during her trial she specified her concern with the damage that the 'Cat and Mouse' process was doing to Emmeline Pankhurst's health. Her statement in court was that:

> [u]nder this Act ... one of the greatest women of the land is going to be done to death. ... I do not think that the Government realises that it is going to kill that woman. If they are willing to kill her, then this is a warning that they can kill me under the same Act, and when I am gone there will be a hundred more able and better women to take my place (*Votes for Women*, 18 July 1913: 622).

This discourse of selflessness was not unique to Mrs Rigby: many suffragettes protested openly against the treatment meted out to Emmeline Pankhurst. But this is often read by historians as 'heroine worship' (D. Mitchell, 1977: 92; Stanley with Morley, 1988: chapters 5 and 6). As described earlier, David Mitchell has argued that women were somehow compelled through infatuation with the Pankhursts to commit militant acts, and certainly it seems that the Pankhursts were an inspiration to many women across Britain. But what were the factors that led so many to respond to them?

Like Edith Rigby, many suffragettes who were arrested for militant action cited the treatment meted out to Emmeline Pankhurst as a reason for their protest. Mrs Rigby's motivations were based upon her respect for Mrs Pankhurst's surrender to the torture of the 'Cat and Mouse Act' and the fact that she was inspired by this to protest against the Act by putting herself through a similar process. Her surrender to the police therefore became part of a public show of strength and solidarity, and her actions suggest a conscious self-sacrifice, rather than infatuation or heroine worship. Mrs Rigby clearly articulated the desire to demonstrate that suffragettes, on both a collective and an individual level, were not prepared to let one of them alone be victimised. Months later, when Mrs Rigby herself was seriously ill from the effects of repeated hunger strikes under the 'Cat and Mouse' imprisonments, a petition was got up by Liverpool and Preston residents to protest against her treatment, as it was realised that it would be impossible for her to serve the whole sentence without it causing her death (*Suffragette,* 19 September 1913: 853). Support was expressed for Mrs Rigby by both suffragettes and local residents alike, and Preston WSPU continued to protest by a variety of means, from interrupting political meetings to attempted arson (*Suffragette,* 8 August 1913: 746; 26 September 1913: 868; 17 October 1913: 12). The editorial pages of the *Suffragette*, the WSPU's newspaper, ensured that her treatment was publicised nationally.

This evidence points to the existence of a community of shared responsibilities and concerns. The intensity of these was lessened by firstly, the fact that only a small number of members were willing to go as far as violent action, and secondly, the indication that comradely commitments extended to *all* suffragettes. Recognising this influence of comradeship and solidarity shows that militant acts were not simply carried out in response to the dictates of the central leadership, and demonstrates the autonomy and commitment of suffragettes on an individual basis.

Although this section has outlined four separate elements within suffragette friendships—shared concerns and experiences, comradeship, self-sacrifice and friendship itself—we have tried to avoid presenting these as mutually exclusive categories, and to suggest that they were instead complementary, as shown by the different ways in which each aspect functioned during the suffrage campaign.

The bonds forged between suffragettes were influential in creating a strong and cohesive movement, and these commonalities were repeatedly reiterated by the 'leaders' as a means of uniting 'their' members (Corbett, 1992: 162). Although the language of comradeship in particular was drawn upon in attempts to transcend differences between women, its primary purpose seemed to be to encourage mutual support and co-operation rather than to strengthen the personal attachments between them. Emmeline Pethick Lawrence, a key member of the WSPU until her expulsion from the Union by the Pankhursts in 1912, viewed the bonds that were forged in terms of women's "new comradeship with each other," which crossed boundaries of class, wealth and education, and in which all that mattered was "devotion to the common ideal" (Pethick Lawrence, 1938: 188). Similarly, Emmeline Pankhurst showed the ILP roots discussed above in one of many speeches which attempted to unite the movement and inspire support: "Women! Comrades! Dear Fellow-workers! I charge you, love this Movement, work for it, live for it" (*Votes For Women*, 2 July 1909: 880). However, despite the lip-service that was paid to 'comradeship', it should be remembered that the Pankhursts devoted much of their energy to trying to ensure that they alone retained power and control over the WSPU.

Drawing out the ways in which these factors worked has shown that while the concept of comradeship was repeatedly employed as a rhetorical device, suffragettes from both the mass membership and the leadership clearly found that their commitment to one another—as members of a political movement with a common aim—was a crucial factor in the WSPU campaign. They stressed that self-respect and equality were needed in political life, and that it was women who could best imbue it with these qualities. There also employed nascent discourses describing how shared beliefs and experiences could bind women together; but there was little public discussion of the friendship element considered in this chapter, which was based primarily on personal affiliations. Evidence of it in the example of Preston WSPU is based on quantifiable details, such as when or for how long known suffragettes kept in touch, or anecdotal details, particularly regarding how and why some women resolved their personal problems with the help of women they had met through public organisations.

Concluding Thoughts: The Significance of Friendship

The study of women's friendships within the suffrage movement can provide valuable insights into the ways in which the campaign was fought. But this chapter has shown that other forms of allegiances are also in need of study, not only because of their importance to the movement, but as a means of avoiding the sentimentalising of friendship. It is not enough to recognise that networks of friendship existed between women, if we do not understand the meanings or consequences of such 'webs'. The context which the suffrage movement offered women provided them with a range of ways in which to negotiate their roles. Suffrage history can only benefit from exposing the myths of the movement, and bringing into focus the many diverse individuals who helped to make up the whole. We hope to have demonstrated the importance of friendship and other forms of mutual support to this particular campaign: close study reveals that for many of its members, it was indeed a movement of women in both social and political union.

Notes

1. The term 'comrade' was in frequent use in British socialist circles from the 1890s. Within the Fabian Society, attempts were made to introduce it as the sole permissible title. See, for example, Thompson, 1971: 68.

2. Julia Dawson soon switched her support to the Adult Suffrage camp (Barrow and Bullock, 1996).

3. The best examples of this sort of rhetoric can be found in the periodicals *The Young Socialist* and *The Labour Prophet*. See also Trevor, 1897.

4. There was a motion at the 1894 ILP conference to form women's sections in connection with the ILP. This move enjoyed very brief success, most notably in Glasgow where a Women's Labour Party emerged. See ILP annual reports, 1894, 1895.

5. Good examples of how early socialist women attempted to square this circle include Enid Stacy, speech to 1894 ILP conference, ILP annual report, 1894; "What can Women Do?" *The Labour Prophet*, August 1893; "Men's Chivalry," *The Clarion*, June 28, 1894; Anon, "The Workman's Wife by One of Them," *Labour Prophet*, March 1892; Isabella O. Ford, "Women in the Labour Movement," *The Labour Prophet*, December 1894.

6. Jackie Scott-Mandeville's conclusion to this book offers a further example of how an interest in women's causes promotes a woman-centred world, where female friendships begin to take priority. The reflexive relationship between the interest in women's suffrage (or the women's movement more generally), and the weight this gives to friendships with women of like mind, is a complex one which would benefit from further study by historians of the women's movement.

7. Stanley and Morley refer to the court cases following a 1911 deputation, when both Mary Leigh and Edith Mansell-Moulin described accompanying Emmeline Pethick Lawrence in order to try to protect her from attack. Mansell-Moulin stated in court that she was "proud to say that in spite of hundreds of police she stayed with her until Mrs Pethick-Lawrence was arrested." Mary Leigh challenged a policeman and demanded to know "what game he thought he was playing at when he jostled Mrs Lawrence ... [she] asked if he could tell her what officer had her by the throat" (1988: 179-80).

8. For example, Liz Stanley and Ann Morley suggest that when Emily Wilding Davison wrote of a "perfect Amazon ... who will sacrifice all even unto this last," she was referring to Emmeline Pankhurst, who was then undertaking repeated hunger strikes under the Cat and Mouse Act (Davison, "The price of Liberty" quoted in Stanley with Morley, 1988: 163).

Heloise Brown completed a D.Phil. in Women's Studies at the University of York, on *Pacifist Feminism in Britain, 1870-1902*. She is a feminist with research interests in Irish Unionism and constructions of whiteness, and is on the steering committees of the Women's History Network and the Women's Studies Network.

Krista Cowman is Senior Lecturer in the School of Cultural Studies, Leeds Metropolitan University. She completed her doctorate with the Centre for Women's Studies at the University of York in 1994. Krista has published widely on suffrage and women's politics, and is author of *Mrs Brown is a Man and a Brother!* (Liverpool University Press, forthcoming), a study of women in Merseyside politics between 1890 and 1920.

Maid and Mistress: Narratives of Friendship in Accounts of Domestic Service

Judy Giles

In her diary for September 1925 Virginia Woolf records:

> it is a curious reflection that a little strain with servants more effectually screws the nerves at the back of my head than any other I am aware of. Now why? It is because it is subterranean partly (Bell, 1977: 41).

Few women in the period 1900-1950 remained untouched by the particular system of domestic service which was the cause of Woolf's tension. Domestic service was one of the ways in which relations between women of different classes were structured, and middle-class women, like Woolf, believed that an unbridgeable gap existed between women who could "stroll through the house and say, that cover must go to the wash or those sheets need changing" and women who cleaned, cooked, ironed, and washed either in their own homes or the homes of the more affluent (Woolf in Davies, 1977, first published 1931: xxiv). For women like Woolf, these social differences between women made informal or friendly relations across the classes impossible and her diaries for the 1920s and 1930s frequently return to the subject of her tortured relationship with her maid-of-all-work, Nelly Boxall. Woolf felt herself to be manipulated and tyrannised by Nelly and the other servants who worked for her, irritated consistently by what she saw as their irrationality, and yet ridden with guilt for her inability to be either a good friend or a tough employer. As she commented in 1929 "[h]ow can an uneducated woman let herself in, alone, into our lives? I could put my theory [of non-residential daily help] into practice by getting a daily of a civilised kind who had her baby in Kentish town; & treated me as an employer, not friend" (Bell, 1977: 220).

This paper explores the ways in which Woolf's problem, the inherent tension in a relationship rooted in economics but experienced as part of private or family life, was explored and questioned within the prevailing discourses of class, femininity and friendships between women. I have chosen to focus on three texts which produce in varied ways different knowledges about how friendships between women of different classes can be understood at a specific moment in history.[1] All three accounts testify to the significance of such relationships in women's lives. Servants were not the invisible hands beloved of some myths of domestic service: they loved, feared, despised their mistresses and in turn were loved, feared and despised. Loyalty, deference, affection, jealousy, irritation, envy, guilt, and duty produced specific experiences of mistress/maid relationships which were then played out within the power dynamics of waged labour and social status. The emotional resonances of such relationships found expression in novels, in diaries and, as Woolf's diaries reveal, through the physical, bodily symptoms of 'nerves' and stress. These accounts not only make visible and raise questions about the forms such friendly relations might take, but they also contest those definitions that represent women's friendships as trivial, peripheral to family and sexual relations, and relatively unproblematic.

The ability to afford a servant was a mark of middle-class status, and domestic service—in all its forms—continued to offer employment to working-class women.[2] The 1931 Census records 1,332,224 'indoor domestic servants', of which 127,647 were classified as "laundry workers, washers, ironers, manglers, dry cleaners" and 140,146 as "charwomen, office cleaners" (HMSO, 1931). Many women performed domestic or personal services for other women more affluent than themselves as daily helps, as maids in schools and nursing homes, as hairdressers, as cleaners in hospitals and hotels, as laundresses, as waitresses, and as step ladies. Step ladies occupied the bottom rung of the domestic service ladder; their job was to scrub the steps and front paths of the homes of the prosperous. Cleaning one's own steps was a mark of declining social status, for as Eileen Elias points out in her autobiography, "no self-respecting housewife would ever be seen on hands and knees in the street" (Elias, 1978: 31). Middle-class women grew up, in the early years of this century, in homes where it was taken for granted that cooking, cleaning, and other domestic chores would be performed by women from a different class, and working-class women were urged to enter domestic service where they could learn the rudiments of 'good' (that is middle-class) housekeeping. The nature of residential domestic service altered in the early-twentieth century, as the large households of indoor and outdoor servants characteristic of Victorian and Edwardian prosperity gave way to single maid households and the practice of employing daily help.[3] It is my contention that these changes in the practices of 'servantkeeping' produced a discursive space in which the conflicts, tensions and possibilities inscribed in the maid/mistress relationship were made visible.

Beneviste has argued that a discourse is produced from the interaction of "the presence of the speaking subject" with the specific spatial and temporal locations in which the communicative exchange occurs (cited in Clifford, 1983: 131). Hence, any particular discursive space is created from the interaction of historical context, the subject positions of the communicating actors, and the cultural narratives available to these subjectivities. In this paper I consider three forms of 'communicative exchange' by women that offer representations of the maid/mistress dyad in order: first, to unravel the prevailing discourses of friendship, class, and femininity within which these women articulated their visions and experience; secondly, to consider how far the characteristic features of the forms in which the authors chose to write were able to produce alternative versions of maid/mistress relations; and, thirdly, to ask whether questions of cross-class friendships between women might be textually negotiated within these forms in ways which destabilised the prevailing discourses of class, sexuality, and friendship. The texts were chosen because they foreground domestic service and, in particular, the question of how far friendly or informal relations were possible between maid and mistress. Celia Fremlin's 'social' survey, *The Seven Chars of Chelsea* (1940), Daphne Du Maurier's novel, *Rebecca* (1938), and the oral life narrative of Doris Arthur, a working-class woman from Birmingham (1988) are all concerned to a greater or lesser extent with the relationships which might exist between women within the system of domestic service. Reading texts from very different genres of writing alongside each other produces a series of reflexive re-interpretations: Doris' account re-interprets Fremlin and Du Maurier, but, in turn, these texts offer knowledges within which Doris' account can be read. Reading across texts in this way can stimulate insights which might otherwise remain hidden. Although none of my chosen texts deals primarily with friendships between women of different classes, the possibility or impossibility of such friendships lies behind the narratives of domestic service around which these texts variously organise themselves. I argue that all three texts are implicated in, yet are able to negotiate, their historically produced discourses of class and gender, in order to contest the inevitability of class division that characterised dominant beliefs about relations between women.

In a letter to her friend, Margaret Llewellyn Davies, a letter which later became the introduction to Davies' collection of life stories by members of the Women's Co-operative Guild, *Life As We Have Known It*, Virginia Woolf identifies the difficulties of representing one class from the standpoint of another:

> [o]ne could not be Mrs. Giles of Durham because one's body had never stood at the wash-tub, one's hands had never wrung and scrubbed and chopped up whatever the meat may be that makes a miner's supper. The picture therefore was always letting in irrelevancies. One sat in an armchair or read a book. One saw landscapes and seascapes (Woolf in Davies, 1977, first published 1931: xxiii).

As Woolf goes on to point out, "the imagination is largely the child of the flesh." 'Mrs Giles of Durham' and Mrs Woolf may share the same ontological status as women, but the meanings attached to their experience of womanhood will vary according to their material day-to-day existence and the historically specific discourses of class which limit the parameters of those meanings. For many middle- and upper-class women, relationships with women from other classes were fraught with difficulty despite a liberal desire on the part of many that this situation should be different.[4]

One of the ways in which continuing concerns about class could be expressed was to focus on the conditions and relations of domestic service, which were constructed as in crisis. The language in which the relations between maid and mistress were represented was often the language of moral panic and social problem: the idea of a 'servant problem', so often complained of during the first fifty years of this century, offered a range of ways to understand the tensions involved in the practice of 'servantkeeping'. On the one hand, it referred to changing occupational and economic structures which meant that the whole system of domestic service was changing from its late-nineteenth-century version in which the large middle- and upper-class home staffed by a hierarchy of servants was giving way to the prevailing norm of the 1920s onward—the one-maid household or the employment of non-residential help (HMSO, 1931; Burnett, 1976: 135-42; McBride, 1976: 111-16; Taylor, 1979: 121-39). The 'problem' identified here was the possibility that the supply of maids might dry up due to the increase in other forms of employment for working-class women. At another level, 'the problem' was perceived as one of suitability and morality. Young girls were increasingly seen as 'unfit' for service: they were seen as "rude, resentful, talkative, and unmannerly" (Fremlin, 1940: 102) and unwilling to demonstrate the degree of commitment and deference mistresses required. In this sense servants, as individuals rather than the system, were the problem. For some, such as Virginia Woolf, "the servant problem" was an unwanted legacy of Victorianism, a system inappropriate to 'modern' life, "a fine rubbish heap left by our parents to be swept" (Bell, 1977: 220). At yet another level, this discourse of problem and crisis around one of the primary markers of social status pointed to a wider discomfort about the emergence of mass democracy and mass culture, which appeared to threaten established hierarchies of social relations. In many minds the threatened collapse of domestic service prefigured the collapse of a social system based on breeding and deference. For women who had not encountered the loosening of social hierarchies that had accompanied many people's experience of the 1914-1918 war, the trend towards one-maid households generated an explosive tension between the recognition that some degree of intimacy and friendship was both necessary and just, and an equally powerful sense of inadequacy about how to set about achieving this.

Reading accounts of 'the servant problem' in this period, there is an increasing sense that the phrase has become drained of any specific meaning at the same time as it signifies an excess of meanings: an empty signifier which can serve as a container for a whole range of issues, from the feared collapse of middle-class society to the moral turpitude of young working-class girls, from a discussion of shifting employment opportunities, to the education of women, from concerns about psychosexual well-being to the design of 'the servantless' house. These and other issues were frequently and vociferously debated under the ample umbrella offered by the idea of 'the servant problem'. This 'servant problem' acted then as a shorthand for talking about, and often displacing, concerns about women's position in the labour force, anxieties about female sexuality, doubts about domestic life, and uncertainty about social status.

The Seven Chars of Chelsea (1940)

In 1940 Celia Fremlin, an Oxford graduate and a Mass Observation observer, wrote an account of how, on leaving Oxford, she 'disguised' herself as a maid of all work in order to discover "what it was like to be a charwoman" (Fremlin, 1940: 1). In doing this she was following in a tradition established in the nineteenth century when young, university educated men would live and work amongst the working-classes in order to 'discover' the lives of the poor and dispossessed, often in order to seek ways of alleviating such social distress (Dyos and Wolff, 1973; Keating, 1976; Walkowitz, 1992). In the 1930s this trend continued and diversified with the emergence of the documentary film movement and Mass Observation, numerous social surveys and the 'condition of England' writings of, for example, George Orwell (1987, first published 1937), J. B. Priestley (1984, first published 1934), and H. V. Morton (1933). Fremlin's book, with its avowed aim of examining the "peculiarities of the class structure of our society" through a study of domestic service, has to be read as occupying the particular discursive space created by documentary realism (Fremlin, 1940: 2). Fremlin wrote for those men and women who in 1930s and 1940s Britain comprised a growing, liberal-reforming intelligentsia (Stevenson and Cook, 1979). The urge, on the part of this élite, to document the experiences of 'the people' manifested itself in John Grierson's documentary films, the anthropological surveys of Mass Observation and the numerous social surveys of the period.[5] Fremlin became an observer for Mass Observation and *The Seven Chars of Chelsea* prefigures MO aims:

> Mass Observation does not set out in quest of truth or facts for their own sake, or for the sake of an intellectual minority, but aims at exposing them in simple terms to all observers, so that their environment may be understood, and thus constantly transformed (Cited in Baxendale and Pawling, 1996: 33).

Despite their laudably reformist aims, MO observers frequently deployed the language of an anthropology which was itself rooted in the imperial project. Tom Harrisson, one of the founders of MO, could speak of the people MO was studying as "the cannibals of Britain" and Orwell spoke of the North of England as "some subterranean place" (Hood, 1983: 107; Orwell, 1987, first published 1937: 18). Whilst Fremlin deploys this discourse of social exploration, expressed in terms of a journey from the familiar to the strange, in *The Seven Chars of Chelsea*, she was aware of the contradictions implicit in such a rhetoric. Fremlin represents her own position ironically, parodying the way her 'upper-class friends' perceive her mission "to act ... as messenger and interpreter between the two worlds" of mistress and servant in terms which not only satirise those friends but the whole rhetoric of 'social exploration':

> [y]et if you were Christopher Columbus returning from the New World, Jules Verne from a voyage to the moon, you could scarcely be received with more amazement, more plied with wondering questions ... The travellers' tales that the Athenians listened to of old; tales of fire-breathing monsters; of three-headed men; of ants as big as donkeys; these tales are as nothing compared with the travellers' tales some of your upper-class friends will expect you to bring back about the 'working classes' (Fremlin, 1940: 3).

Fremlin's hypothesis, set out in her introduction, is that the worlds of mistress and servant are so enormously divided that any informal or friendly relationship between the two is impossible, "you speak two different languages; you think different thoughts; you live in different worlds" (1940: 2). The narrative practice of representing the study of the working class as a journey from civilisation to the 'dark' reaches of the East End or the urban wastelands of the North of England had produced a discourse of class in which the 'ordinary people' of Britain could be viewed, very much as Fremlin suggests, as a separate tribe with its own rituals, totems and language, a tribe which might be visited, scrutinised, reformed, and exhorted to revolution but which remained forever 'foreign', distanced from the heartland of middle-class identity—the domestic home. The 'problem' with domestic service was, of course, that this distancing was not possible. Servants, increasingly in one-maid households, could know and share in the daily details and intimate interactions of their employers' lives:

women's experiences *of class* were frequently located in the very sphere which defined them *as women*—the private sphere of the emotions, of nurture and of relationship. *The Seven Chars of Chelsea* does not, and cannot, represent its subjects simply as objects of voyeuristic fascination—unfamiliar, other: the effect of documenting the lives of servants in the rhetoric of anthropological ethnography is to destabilise and problematise the fundamental terms of the opposition, 'familiar/strange'.

Fremlin concludes her study with a utopian vision of a social democratic future in which maid and mistress "can work and laugh and struggle together," happily unaware of how many hours they have worked because "both will be too much interested in the job for its own sake" (1940: 176). This political vision of cooperation and equality is rooted for Fremlin in the 'feminine' values of the domestic sphere, which she describes as "friendly, informal co-operation, the casual give and take that should form the basis of home life" (1940: 174). The industrial workplace as the centre of conventional Marxist analyses of the period is displaced by Fremlin's focus on the bourgeois home and the system of domestic service as the starting point for an attack on the "antagonisms of class." At the same time her text implicitly posits her vision of female friendship and cooperation in the maintenance of domestic order as a model for workers' solidarity and as the key to social transformation. In 1945, the newly established Welfare State embodied many of the 'feminine' principles which also inform the utopian future argued for in *The Seven Chars of Chelsea*.

However, Fremlin's socialist solution to the gap she perceives as existing between women of different classes remains as fragile in the text as it is as a political strategy. *The Seven Chars of Chelsea* is a mixture of social survey, anecdote and storytelling. It starts with accounts of three different situations taken by the author in her 'disguise' as a maid-of-all-work: general maid in a residential upper-middle-class home with a large staff; general maid in a boarding-house run by a working-class woman, and cleaner in a hospital. These chapters are written in the style of a short story or fiction with a cast of characters, invented dialogue and narrative plots which encode a moral message. The book's central chapter, entitled "The Seven Chars of Chelsea", is a comic account of Fremlin's time as a cleaner in a hospital. The 'chars' are represented as choric figures whose circular, sometimes meaningless, dialogue acts as a commentary on the society Fremlin attacks. Fremlin's 'chars' are the 'salt of the earth'. They demonstrate an apparent indifference to the appalling conditions of their lives through their humour and fatalism, they act and move in chorus and they bicker good-heartedly throughout the day. In the sections which follow no attempt is made to link the 'chars' to economic structures or the social analysis which concludes the book. However, much is made of the isolation and the psychological effects of the structures of deference which characterise an older form of residential service and the 'chars' come to stand as expressions of a romanticised working-class female vitality which is being sapped from within its own class by the continuation of Victorian modes of residential service. The ideal of residential service, represented by the figure of the faithful retainer, loyal, devoted, deferential, and celibate, is critiqued by Fremlin for its potentially damaging effects on a femininity defined in terms of wifehood and motherhood.

When it turns to examining residential service, *The Seven Chars of Chelsea* has some sharply Gothic moments. The servants whom Fremlin meets in the households she observes are represented as occupying a psycho/sexual landscape of repression and waste. Trapped in the structures of deference and duty, intimacy and isolation which could constitute the relations between a mistress and her servants, these young women are described as psychologically damaged by their experience. They live, according to Fremlin, sterile and purposeless lives, in which an obsessive devotion to cleanliness and order has replaced the 'natural' outlets for womanly energies. In this Fremlin draws on the Freudian discourses of sexual repression and hysteria which dominated discussions of sexuality in the period. Her description of a retired family servant is illustrative:

> [i]nside the house was silent. No wasps were ever heard buzzing after Agnes's jam; no flies hummed hopefully round her larder door. The wire netting on her windows was completely effective. The last mouse had been trapped years ago, and now the whole house stood trim and silent. Its barricades against the surge of life were impregnable.
>
> We knocked on the brass knocker, and Agnes came to the door. She was tall and erect, and her face was clammily white, with few wrinkles for her seventy years. She wore an old-fashioned black dress of very good material, a tight lace front and choker, and her hair was grey and wisp-like. You could not tell what colour it had once been (1940: 151).

A whole chapter is devoted to the difficulties for residential servants in finding suitable marriage partners and the social tragedy this represents for hundreds of young women. Young women entering service, according to Fremlin, are in danger of wasting their femininity to the point at which they become, like Agnes above, faded and unused, alone "with her furniture, polished, firm and shining; shining like living coals, but silently" (1940: 156-7). Fremlin concludes this chapter by asking rhetorically what Agnes and her seven 'chars' could possibly "have to say to each other." It is difficult for the reader to avoid concluding that Fremlin is advocating non-residential 'charring' as a preferable mode of working-class femininity than that learned in dependent service to the middle-class household. This may be a radical proposition in 1940 and is certainly appropriate to the wartime rhetoric of egalitarianism and 'the people's war', but it does little more than celebrate a certain version of working-class womanhood and nothing to dismantle the classed opposition—lady/woman—which secured the mid-twentieth-century hierarchy of white femininities. Unable to locate the residential servant as 'out there' in the way she can the 'chars' who clean public places like hospitals, Fremlin is forced to draw on the discourses of Freudian popular psychology in order to maintain the distance between one class of woman and another. Despite Fremlin's attempt to draw attention to the barriers and exploitations between servants and employers, this is undercut by the psychological narratives which reinforce the text's determination to maintain a distance between servants and mistresses. The 'seven chars' can be afforded a measure of dignity because they remain employees with a definable workplace: the residential single maid is problematic because her workplace is also her home and is shared with her employer. She can only be held at a distance by pathologising the very qualities which mistresses demanded—deference, loyalty, and celibacy. The utopian narrative of a home in which maid and mistress "work and laugh and struggle together" is constantly questioned by a parallel narrative of emotional waste and repression, linked to contemporary discourses on female sexuality that celebrated heterosexual marriage as the only location for emotional and sexual fulfilment. Within such discursive practices the possibilities for creating narratives of friendship remain curtailed. None the less precisely because Fremlin's text struggles to hold in place the prevailing discourses of class at the same time as deploying a reformist rhetoric, the possibilities of domestic service as a site wherein ideas about cross-class friendships could be negotiated and debated are rendered visible.

REBECCA (1938), DAPHNE DU MAURIER

As Alison Light has argued, Daphne Du Maurier wrote romantic novels for those 'superior' readers like herself who "despised the Barbara Cartland school of romance" and the sentimental 'gush' of some Victorian fiction (Light, 1991: 158-166). Her fiction functions to create a discursive space in which one 'superior' woman (herself) communicates with other 'superior' women. Du Maurier's novels assume a middle-class, middle-brow female readership who were contemptuous of the kind of romantic fiction with its emphasis on exotic locations and sensationalised plots that was read by working-class women.[6] *Rebecca*, Du Maurier's most well known fiction, revives the Gothic romance as a form in which anxieties about female sexuality, marriage, and class can be pleasurably explored by her middle-class female readers without recourse to the, so-called, 'pulp' romances of magazines like *Peg's Paper* which were targeted at working-class women. Despite the novel's relatively conventional resolution of the relationship of the unnamed narrator with her brooding, enigmatic husband, the heterosexual romance narrative of *Rebecca* is fatally undermined by parallel narratives of lesbian constancy and female sexual independence. The unnamed heroine's struggle for a bourgeois feminine identity is positioned between the amoral sexual hedonism of her rival, the dead Rebecca, and the disturbingly obsessive devotion of the housekeeper, Mrs. Danvers, for Rebecca. At the novel's climax the heroine experiences a hysterical inertia during which she almost succumbs to the seductive exhortations of Mrs. Danvers to accept both literal and psychic annihilation. Mrs. Danvers urges suicide in language which insists on the links between social position, female identity and sexual love.

> She's still mistress here, even if she is dead. She's the real Mrs de Winter, not you. It's you that's the shadow and the ghost. It's you that's forgotten and not wanted and pushed aside. Well, why don't you leave Manderley to her? Why don't you go? ... We none of us want you. He doesn't want you, he never did. He can't forget her (Du Maurier, 1975, first published 1938: 257).

Mrs. Danvers' function in the text has similarities with the displaced Bertha Mason in Charlotte Brontë's *Jane Eyre*: she can be read as voicing the suppressed fears and desires of the heroine whose narrative is constantly disrupted and threatened by her intrusions (Brontë, 1966, first published 1847).[7] Mrs Danvers is, however, a residential housekeeper, neither one of Fremlin's 'chars', nor the Creole, exoticised wife from the West Indies, but a hitherto overlooked member of the bourgeois household, distinguishable only from the narrator's white femininity by her servant status. That such a figure should be chosen, along with the promiscuous Rebecca, to voice that which is unspeakable by the text's narrator, speaks directly to middle-class women's profound anxieties about female sexuality and their relationships with their servants.

Mrs Danvers, like Fremlin's Agnes, is presented as the product of a female sexuality turned obsessive as a result of the enforced celibacy of domestic service. However, whilst the reader is invited to pity and patronise Fremlin's 'neurotic spinster', Mrs Danvers represents a powerful anger which, rather than turning inwards to self-destruction, focuses its energies on the manifestations of its hatred. At the end of the novel, Manderley, the symbol of aristocratic and upper-middle-class England, is destroyed by fire at the hands of the servant whose existence once allowed it to flourish.

The form and genre of Du Maurier's narrative allowed her to represent relations between women of different classes in ways that make visible the ambiguities for a specifically female readership. The text is neither constrained by the social or political conventions required when addressing a mixed-sex readership of reformist leanings that characterise Fremlin's study nor the demands of fictional domestic realism. E. M. Delafield's *Diary of a Provincial Lady* (1984, first published 1930), for example, written as it is within the conventions of fictional realism, can only treat relations between mistress and servant as a source of wry comedy; a mode of writing which, whilst raising the impossibility of friendly intimacy between women in such situations, can neither probe the reasons for this nor offer alternative narratives. For Delafield's narrator, better relations might be desired but the comic mode determines the parameters in which such relations can be imagined. In the end the Provincial Lady can only take refuge in ironic resignation. As Tania Modleski has observed:

> because [Gothic] novels so radically displace reality by putting the action in distant times and strange and ghostly lands, they are uniquely equipped to become a site for the displacement of repressed wishes and fears. In other words, Gothics can present us with the frighteningly familiar precisely because they make the familiar strange—which is, it will be recalled, the way Freud said the uncanny sensation in literature is produced (Modleski, 1984: 20).

Leaving aside the fact that *Rebecca* can hardly be said to be located in "distant times and strange and ghostly lands", its Gothic elements produce precisely that sensation to which Modleski, following Freud, refers. Indeed, the 'frighteningly familiar' terrain of the English country house is made surprisingly strange and threatening. And this is because the familiar relations of mistress and servant, as well as husband and wife, are rendered threatening, even murderous. Home for middle-class women of this period was inextricably linked with their role as mistress of a household—maturity and selfhood meant not only wifehood and motherhood but the ability to achieve authority over servants. Hence the inability to retain a traditionally authoritarian mistress/servant relationship or to sustain a more informal, friendly relationship could be felt not only as a problem of domestic organisation but as a threat to a vital and constituent element of a mature, middle-class, female identity. To be accused of being 'ruled by your servants' was to attack the basis of this identity, rooted as it was in the ability to control, organise and create a harmonious domestic life. The power of *Rebecca* is that it makes visible the paranoia which underpinned the middle-class woman's relations with her servants: a paranoia the more disturbing for its location in the familiar heartland of private relations—the bourgeois home. When the narrator of *Rebecca* remembers her first meeting with the servants of Manderley, she does so in language that, in its excess, produces the paranoia which so nearly paralyses her: "they were the watching crowd about the block, and I the victim with my hands behind my back" (1975, first published 1938: 72). Equally, the narrator's transition from gauche young woman to mistress of Manderley is marked by her almost magically conferred ability to deal with the Manderley servants and, in particular, the terrifying Mrs Danvers.

This moment of precariously achieved maturity is also a moment of sexual awakening. It is her husband's desire for her as a woman rather than a young girl which propels her into maturity and enables her to perform her role as mistress of Manderley. In doing so she escapes the paralysis of her desire to emulate the erotically powerful Rebecca. Given the novel's lesbian sub-text, this final refusal to identify with Rebecca and the narrator's confrontation with Mrs Danvers constitute, at one level, a rejection of homoerotic pleasure in favour of the heterosexual narrative.

At another level, however, the text's linking of female sexuality with class and social status through the unspoken suggestion of a lesbian relationship between Mrs Danvers and Rebecca, produces the possibility of a narrative for cross-class relations between women that was unimaginable in other forms of writing. Many of the period's anxieties about female sexuality focussed on the celibacy of women but much of this concerned itself with the 'dangers' of celibate professional women:

> We do not yet have the means to investigate the psychological effects of permanent virginity in great detail but enough is known to make us aware that in entrusting responsibility towards individuals and the State to elderly virgins we may be acting unwisely (Charlotte Haldane cited in Jeffreys, 1985: 174).

As Fremlin's text suggests, the mistress/servant relationship could, in its demand for deference and loyalty, only produce narratives of 'neurotic' obsessive spinsters. Whilst *Rebecca* at one level appears to confirm this narrative, at another it opens up for its female readership the possibility of seductive pleasures derived from the lesbian sub-text.

Rendering and reading Mrs Danvers as villain and destroyer of Manderley may have enabled a middle-class female readership to entertain their own fantasies of destroying the social structures that 'forced' them into maintaining the divisions between women of different classes and created the emotional tensions so eloquently expressed by Woolf. In order to entertain such fantasies women readers would be required to undergo an act of identification with an obsessive servant, a textual strategy and subject positioning that was unavailable to the readers of *The Seven Chars of Chelsea*. Equally, Mrs Danvers' unqualified acceptance of Rebecca's sexuality might speak to female fantasies of caring friendships that were neither constrained by the demands of an unattainable femininity nor limited by the conventions of middle-class life. *Rebecca* draws on the same discourse of celibacy and neuroticism that informs *The Seven Chars of Chelsea*, but is able to re-interpret this so as to offer its female readers a variety of potentially liberating positions to read from. This is achieved as a result of Du Maurier's choice of form and genre: the melodrama of the Gothic romance, freed from the requirements of social realism or documentary, can represent the sexual yearning and eroticism that could motivate the devotion and loyalty of servants towards their mistresses as an active, rebellious force rather than as passive neuroticism.

Doris Arthurs

The *Seven Chars of Chelsea* and *Rebecca* are both published texts produced for a middle-class readership. Doris' narrative is an oral account heard only by myself and certainly not produced for a wider audience.[8] The reading of Doris' narrative which follows is not intended as a 'truer' account simply because it draws on first-hand experience. It remains one possible version of Doris' experience. Indeed, as Katherine Borland has pointed out, readings of oral narratives are produced from different standpoints and for varied purposes (Borland, 1991). I am using Doris' story here as a way of commenting on the narratives by Fremlin and Du Maurier rather than as an authoritative interpretation of the 'servant voice'.

When I visited Doris in 1988 she was eighty, and lived with her husband, Jim, in the same council house on an estate in Birmingham that they had first rented in the 1930s. Doris has not had an easy life. Born near Cannock in Staffordshire in 1908, Doris was one of ten children, of whom six survived. Her father was a miner and the family rented a cottage in the village of Hednesford. Like her three sisters, Doris left school at thirteen to begin work as a domestic servant in the local vicarage, cleaning the brasses and serving meals. Once she was old enough, Doris, like many young women, moved to Birmingham in search of more lucrative work to supplement her family's meagre income. Jobs in domestic service were plentiful in a large city like Birmingham and provided a respectable occupation as well as board and lodging for a young woman from the countryside. After a series of jobs Doris went to work as a housemaid in the home of the Mayor who lived in a wealthy suburb of Birmingham. When she was sixteen she met Jim and, after a long courtship, married him when she was twenty-four. Jim and Doris had one child, Valerie, whose life has been an unhappy one. They moved into their present home when it was built as part of the house building programme of the 1930s and Doris found part-time employment as a non-residential cleaner for a childless couple in order to help with the increased rent. Mr P and, particularly, his wife Jessie came to play a central role in Doris' life both emotionally and materially: Mr P sent a car to fetch her to work, she and Jim were taken on holiday and Jessie left Doris a small legacy. Doris was to say of them "they were ever so good to me they really gave me a good start in life." Mr P died shortly after the end of the Second World War and from then on Doris devoted herself to caring for Jessie, "who couldn't have enough of my company." When Jessie died it was Doris who made the funeral arrangements and it is Doris who continues to grieve for Jessie.

I resisted hearing Doris' story for a long time. I was researching home life and wanted to hear about relations with parents, spouses and children. Equally, I was uncomfortable with Doris' deferential and admiring account of her employer. I wanted to hear stories, such as those of Jean Rennie or Winifred Foley (Burnett, 1976), which celebrated overt acts of resistance to the exploitations of domestic service. When at last I acknowledged how important Doris' relationship with Jessie was to her I was forced to re-think my own understanding of deference and class in light of Doris' experience.

Doris' story is in some ways not unlike those of Fremlin and Du Maurier. The narrative includes the deference, the life devoted in service to another, the loyalty and the fidelity and the attachment to the material belongings of the mistress.[9] I want to suggest, however, that the language of Doris' narrative produced the possibility of understanding her relationship with Jessie as one in which her deference was balanced by Jessie's need. Doris' account re-constructs conventional understandings of the relations between the two women by configuring it as a family relationship. She spoke of Jessie as "being a sister to me" and this is reinforced by her use of Jessie's Christian name—Jessie's husband is always referred to as 'Mr P'. Yet, despite the apparently democratic, and at times intimate nature of their relations, Doris recalled it in the language of economics and materiality. Jessie gave Doris clothes for her daughter, Valerie, and cast-off household items whenever she moved house; Jessie left Doris a legacy and Doris inherited furniture when Jessie died. Jessie paid for a holiday for Doris and Jim and, as we have seen, Doris believed the couple "gave her a good start." Doris told me "I shall never be out of her debt." In return

Doris gave Jessie her time and her care, for, according to Doris, Jessie "couldn't have enough of my company. I used to hurry up and get my jobs done and race up there." For Doris, as for many working-class women of the period, love, caring, and nurturance were understood as a series of reciprocal relations, deeply rooted in economic as well as emotional needs. Emotional commitment is expressed through and co-terminous with material and economic realities: husbands, for example, are loved for their ability to provide the economic security missing from so many women's childhoods (Giles, 1995: 61-63). This is completely unlike the structures of meaning found in writings by middle-class women like Fremlin and Woolf, where affective and spiritual needs are perceived as distinct from and superior to bodily and material needs. Indeed, for writers like Woolf the material and physical needs which underpin each individual's existence are often treated as intrusions which threaten the 'inner life' that sustains creativity and the supposed superiority of middle-class life.[10]

When Doris went to work for Jessie she went as a married woman with a child, non-residential and employed as the only servant. This was very different to her experience as a housemaid in the Lord Mayor's household, where her relations with her employer would have been through the mediations of more senior servants. As a result Doris may have experienced her position *vis-à-vis* Jessie as more egalitarian than the rigid hierarchies to which she had been accustomed and this, in turn, produced a sense of confidence and autonomy about her employment, particularly when she was able to understand her relationship with Jessie within the familiar and familial discourse of economics. Jessie provides much needed material help, Doris 'pays' for this with her labour as well as her emotional care and support. Jessie is childless and later widowed: she 'buys' herself a sister and a friend. Jessie needed Doris, Doris needed the material benefits but she also needed to experience the power of being needed which Jessie's dependence might bestow. Doris may have experienced the envy and resentment endemic to the situation of a servant but equally she was able to balance this against the satisfaction and pride she felt about her friendship with a woman like Jessie. Doris' account of her friendship with Jessie expresses a belief that the barriers of class are not as impregnable as Fremlin would have it, neither do such friendships need to remain trapped in a refusal to acknowledge the material and economic realities which structure them.

Conclusion

The three texts examined here produce very different narratives of class relationships between women even when they draw on similar discourses. The texts of Fremlin and Du Maurier are both located in the early-twentieth-century discourse of Freudian psychology, but these texts, through a process of negotiation with other discourses and genres—in Fremlin's case the discourse of documentary realism, in Du Maurier's the genre of Gothic romance—produce different meanings. Ultimately, however, both *The Seven Chars of Chelsea* and *Rebecca* succumb to the heterosexual narrative of marriage, in which a woman's 'real' fulfilment is to be sought. Working-class women's devotion to their mistresses, however admirable or powerful, is not to be encouraged lest it lead to so-called morbid and unhealthy obsessions. Fremlin prefers her safely married 'chars' to the dangerous spinsterdom of her housemaids and Du Maurier's discomfort with the myths of heterosexual romantic love can only find expression in the sense of nostalgia and loss evident in the opening and closing pages of the novel. Yet both these texts testify to the sense of fear, desire, and fascination with which middle-class women of the period regarded relationships with their female servants, which in itself speaks to the centrality of such relationships in women's lives. Doris Arthurs' reminiscences were recorded long after the event and were listened to in a context which permitted a degree of intimacy between two women but which also focussed on family and economic relations.[11] The discursive space thus created produced a narrative of friendship between employer and servant that challenges those understandings of deference and loyalty which define 'service' as either straightforward oppression or an oblique manifestation of psycho/sexual repression. All three texts question those discourses of women's friendships that define heterosexual and familial relationships as the sole locus of women's emotional fulfilment. All three texts, in the ways discussed above, accord a significance and centrality to those relationships women negotiate with other women, outside the sphere of kinship and marriage. In doing so they not only render visible the complexities of such relationships but refuse the marginality which has so often attended discussions of women's friendships.

Notes

1. Celia Fremlin (1940), *The Seven Chars of Chelsea*; Daphne Du Maurier (1938), *Rebecca*; and transcript of interview between Doris Arthurs and Judy Giles (1988).

2. Rowntree in his 1901 survey of York drew the boundary between the working and the middle class at the point of servantkeeping, "the keeping or not keeping of domestic servants has in this inquiry been taken as marking the division between the working classes and those of a higher social scale" (Rowntree, 1901: 14).

3. The National Union of Women Workers noted as early as 1900 that 60 percent of the 'servantkeeping classes' kept only one servant and another 20 percent kept no more than two servants (cited in Dyhouse, 1989: 109).

4. See amongst others Delafield (1984, first published 1930); Brittain (1928); Mitchison (1979); Hughes (1979, first published 1940).

5. See for example The Pilgrim Trust (1938); Seebohm Rowntree (1941).

6. Pearl Jephcott, a youth work and educationalist, condemned those "stories of sex and sentimentality" in which "'[t]he kisses, the love stuff' are thrown at the readers" and "[e]very page is sickly with them." (Jephcott, 1942: 110).

7. In *Jane Eyre* Mr Rochester's wife, Bertha Mason, a Creole woman from Jamaica, has been confined to the attic of Thornfield as a lunatic. At crucial moments in the courtship between Rochester and Jane, Bertha, as madwoman, enacts the emotions which are unavailable to the modest, chaste Jane. In *Rebecca* Mrs Danvers is represented as 'neurotic'; her presence, like Bertha's, is sinister; her intrusions are dangerous.

8. 'Doris Arthurs' is an assumed name for one of the women I interviewed as part of the oral history research I undertook for my doctorate. See M. J. Giles (1989) '"Something that bit better": working-class women, domesticity and respectability, 1919-1939', unpublished D. Phil, University of York, for details of this research. For a fuller discussion of the ways in which subjectivities are represented in oral narratives, see Giles, 1995: 26-28.

9. In Fremlin's account of Agnes there is a section devoted to a long anecdote apparently recounted by Agnes in which she 'saved' a valuable piece of her mistress's furniture by her loving attention and care. In *Rebecca* readers will recall the scene in which Mrs Danvers conducts the narrator on a tour of Rebecca's bedroom, maintained by Mrs Danvers as a shrine to her dead mistress. The erotic undertones of this scene are strongly emphasised in the 1940 Hitchcock film of *Rebecca*. Doris insisted on showing me the furniture left her by Jessie and a photograph of the cottage in the country which belonged to Jessie and her husband.

10. Particularly relevant here is Virginia Woolf's distinction between women who "desire Mozart and Einstein" and those who "need baths and ovens" (Woolf in Davies, 1977, first published 1931: xxviii).

11. This is not to disregard the debates around feminist ethics of interviewing and research but to draw attention to one of the various positions Doris and I were able to take during the process of talking and listening. These positions included researcher/researched, young woman /older woman, visitor/host, woman/woman. For a fuller discussion of these issues, see Forrest and Giles (1999).

Judy Giles completed her doctorate with the Centre for Women's Studies at York in 1989. She is the author of *Women, Identity and Private Life in Britain 1900-1950* and co-author, with Tim Middleton, of *Writing Englishness 1900-1950: An Introductory Sourcebook on National Identity*. and *Studying Culture: A Practical Introduction*. She has contributed articles to *Women's History Review* and *Women's Studies International Forum* and is currently working on discourses of domesticity in the period 1945-1960. Judy teaches Women's Studies and Cultural Studies at the College of Ripon and York St John. Her friendships with women have inspired, supported and provided her with great joy.

Problems with (Girl)Friends? Contemporary women poets and tensions in female friendship

Vicki Bertram

> *"Where my Hands are cut, Her fingers will be found inside"*
> *Emily Dickinson*[1]

'Friend' seems such a little word. Nor does it get bulkier if I add an adjective: 'best friend' carries connotations of the playground, and fails to convey anything of the significance and intensity of the relationships I have in mind. Even that word 'relationship' is wrong; it is used almost exclusively nowadays to imply sexual contact between people. Often there's an unspoken 'only' lurking somewhere in conversations about friends, immediately signalling the lesser weight attributed to friendship. Language seems geared to sexual (usually heterosexual) bonds; I can't find adequate words for experiences that have absorbed far more of my life, and exerted a far greater influence over me, than my love affairs and 'relationships'. I think there is a hole in the English language. We resort to weak analogies: she is 'like a sister to me'—but that only underlines the lack of alternatives, and also implies the greater importance attributed to blood ties—an issue I shall return to. I am only in the first paragraph of this chapter and already I have run out of synonyms. Even *Roget's Thesaurus* seems to have difficulty:

> **friend**, girl-f., boy-f. *[not a promising opening]* 887 n. **loved one**; *[doesn't this have connotations of blood ties?]* acquaintance, intimate a.; gossip, *[ahh...]* crony (see **chum**); neighbour, *[not, I believe, necessarily the same thing at all]*, fellow-townsman, fellow-

> countryman; *[ditto, not to mention the generic]* well-wisher 707 n. **patron;** fellow, brother 707 n. **colleague**; ally, brother-in-arms 707 n. **auxiliary**; friend in need; invitee, guest, persona grata; host 882 n. **social person.**
> *[now it gets warmer]* **close friend**, best f., next f.; best man 984 n. *[what?]* **bridesman**; dear friend, intimate, bosom friend, *[from Shakespeare, sadly not born of a recognition of the power of* ***female*** *friendships]* confidant; alter ego, other self, shadow; comrade, companion, boon c.; good friends all, happy family; *[oh no, the blood again...]* inseparables, band of brothers; birds of a feather.
> **chum**, gossip, crony; pal, mate, bully, buddy, sidekick; fellow, comrade, shipmate, messmate 707 n. **colleague**; playmate, schoolfellow (352).

Many of these words seem more appropriate for men. But then, women aren't supposed to like other women. Literature offers countless examples of comradeship between men but, until very recently, almost no accounts of female friends' loyalty. Seventy years ago Virginia Woolf observed that women were always depicted in relation to men in the English novel, leaving the nuances and complexity of their connections with other women entirely unexplored: "All these relationships between women, I thought, rapidly recalling the splendid gallery of fictitious women, are too simple. So much has been left out, unattempted" (Woolf, 1977, first published 1929: 79). Towards the end of this lecture on women and fiction (published as *A Room of One's Own*) Woolf slips into her most arch irony to relate her experience of reading an unusual first novel by one Mary Carmichael:

> determined to do my duty by her as reader if she would do her duty by me as writer, I turned the page and read. ... I am sorry to break off so abruptly. Are there no men present? Do you promise me that behind that red curtain over there the figure of Sir Charles Biron is not concealed? We are all women you assure me? Then I

> may tell you that the very next words I read were these—"Chloe liked Olivia ...". Do not start. Do not blush. Let us admit in the privacy of our own society that these things sometimes happen. Sometimes women do like women (78).

Woolf makes a big to-do about the secrecy and potential embarrassment surrounding this revelation of female friendship (or 'more'?), and goes on to suggest that what happens between women alone together is so sensitive to the intrusion of male observers that it actually *requires* this secrecy. In addition, because her subject is fiction, Woolf is interested by the changes in form and structure that accompany this radical departure. She implies that this new focus—on Chloe and Olivia rather than Chloe and Roger—necessitates a new kind of sentence. Instead of the gentle rhythms of Jane Austen's prose, the sentences lurch and jar: "to read this writing was like being out at sea in an open boat. Up one went, down one sank" (77). She thinks Carmichael has set herself a tricky task:

> The only way for you to do it, I thought, addressing Mary Carmichael as if she were there, would be to talk of something else, looking steadily out of the window, and thus note, not with a pencil in a notebook, but in the shortest of shorthand, in words that are hardly syllabled yet, what happens when Olivia—this organism that has been under the shadow of the rock these million years—feels the light fall on it, and sees coming her way a piece of strange food— knowledge, adventure, art (81).

The densely figurative language points to the problem Woolf shares with her novelist: how to imagine—or more accurately, how to find words to describe—the behaviour and interaction of two women, when Literature has never looked in their direction, but carved its plots out of the stuff of wars or romantic love. *A Room of One's Own* was published in 1929; since then women writers, inspired or challenged by 'second wave' feminism, have done much to address this silence. But when I set out to consider contemporary women poets' treatment of friendship, I was surprised at the lack of examples I could find.

This seems particularly strange in an era in which feminism and female solidarity have done so much to encourage the publication of women poets' work, and when the poets themselves frequently testify to the importance of other women's encouragement, critique and emotional support. During the last two decades there have been countless anthologies of women poets, as well as individually-authored collections. Many of these women have recorded their gratitude to other women writers, the confidence and skills they learned or honed together through workshops or—more generally—the value of the support of women in their lives. So I expected to find some record in the poems of the significance of friends: poems addressed to friends, or about them, celebrating particular friendships.[2]

I have found only a handful. There are endless poems *about* women: observed by the poet on the street, in the park, at bingo; historical or mythical women imagined or invoked; poems about women subjects in paintings; and poems about daughters, mothers and grandmothers. But there are very few about friends. This raises the issue of how 'friend' is defined. Does it only refer to closeness between two people unrelated by blood, or can, say, sisters be included? Can it be used to include those relationships that also have a sexual intimacy? Conventionally, I would suggest, the answers to these questions are 'yes' and 'no', respectively, although the poems I'll discuss go some way towards challenging this. Societies across the world regulate human relationships according to two systems: blood ties, and marriage. Friendships are unrecognised by legal, economic and social systems although for women especially, I would argue, the amount of time, and the nature of the support (practical and emotional) gained from friendships often exceeds that of other, more publicly-celebrated relationships.

In those poems I have found, the friend remains a shadowy presence. She rarely emerges as an individual with a clear personality or existence separate from that of the poet. In the remainder of this essay I shall consider some possible reasons for this state of affairs. Rather than an explanation, this is a speculative piece, and it draws upon an eclectic mixture of fields of knowledge—psychological, literary and cultural. What has interested me throughout is the very close identification, the mirroring, that often seems to characterise women's friendships.[3] The Dickinson quotation in my epigraph—in which the poet is describing her feelings for her closest lifelong friend and sister-in-law, Sue Gilbert— conveys the intensity of this experience of a merger which is not figured as fleeting (as in sexual union), but disturbingly constant. A disproportionate number of the poems I *have* found tackle this theme of overlapping identities between women, of a confusion of boundaries between self and other. Sometimes these poems are marked by anxiety, and an almost obsessive effort to demarcate differences between poet/narrator and friend. Others revel in the confusion of identities, recognising the subversive impact of such a fierce conjunction. Taken collectively, the relatively few contemporary poems about women's friendships also highlight the constraining effects of social expectations and language-usage. In other words, I am suggesting that the problems that poets appear to encounter when approaching this subject-matter may stem partly from the inadequate recognition accorded to friendship in women's lives. As I've argued, these crucial relationships are nameless and invisible, not formally recognised by any legal, social or religious code. This causes specific problems for the poet who wishes to record and explore their place in her life. The poems she creates may—like Mary Carmichael's novel—break the familiar mould. Interestingly, today's poets don't seem to be taking Woolf's advice (quoted above) about pretending not to look, jotting the briefest of shorthand notes while cultivating an air of studied indifference. Their poems record their own entangled involvement, and are far from being portraits of the friends in question. Instead, they seem to record and probe a tension in the friendship between identification and difference. "I will wrestle you to the end / for our difference (as you have wrestled me"—a line from Adrienne Rich's poem "Sleepwalking Next to Death" (Rich, 1989)—offers a succinct illustration of this theme. A little later in the same poem, she broaches a related issue about whose version of the relationship gets articulated:

> Calmly you look over my shoulder   at this page   and say
> *It's all about you*   *None of this*
> *tells my story*

It is important to note that the poetry I am familiar with (and which I have studied while researching this chapter) is predominantly text-based rather than performance work. Most of this writing is by white, middle-class heterosexual women poets from Britain, Ireland and the United States. It is likely that the characteristics I identify are specific not only to this historical moment, but also to this cultural group who, while obviously differing in many ways, probably do share a common experience of the place of female friendship in their lives. Certainly the current low status and invisibility of women's friendship is not a historical constant. As feminists have shown, in the nineteenth century 'romantic friendships' between women were encouraged and recognised as an important part of girls' maturation (Smith-Rosenberg, 1975; Faderman, 1981, 1992). Faderman suggests that the demise of the acceptability and recognition of romantic friendships is the result of our late-twentieth-century obsessive sexual awareness:

> It became so incredible to our century that passionate love could occur without genital sexual expression that the term 'romantic friendship' dropped out of the language .... Whatever wide spectrum of subtleties, gradations, or varieties that were once possible in women's love relationships with each other became much more circumscribed (Faderman, 1992: 305-6).

Genital sexual activity has become a—if not *the*—central determinant of human identity, and the marker of significance in relationships. Even the progressive vocabulary of someone's 'significant other' affords pre-eminence to the sexual partner. (Are other 'others' insignificant?) Is it inevitably the case that a genitally-sexual relationship is *necessarily* more intimate than one that is not? I think not, but our culture imbues sexual connection with a romantic mystique that implies that it is. This intensifying focus on the couple prioritises exclusivity and the tight-knit, essentially private, independent nuclear family unit. Whether this unit is composed of a man and a woman, two men, or two women seems less important than that they be in a sexual relationship, which is then automatically viewed as conferring a stable sexual identity on its participants, despite all evidence to the contrary.

To turn now to poetry. I have chosen to discuss five poems. One presents a conventional scenario, in which a woman comforts her friend after the painful ending of her relationship with a male lover. The next two illustrate a preoccupation with the tension between sameness and difference that I have already mentioned. Finally, I look at two poems that self-consciously situate themselves outside the orthodox social structures that relegate friendship between women to the margins, unnamed and unrecognised. In the course of my discussion I hope to make connections between contemporary poetry and the social and cultural climate. Here I take my cue from Rachel Du Plessis, who argues for a more culturally-attuned approach to lyric poetry:

> ... lyrics have often been privileged by the critical assumption of their timeless, universal emotions and nonparticipation in historical debate .... It has been relatively difficult to make them "telling", to have them tell tales of embedded ideologies and debates in the same ways that narrative has. Both the privileges of poetic genius and assumptions of a transcendent "beyond" of art cling to lyric poetry in ways that make it difficult to see the cultural work done by poems. To counter this devastating assumption of poetic neutrality or specialness, I now simply assume that all kinds of social materials and cultural narratives saturate poetic texts: the question is not whether they are there, but how to find them and what they mean (Blau DuPlessis, 1994: 70-1).

It is precisely this 'cultural work' done—or, as in this case, not commonly done—by poetry that interests me. The fact that almost all poetry published today comes under the generic heading 'lyric' is not mere chance, but is intricately related to the kinds of relationship that are given status and value in contemporary Western culture. Lyric poetry, originally a term for poems accompanied by music, is now loosely-used to describe:

> any fairly short poem expressing the personal mood, feeling, or meditation of a single speaker (who may sometimes be an invented character, not the poet) ... Lyrics may be composed in almost any metre and on almost every subject, although the most usual emotions presented are those of love and grief (Baldick, 1990: 125).

The lyric is thus well-suited to the expression of an individual's emotion, whose source often lies in the behaviour or fate of an other. It invariably takes the form of a monologue: no other voice—including that of the other who forms the subject of the poem—speaks.[4] As a short, intimate address, the lyric side-steps the dilemma of audience: how to find, or rely upon, a common currency of language and allusion. (The poetry-reading public used to be a tight-knit élite: sharing educational background, knowledge of the Classics and other literary canonical works. Today, the number of poetry readers is still very small, but poets can no longer rely on their shared knowledge.) It also offers up intimacy to public consumption, and our thirst for this kind of insight currently seems unquenchable. Lyric poetry is frequently addressed to a particular individual, even though it may—as the poet hopes—resonate with the experiences of others. In these ways it seems the form most suited to an age of extreme individualism.

But if lyric poetry is so well-suited to relationships, why not to women's friendships? Partly, I suspect, because Western culture's preferred version of "love" is the romantic—and potentially sexual—variety. The low status afforded friendship provides the poet with little incentive to celebrate it. Poetry absorbs and grows out of the cultural climate, so in poetry—as in society—romantic heterosexual union is championed as the 'natural' endpoint of maturation, despite the wholly-constructed (if ancient) ideology of romance. The lack of models from poetry of the nineteenth and twentieth centuries may also play a part in discouraging poets from this subject. In the eighteenth century, friendship poems were common, but that era's public, formalised poetic is not attractive to today's neo-romantic expectations of poetry.[5] It is extremely difficult to open up new areas of experience to poetic treatment, particularly when there are so very few commonly-recognised myths or stories about female friendship upon which to draw.[6] But in addition to these obstacles, I suspect part of the reason lies in the troubling nature of the subject matter itself: that the closeness of identification between women may be experienced by the poet as a threat to her own identity. In order to explore this further, I will make use of the theories of Nancy Chodorow and other feminist-orientated object relations psychologists. If 'sisterhood' is powerful, as one feminist slogan put it, it is also competitive and antagonistic. These more difficult dimensions of relationships between women are still under-acknowledged and under-researched, but their impact can be felt in some of the poetry that tackles this material.

Many of the poems I have found about friendship are written from a lesbian perspective. Lesbians obviously have a more urgent interest in delineating the varieties of woman-to-woman relationships. For them, the heterosexual love lyric simply does not fit, as poet Suniti Namjoshi explains:

> Sex itself is an image and in lyric love poems is a central metaphor for figuring the relation between the "I" and the "you". In other words it embodies an entire ideology, and in the lyric tradition this ideology is the ideology of patriarchal heterosexuality .... a lesbian writing a love lyric in her own voice, ie. not in an encoded voice, necessarily either subverts the lyric tradition or ruptures it every time she writes such a poem, because she is the unimaginable: the woman speaker as lover addressing a fellow woman lover (Hanscombe and Namjoshi, 1991: 157).

While Namjoshi's unfashionably essentialist claim may be open to criticism, it seems to me that precisely because of their lack of investment in this tradition, lesbian poets are in a better position to push poetry into new areas and, at the same time, to tackle the challenging terrain of identification and differentiation between women, whether lovers or friends. From this oblique perspective, and by dissolving the rigid demarcations between lover and friend, they can create alternative conceptualisations of self, other, intimacy, and love. The two poems I discuss last offer examples of such possibilities.

I'll start with two poems whose settings are more orthodox: in both, female friendship and heterosexual relationship are presented as mutually exclusive. In Michèle Roberts' "Magnificat", the speaker's friend brings comfort at the traumatic end of a love-affair. It is a bold attempt to commemorate a friendship, and is dedicated to "Sian, after thirteen years":

> oh this man
> what a meal he made of me
> how he chewed and gobbled and sucked
>
> in the end he spat me all out
>
> you arrived on the dot, in the nick
> of time, with your red curls flying
> I was about to slip down the sink like grease
> I nearly collapsed, I almost
> wiped myself out like a stain
> I called for you, and you came, you voyaged
> fierce as a small archangel with swords and breasts
> you declared the birth of a new life
> in my kitchen there was an annunciation
> and I was still, awed by your hair's glory
>
> you commanded me to sing of my redemption
>
> oh my friend, how
> you were mother for me, and how
> I could let myself lean on you
> comfortable as an old cloth, familiar as enamel saucepans
> I was a child again, pyjamaed
> in winceyette, my hair plaited, and you
> listened, you soothed me like cakes and milk
> you listened to me for three days, and I poured
> it out, I flowed all over you

like wine, like oil, you touched the place where it hurt
at night we slept together in my big bed
your shoulder eased me towards dreams

when we met, I tell you
it was a birthday party, a funeral
it was a holy communion
between women, a Visitation

it was two old she-goats butting
and nuzzling each other in the smelly fold
(Roberts, 1986: 70)

With characteristic verve, Roberts usurps the Virgin Mary's praise hymn, infusing it with an earthy realism and borrowing religious vocabulary in order to assert the solemnity and resonance of bonds between women. She juxtaposes the language of the Bible with domestic banality, deliberately jumbling up sacred and profane: angels and kitchen grease, saucepans and psalm-like cadences. Women are put back into the religious story: flesh-and-blood women with sexy red hair and failed love-affairs. This is a project Roberts has pursued in her fiction too, but here what interests me is the way in which the healing role of the friend is sanctified. Her presence signals a profound change; she seems to have a spiritual aura about her, and her touch is healing. The speaker regresses into childhood and is cared for by her nurturing friend who, like a religious appointee, hears her friend's confession, and helps restore her sense of self, which has come so close to dissolution. But this is conveyed via images of mothering and of birth: metaphors that strike me as somehow worn out or inappropriate. The poem seems aware that neither quite catches the essence of the relationship. Hence the closing stanzas, heaping up examples of public events granted a comparable significance: a list of religious and cultural events imbued with a special aura. In this way the poem (intentionally?) draws attention to the lack of vocabulary or recognition for women's friendship. It is the closing lines that offer the most arresting image. Here, in a pointed analogy with animals—outsiders to the social order—Roberts suggests the existence of an instinctive complementarity between the two women. Rather than shaping their behaviour according to the other's mood, they are free to be as they feel: tender and solicitous, or impatient and irritated, by turns. Such spontaneous, freely-chosen behaviour contrasts strongly with the mirroring and projection of mood identified by Chodorow and others.

As Woolf feared, reactions to such an account of women's friendship have been strong. In a disparaging review of *The Virago Book of Love Poetry* (Mulford, 1990), which bravely attempted to broaden notions of love to include friendship, and reproduced "Magnificat", Zoe Heller dismissed it as "a mimsy eulogy" (Heller, 1990). Mimsy carries connotations of something over-prettified or twee. Certainly the poem concentrates on one particular incident in its celebration of a long friendship, but the closing lines guard against accusations of idealisation.

The second poem, "The Choosing", is by the Scottish poet Liz Lochhead:

> We were first equal Mary and I
> with same coloured ribbons in mouse-coloured hair
> and with equal shyness,
> we curtseyed to the lady councillor
> for copies of Collins' Children's Classics.
> First equal, equally proud.
>
> Best friends too Mary and I
> a common bond in being cleverest (equal)
> in our small school's small class.
> I remember

the competition for top desk
or to read aloud the lesson
at school service.
And my terrible fear
of her superiority at sums.

I remember the housing scheme
where we both stayed.
The same houses, different homes,
where the choices got made.

I don't know exactly why they moved,
but anyway they went.
Something about a three-apartment
and a cheaper rent.
But from the top deck of the high-school bus
I'd glimpse among the others on the corner
Mary's father, mufflered, contrasting strangely
with the elegant greyhounds by his side.
He didn't believe in high school education,
especially for girls,
or in forking out for uniforms.

Ten years later on a Saturday -
I am coming from the library -
sitting near me on the bus,
Mary
with a husband who is tall,
curly haired, has eyes
for no one else but Mary.

Her arms are round the full-shaped vase
that is her body.
Oh, you can see where the attraction lies
in Mary's life -
not that I envy her, really.

And I am coming from the library
with my arms full of books.
I think of those prizes that were ours for the taking
and wonder when the choices got made
we don't remember making.
(Lochhead, 1984: 151)

As its title indicates, this poem confronts the different life trajectories of the narrator and her childhood friend Mary—though its scepticism about the freedom of that "choice" is heavily underscored by its location of blame and responsibility on Mary's father. Nevertheless its treatment of childhood friendship between girls is interesting because it emphasises the similarity of the two girls, and their own attempts to enhance this identification: they wear their mouse-coloured hair in exactly the same style, "with same coloured ribbons." The friendship seems to depend upon their sameness ("a common bond in being cleverest (equal)"), as though the intrusion of difference—in the guise of one edging ahead of the other—would destroy the grounds of their mutual affection. Their liking depends upon this narcissistic mirroring (I am using the phrase in its psychoanalytic sense, as descriptive of a vital stage in human development). The narrator recalls being hyper-conscious of this tense poise, continually fearful lest Mary would pull ahead in Maths, and thus force the fact of their difference into the open. At the same time, there is a hint of her sense of constriction and claustrophobia in the relationship. Class and patriarchy intervene, imposing different futures upon the two girls, but also forcing the inevitable fact of their separateness upon them. Profound differences may be concealed beneath an appearance of sameness. While the poem makes a sharp political point about the illusory nature of 'choice' in many women's lives, the patriarch's action saves the girls from having to actively relinquish their merger, and experience the pain of willed separation as the result of their own choice. A decade later the narrator seems to have no more sense of agency than Mary, despite her avid studying; when she sees her old friend, she starts mirroring her once again, substituting the books in her arms for the contours of the baby in Mary's womb. Now the two women encounter one of the most profound differences: between women with, and without, children. The narrator is not convincing in her denial of envy: that "really" qualifies her claim of indifference, and the final lines' admission of her own lack of conscious choice underlines the self-doubt. Beneath the poem's political edge lie disturbing hints of the elusive and difficult quest for female autonomy. Sylvia Plath's poem, "The Babysitters" also reminisces about a close youthful friendship, revealing a much stronger sense of bewilderment at the transformations that have taken place in the interim. The narrator recalls a day trip by rowing-boat, and a swim:

> We kicked and talked. The thick salt kept us up.
> I see us floating there yet, inseparable - two cork dolls.
> What keyhole have we slipped through, what door has shut?
> The shadows of the grasses inched round like hands of a clock,
> And from our opposite continents we wave and call.
> Everything has happened.
>
> (Plath, 1981:174)

Distance and separation—both temporal and geographical—account for the failure of communication. Again, circumstances, rather than a willed break, seem to have caused the end of intimacy. Where Lochhead opts for a politicised analysis of this, Plath's poem is unambiguous in its anguished sense of isolation and the loss of friendship's intimacies.

All three of these poems remain silent on one crucial facet of the scenarios they depict: female friendship flourishes in the absence of males. "The Choosing" indirectly makes the father responsible for the break between the girls; "Magnificat" focuses on a friend's rescue work after a traumatic mauling from a male lover. "The Babysitters" offers no information about the speaker's present circumstances, but her memories of that summer cluster round her relationship with the other *au pair*. This is uncannily reminiscent of Woolf's point about the surreptitious nature of female friendship, flourishing in women-only spaces, destroyed by the appearance of men.

The next poem explores similar territory to that in Lochhead's. In "Got You" Jackie Kay returns to the scene of childhood friendship, although instead of the retrospective viewpoint of the adult, she offers the child's perspective. The poem explores the most intense version of identification between girls by depicting near-identical twins:

> You know I am the shy one really, don't you,
> not you; that your maths have my answers,
> then how come I am the slow one
>
> and you are the one who shines. School Dux.
> Prefect. Your blazer is shabbier than mine
> but Gran from Dornock loves you better
>
> than me and so does our mother. The dog
> licks you. People who say they can't tell
> the difference drive you crazy: your skin is creamier,
>
> your nose less wide; your hair loose floppy
> curls, not *frizzy*, not *sheep's wool*. I know,
> I know like I know the back of my hand. Last night
>
> in the top bunk, I wanted to climb down
> and do something. Can't tell what. Not even in our tongue.
> I swallowed hard listening for the sound of real sleep

till I must have given in again.
You know me better than I know you.
Always get me. I sat bolt upright, my heart

flapped like our bedroom curtains, your night-time
laughter, soft, squeezed to your chest, doubled-up:
"Got you. Didn't I. Got you again."

(Kay, 1993: 53)

This poem captures the extreme complicity between the girls, as well as describing the pressure it produces. Not only do they appear virtually identical, they also share their own, secret, language. The narrator struggles to preserve—or create—her own identity, feeling overshadowed by her twin, who seems to try less hard and yet to possess a far stronger sense of self. This is proved, in the narrator's eyes, by the greater recognition she wins: more love and admiration from both public and private spheres represented by school, granny, even the dog's preference. Her predominantly monosyllabic sentences are littered with first and second person pronouns, and circle obsessively around registering the distinction between the two:

You know *I* am the shy one really, don't *you*,
not *you*; that *your* maths have *my* answers,
then how come *I* am the slow one

and *you* are the one who shines.

Her vocabulary seems to reflect the weakness in her sense of self; she takes refuge in an adult's idiom that sounds forced and secondhand ("I know, / I know like I know the back of my hand."), but also introduces an unsettling image of her studied, almost obsessive self-scrutiny. Her twin guards her individual identity fiercely, rejecting any suggestion that she looks like her sister. Instead, she strengthens her own sense of self by insulting her sister's hair, defining herself against this threateningly similar other. The girls' night-time game symbolises the struggle between them and the narrator's dilemma. Falling asleep entails a very literal loss of self-presence, and yet once again she fails to hold on to her conscious selfhood, slips into oblivion and is taunted back to wakefulness, and her sister's dominating presence.

Both Lochhead and Kay depict relationships in which the other girl is so close to the narrator that she appears both to threaten her sense of independent selfhood and yet, paradoxically, also to offer some kind of desirable and strengthening affirmation. This is very close to the scenario first described by psychologist Nancy Chodorow in her famous study, *The Reproduction of Mothering* (1978) which has been taken up, challenged and refined by many commentators since its first publication. For my purposes here, the relevance lies in Chodorow's psychoanalytically-oriented argument that the female child has difficulty establishing firm ego boundaries, due to the closeness of her relationship with her mother, who "cathects her daugher as a narcissistic extension of herself" (Abel, 1981: 417). The daughter retains her preOedipal bond with her mother, and thus, in maturity, continues to define herself "relationally," or in relation to others.

Chodorow's ideas have been popularised by feminist psychologists Susie Orbach and Luise Eichenbaum. Their study of the tensions and conflicts arising between close women friends arose from work at the Women's Therapy Centre in London. First published in 1987, *Bitter Sweet: Love, envy and competition in women's friendships* is a response to difficulties between women which they connect to the growing achievements and freedoms in contemporary women's lives. Like all such theories, it risks homogenising women's experiences, and overlooking the mediating effects of class and race. Nevertheless, the pattern of female relationships that Orbach and Eichenbaum describe does resonate with what I have found in these two poems.

They argue that the mother/daughter relationship sets the pattern for all future adult relationships. This formative relationship is characterised by what they call "merged attachment" between mother and daughter (their version of Chodorow's ideas):

> The mother's need for attachment, combined with her identification with her daughter, creates a fusion between the two of them. The mother is not separate from her daughter and, as her daughter expresses her needs, the mother experiences them *with* her, almost as though they were *her own*. She feels them too (Orbach and Eichenbaum, 1987: 53) [their emphasis].

This intimate connection has double-edged effects: it is the source of women's capacity to nurture and establish close relationships, but it also encourages a fluidity in women's boundaries. Merged attachments are marked by three characteristics: compulsive attendance to the needs of the other; the repression of one's own initiatives, and the denial of difference. Orbach and Eichenbaum suggest that women therefore find it particularly difficult to create relationships based on an acceptance of their separateness from one another:

> In adult relationships she is searching to find herself. But because the only mechanism she has for doing so is through merging and identifying with others, she comes to these relationships with emotional malleability. She comes with her emotional antennae ready to tune into the needs of the other. She is ready to adjust herself, deny herself, indeed lose herself (in order to find her 'self') in the attachment. But this process means that she loses sight of her own separate needs and desires. A search begins to find them in the other. ... Her adult relationships are woven with the threads of merged attachments (1987: 53-4).

Related to this is the tendency to over-identify with others: "women often fall into an experience of identifying with one another rather than seeing objectively the other's experience and empathising with it" (59). Empathy requires making a conscious effort to understand the other, as other, and different; it is a process characterised by compassionate detachment.

In their articles on female friendships in fiction (see note 3), both Elizabeth Abel and Judith Gardiner make use of Chodorow's ideas about women's relational self-definition. Gardiner also comments that the intense ambivalence of the mother / daughter relationship colours all future female friendships, and that the model is one of a continuum from mother / daughter on to friend / friend. Considering these theories in relation to the poems I've looked at so far, only "Magnificat" (in its closing lines) presents a friendship that seems wholly free of the characteristics of merged attachments. In "The Choosing" and "Got You", intimacy seems founded on sameness and identification.

These ideas are theories, they are not determinist: not all daughters will inevitably have such an experience. Nor, indeed, is it only mothers who can project their unmet needs onto and into their daughters; fathers can do it too, and of course sons may find themselves in the receiving position, as well as daughters. But as a generalisation, extrapolated from the experiences of a large number of women from similar cultural backgrounds, they do offer some further insight into why this territory should be so difficult for the woman poet. They suggest a way of knowing that entails what could be seen as parasitic intimacy: by reaching out, into the other, the woman tries to understand and to know her. But this apparent incorporation of the other's experience risks denying her separate, distinct and different existence. In Emily Dickinson's startling metaphor, Sue Gilbert has been ingested: cut the poet's flesh, and you will find *her* fingers within. This disturbing image, with its implied violation of both women, is an extreme example.[7] But it is this erasure of the other woman that Helena Michie identifies in the research work of well-known feminists. She points out that, however determinedly feminists seek to acknowledge the limits of their own knowledge and experience, and to leave space for 'the other woman', we fail to do so. She concludes her article with a description of the feminist "self" that has haunted me since I first read it:

> many rhetorical and political gestures that begin as explorations of Otherness, end by absorbing Otherness into an increasingly capacious notion of self. It is this capacious and hungry self—most benignly embodied in the metaphor of sisterhood—that feminists must learn to recognize so that they can ultimately recognize the face outside the mirror: the face of the Other woman (1989, in Warhol and Herndl, 1991: 67).

The Dickinson quotation is used by Betsy Erkkila in her fascinating study *The Wicked Sisters: Women Poets, Literary History, and Discord* (1992). In it she focuses on important female relationships in the lives of Elizabeth Bishop, Gwendolen Brooks and other twentieth-century poets. Rather than idealising sisterly solidarity, Erkkila uncovers the (often creatively fruitful) tensions between these women.[8] What emerges is a version of Michie's "hungry and capacious self": friendships that are characterised by their demanding, possessive quality. Erkkila argues that Chodorow's work has been used to emphasise the positive, mutually-nurturing qualities of female relationships. She points out that "the bonds of assistance and resistance that women poets have formed with other women have also been bonds formed by exclusion, silencing or demonization of other women" (1992:14-5).[9] Writing of Dickinson, Erkkila claims that her circle of close women friends was a vital source of support as she worked out her own defiant position as an unmarried woman. She also suggests that Dickinson conducted these friendships mainly by letter, so as to avoid having to confront the disruptive reality of her friends' separate physical existence. At the same time, she notes that the poet "is most potent when she defines herself not *apart from* but *in relation* to others .... She wanted her friends to mirror and affirm her own needs and desires" (Erkkila, 1992: 18, 26). Abel finds something similar in the fiction she examines: "Because this identification process can engulf as well as shape identity, its course is smoothest when the object of identification is remembered or imagined rather than physically present" (Abel: 1981: 426). Several feminist critics have produced sharp-eyed analyses of traditional, male-authored love lyrics (especially sonnets), showing how the female love object functions as a cypher against which the male poet defines himself (Homans, 1981; Montefiore, 1987). Perhaps women use their friends in a similar way.

Michie points out that the feminist movement has absorbed, and in its turn replicates, a Freudian model of human relationships, centred on the family. As a consequence, feminist discourse employs familial metaphors, without even noticing how this hinders our efforts to find new ways of relating to other women. Michie draws attention to the constraining effects of feminism's preoccupation with the family drama. She tries to think outside what Jane Gallop has described as "the pitfalls of familial thinking" (1989, in Warhol and Herndl, 1991: 60), and describes how feminists have:

> turned their gaze horizontally and have chosen—or tried to choose— to mirror each other and not the father. The axis of symmetry, the mirror of likeness upon which the Oedipal triangle is based, moves, then, from the space between father and daughter to the space(s) between sisters (58).

The possible configurations of relationships between women are, to a large extent, determined by these familial metaphors:

> No matter how problematized, metaphors of sisterhood and motherhood remain central to the feminist project. "Sister" and "mother" become the vessels that contain, shape, and delimit feminist discourse just as the family as it is now construed contains and shapes the roles and bodies of "real" mothers and sisters (59).

It seems to me that the effects of the structural centrality of this model have been overlooked; we have inherited it, and reproduced it, without question. But if the nuclear family is placed at the heart of analysis, then relationships that fall outside it are inevitably marginalised, seen as less significant, placeless, even illegitimate. Once this scene is accepted as central, there becomes no way of thinking outside it. The meanings of roles like mother and daughter are overdetermined. The family romance is powerfully seductive, so much so that feminists can't break away from it. And our poetry reflects this love affair: overpopulated with poems to / about mothers and fathers, and to / about lovers. As O'Connor and Ryan (1993) demonstrate in their study of the failure of psychoanalytic theories to account for lesbianism as anything other than pathology, it is the acceptance of this nuclear family scenario as primal and determining that lies at the heart of the difficulty of developing alternative roles and identities that would no longer be defined always in relation to the norms of the nuclear family.

This is what is beginning to be done, particularly by lesbian poets. In their work familial roles get shaken up, and take on new meanings; the conventional chronology of the young woman's growth away from mother and father towards an adult male and the reproduction of the family unit, is rejected. Freeing up space in this way, there is suddenly room for a different kind of encounter with, and recognition of, the friend. No longer the 'other woman', she can emerge from the sidelines, and even take centre-stage as a significant presence in the poet's life.

"An Anointing" by an African-American poet, Thylias Moss, attempts just such a realignment. It is a feisty, exuberant account of the friendship between two young women:

Boys have to slash their fingers to become brothers. Girls trade their
Kotex, me and Molly do in the mall's public facility.

Me and Molly never remember each other's birthdays. On purpose. We
don't like scores of any kind. We don't wear watches or weigh our-
selves.

Me and Molly have tasted beer. We drank our shampoo. We went to the
doctor together and lifted our specimen cups in a toast. We didn't
drink that stuff. We just gargled.

When me and Molly get the urge, we are careful to put it back exactly
as we found it. It looks untouched.

Between the two of us, me and Molly have 20/20 vision.

Me and Molly are in eighth grade for good. We like it there. We adore
the view. We looked both ways and decided not to cross the street.
Others who'd been to the other side didn't return. It was a trap.

Me and Molly don't double date. We don't multiply anything. We don't
know our multiplication tables from a coffee table. We'll never be
decent waitresses, indecent ones maybe.

Me and Molly do not believe in going ape or going bananas or going
Dutch. We go as who we are. We go as what we are.

Me and Molly have wiped each other's asses with ferns. Made emergency tampons of our fingers. Me and Molly made do with what we have.

Me and Molly are in love with wiping the blackboard with each other's hair. The chalk gives me and Molly an idea of what old age is like; it is dusty and makes us sneeze. We are allergic to it.

Me and Molly, that's M and M, melt in your mouth.

What are we doing in your mouth? Me and Molly bet you'll never guess. Not in a million years. We plan to be around that long. Together that long. Even if we must freeze the moment and treat the photograph like the real thing.

Me and Molly don't care what people think. We're just glad that they do.

Me and Molly lick the dew off the morning grasses but taste no honey till we lick each other's tongues.

We wear full maternity sails. We boat upon my broken water. The katabatic action begins, Molly down my canal binnacle first, her water breaking in me like an anointing.

(Sherman, 1995: 163)

The poem is interesting for its refusal to define the girls' relationship within traditional categories: whether theirs is a sexual relationship or 'just friends' is not clear. But as Eve Kosofsky Sedgwick has pointed out, the rigid opposition that exists between "homosocial" and "homosexual" behaviours amongst men is not there for women:

> At this particular historical moment, an intelligible continuum of aims, emotions, and valuations links lesbianism with the other

forms of women's attention to women ... (1985, in Warhol and Herndl, 1991: 464).

Eschewing the widespread belief that sexual behaviour constitutes an identity, Moss effectively refuses to let these women's behaviour be seen as aberrant. Her youthful iconoclasts also reject other constraining modes of classification and competitiveness—age, time and weight, for example —which operate as crucial factors in women's lives and the ways in which they are defined. These two not only dispense with the decorum of femininity, but break the taboo on physical intimacy between women. They are determined to be 'indecent', and signal their distance from traditional femininity in every action, including refusing to care for, or about, others: "Me and Molly don't care what people think. We're just glad that they / do." Their relationship shows none of the characteristics of merged attachment identified by Orbach and Eichenbaum: they certainly don't attend to the needs of others, nor repress their own desires. Nor, surprisingly, do they deny their difference: in place of the anxious demarcation of differences in the last two poems, Moss depicts two women who are extremely close, who share values, aspirations and activities, but nevertheless remain distinct: the phrase "me and Molly" is reiterated endlessly to force home the point. Where boys engage in a rather forced ritual of flesh-cutting and blood-sharing, girls—in this subversive scenario—fall into intimacy effortlessly. In this way the common belief that boys are loyal mates, and girls sneaky rivals, is undermined. The poem also flouts chronology; with the euphoric omnipotence of youth, these two want to stop time, to postpone indefinitely the passage into adulthood and old age. I believe this is an attempt to depict women outside time, and to show how thoroughly time itself is culturally-determined, and operates to fix and limit women's freedoms. The closing image, of a mutual giving birth to both self and other simultaneously, implies a radical rewriting of woman's life-cycle. It is no coincidence that the poem avoids analogies to motherhood, a role so frequently associated with ideas of self-sacrifice and the loss of independent selfhood. There is little evidence here of the nurturing, maternal quality celebrated by Roberts in "Magnificat", but to my mind this is part of what makes the poem and its characters so vigorous and original. Rather than presenting the friendship as a practice-run for adult heterosexuality, this poem rejects the plot and, in so doing, breaks out of the familial scene that relegates the friend to a position outside its hallowed circle. Instead, these two are determined to make their own rituals with gleeful inventiveness, unfazed by the lack of precedent.

Perhaps it is because they position themselves outside heterosexual norms that their closeness does not produce the familiar tension. By avoiding the fixed dynamic of the mother/daughter analogy, the narrator insists on the determined mutuality of the relationship. As with Dickinson, what is particularly striking is the way that this friendship is figured by the image of one woman's body being taken inside the other's. Here, though, the poet certainly *claims* a mutuality about that intimacy; as we hear nothing from Molly, it is impossible to evaluate the claim.

The last poem I want to look at, 'Towards Autumn', is by another American, Marilyn Hacker:

> Mid-September, and I miss my daughter.
> I sit out on the terrace with my friend,
> talking, with morning tea, coffee, and bread,
> about another woman, and her mother,
> who survived heroism; her lover
> who will have to. I surprise myself

with language; lacking it, don't like myself
much. I owe a letter to my daughter.
Thinking of her's like thinking of a lover
I hope will someday grow to be a friend.
I missed the words to make friends with my mother.
I pull the long knife through the mound of bread,

spoon my slice with cherry preserves, the bread
chewy as meat beneath, remind myself
I've errands for our ancient patron, mother
of dramas, hard mother to a daughter
twenty years my senior, who is my friend,
who lives in exile with a woman lover

also my friend, three miles from here. A lover
of good bread, my (present) friend leaves this bread
and marmalades *biscottes*. To have a friend
a generation older than myself
is sometimes like a letter for my daughter
to read, when she can read: What your mother

left undone, women who are not your mother
may do. Women who are not your lover
love you. (That's to myself, and my daughter.)
We take coffee- and tea-pot, mugs, jam jars, bread
inside, wash up. I've work, hours by myself.
Beyond the kitchen, in her room, my friend

writes, overlooking the same hills. Befriend
yourself: I couldn't have known to tell my mother
that, unless I'd learned it for myself.
Until I do. Friendship is earned. A lover
leaps into faith. Earthbound women share bread;
make; do. Cherry compote would please my daughter.

> My daughter was born hero to her mother;
> found, like a lover, flawed; found, like a friend,
> faithful as bread I'd learn to make myself.
>
> (In Mohin, 1986: 49)

In a rather different way this poem also attempts to move beyond conventional configurations of relationships between women. Unlike the others, this one is concerned to re-examine the mother / daughter relationship by approaching it from outside the family unit, and setting it within the broader context of relationships between adult women. It is about the difficulty of finding a language in which to express the subtle transformations and nuances of which friendships are capable. The speaker needs to communicate knowledge about this potential to her daughter, knowledge that she herself has gained only through experience, and that was not available to her own mother. The poem plays with the roles of mother, lover and friend, repeatedly and confusingly using the last word as if to draw attention to the lack of available alternatives ("friend" appears eleven times). The witty linebreak in the fourth stanza makes this mischievous play with language explicit: "A lover / of good bread," leads the reader to expect another kind of lover altogether. Language is ill-equipped to meet the poet's challenge and while she acknowledges the temptation to blame herself, the poem implies it is not her fault. Women of previous generations have not been able to redefine their relationships with their mothers outside the family unit: "I missed the words to make friends with my mother." Now, perhaps, the possibility exists, but language is still inadequate to the task.[10] In Hacker's treatment friendship spans generations, and transcends blood ties, even replacing them: as daughters grow up and the merged attachment between mother and daughter is broken, their relationship can develop into a friendship between two separate adults. In this way the poem is concerned to show that mothers exist outside that role, and to stress its transitory quality: rather than a fixed identity immune to the effects of time, mothering is seen as a position very much *within* time. The mother must move from her initial idealising love-affair with her child to a more detached, 'earned' perspective. Like "An Anointing", this poem rejects the conventional time frame, in which the mother fades from the scene as the daughter comes into her own; instead it embraces the hope that mother and daughter can create a new relationship beyond the constraining roles of the family unit.[11]

Hacker's narrator possesses a solid sense of self: her tone is quiet, but assured, with an unfaltering sense of her own agency and responsibility. She is not threatened by the close proximity of her friend writing "overlooking the same hills"; their separate rooms, but similar activity, symbolise this easeful acceptance of the friend as other. In these last two poems, there is a clear sense of the potential for new configurations of friendships between women. Their efforts to map out relationships that avoid the conventional options of fusion or violent separation remind me of Irigaray's clever use of the placenta as a metaphor for new, female ways of relating. Commenting on the general misconception that mother and child *in utero* are in a state of fusion, she quotes a French biologist, Helene Rouch, who has researched the role played by the placenta. Rouch explains that, while it is created by the embryo, it behaves like an independent organ:

> it's the mediating space between mother and fetus .... there's never a fusion of maternal and embryonic tissues .... what we have here is an organ that, although anatomically dependent upon the embryo, secretes maternal hormones that are essential during gestation when the maternal organism finds itself unable to continue its usual ovarian function owing to the state of pregnancy. This relative autonomy of the placenta, its regulatory functions

> ensuring the growth of the one in the body of the other, cannot be reduced either to a mechanism of fusion (an ineffable mixture of the bodies or blood of mother and fetus), or, conversely, to one of aggression (the fetus as foreign body devouring from the inside, a vampire in the maternal body). These descriptions are of imaginary reality and appear quite poor indeed— and obviously extremely culturally determined—in comparison to the complexity of biological reality (Irigaray, 1993: 39).

In other words, conventional models are inadequate to articulate a strange relationship of extreme intimacy existing alongside separateness: just the kind of relationship women, on the evidence of these poems, seem to find so necessary, and yet so troubling.

These poems take lyric poetry into new areas where there are no familiar signposts to guide us. As Virginia Woolf discovered on first reading fiction about women's friendship, the topic upsets the conventional plot; these poets, like Mary Carmichael, have "gone further and broken the sequence—the expected order" (Woolf, 1977, first published 1929: 87). Though they have come to it later than the novelists, women poets are currently broadening the range of relationships capable of exploration in lyric poetry and, in so doing, loosening the ideological roles that delimit and constrain female experience. Woolf recognised in Carmichael's novel the first stirrings of a new sensibility, and she prophesied that "in another hundred years' time," Mary Carmichael would be a poet (90). The next thirty years look set to be interesting.

Notes

1. Quoted by Betsy Erkkila (1992: 30).

2. The influence of friends may, of course, be less obvious—a sensibility, or tone in the poetry, or a preoccupation with certain issues. These subtler traces of the significance of friends are beyond the scope of this essay.

3. Women's friendships have been the subject of several other inquiries, but the critics involved have chosen to concentrate on fiction. See, for example, Janet Todd (1980); also Elizabeth Abel (1981) and Judith Kegan Gardiner (1981).

4. Although the work of Suniti Namjoshi and Gillian Hanscombe subverts this monologic tradition; in *Flesh and Paper*, a co-authored collection, individual poems are unsigned and form a dialogue as the two women respond to one another's words, thus avoiding the objectification of the other (Hanscombe and Namjoshi, 1986).

5. Having said this, the very public way in which Adrienne Rich and Audre Lorde have conducted dialogues through their published poetry does, in a strange way, have similarities with this earlier period. "Negotiations", by Rich, provides a good example of such a public account, and also raises some of the themes I have identified. It includes the lines: "keeping faith is not about deciding / to clip our fingernails exactly / to the same length or wearing / a uniform that boasts our unanimity" (Rich, 1989: 8).

6. Adrienne Rich has pointed out the comparable absence of myths or stories about mother/daughter relationships in *Of Woman Born: motherhood as experience and institution* (1977). This forms a stark contrast with the wealth of examples of bonds between fathers and sons that can be found in myths and literature. The fairy godmother figure is one of very few enduring and commonly-recognised benign female influences, but because of the implied age-gap, it is of little use as a metaphor for friendships.

7. Although when this image is compared with the metaphorical depiction in Roberts' poem of being 'eaten up' and spat out by her lover, Dickinson's image suddenly appears less an act of aggression, more a quiet statement of an intimacy that is fierce and potentially claustrophobic. The fusion may still be harmful.

8. Joanna Feit Diehl has also found evidence of the tensions accompanying influential friendships between women authors. She, too, has used object relations theory to explore these relationships. See *Elizabeth Bishop and Marianne Moore: the psychodynamics of creativity* (1993).

9. Erkkila also offers a fascinating reading of Bishop's poem, "Invitation to Miss Marianne Moore". In it, the younger poet expresses her need to distance herself from her mentor, poetically, publically and privately. Erkkila draws out the extent of the ambivalence in the poem, which is usually read as a straight praise poem (Erkkila, 1992: 31-7).

10. This effort to create, and acknowledge in language, new relationships amongst women is the subject of Helena Michie's *Sororophobia: Differences among women in literature and culture*. She coins the term "sororophobia" to express "negotiation of sameness and difference, identity and separation, between women of the same generation, and [it] is meant to encompass both the desire for and the recoil from identification with other women" (1992: 9).

11. Comparison with Irigaray's famous meditation on the mother / daughter relationship is inevitable: "Put yourself less in me, and let me look at you ... I'd like you to remain outside, too. Keep yourself / me outside, too. Don't engulf yourself or me in what flows from you into me. I would like both of us to be present. So that the one doesn't disappear in the other, or the other in the one" (1981: 61).

Vicki Bertram is a Senior Lecturer in English Studies at Oxford Brookes University, where she teaches courses on modern and contemporary literature. She organised *Kicking Daffodils*, a simultaneous conference and festival of women poets, held in Oxford in 1994, and edited *Kicking Daffodils: Essays on Twentieth-Century Women Poets* (Edinburgh, 1997). Her main research interests are in feminist theory and practice, and contemporary poetry. She is currently working on a study of gender and recent poetry, *Gendered Poetics*.

'She says she's a woman': Feminine Friendships in Virtual Reality

Ann Kaloski
with Francesca de Rimini and Sue Thomas

> Not only hackers, computer addicts, adolescents and children, but even ostensibly sober adults with "serious" commitments in the REAL WORLD are learning to play in new ways (Danet, 1994).

> Who we are, what we know, and how we think, are all being changed as we move from a print-based society to a computer-based world. We are becoming different people: we are creating a new community (Spender, 1995).

> In the talk of women friends, new selves are forged and new knowledges are developed (Coates, 1996).

Two in the morning. I am awake. I've tried daydreams and counting sheep; I've decided to give up coffee for a month; I've finally won that argument I had with my sister four years ago, this time slipping in an ironic but cutting remark at the appropriate moment. My sister storms off and I have nothing left to do. I am wide awake. I feel like dancing, but this is suburban England and the 'Seventies Night Disco' (free entrance to those wearing flares) is long over. I want company. I could phone a friend, or my sister, but I am awake and energetic, not depressed, not lonely. This isn't an emergency which justifies waking up even those close to me. A book? Behind the Scenes at the Museum *is by my bed, and I stroke it longingly.*[1] *But I have one chapter to go, and I don't want the story to end for me. Letters? I could write to Sandy and let her know that I've finally found a comfortable bra that gives me cleavage—should I buy the black or the purple? I need her advice. It's two-fifteen and I want to talk.*

My computer squats in the corner of my bedroom, plugged into the electricity outlet and the phone socket. A few keystrokes and I will be transported out of a fallow bedroom and into a busy city. I think I grin with delight. Soon I'm in the corner of my room with a mug of tea, about to enter cyberspace.

I decide to visit LambdaMOO, one of the virtual cities of cyberspace. I type in the address easily, without thinking, like dialling a close friend's telephone number.

Contact is made, and I am faced with this screen message:

```
* * * * * * * * * * * * * * * * * *
*   Welcome to LambdaMOO   *
* * * * * * * * * * * * * * * * * *
```

I am in a cybercity.

\\W/

This article considers one area of cyberspace, that of text-based virtual reality, and appraises ways that affectional relationships emerge among computer users who 'say they are women'. This CMC (computer mediated communication) is a form of exchange that is developing fast, and in order to make the new technology more accessible I deploy two illustrative strategies. First, I structure the article around multiple narratives: autobiography, discussion, cultural theory, fantasy, and the instruction manual. Second, I introduce and use some common terms of virtual reality to draw in readers who have not yet encountered virtuality, and to open up the jargon to a wider audience. In addition, I attach an appendix which presents simple instructions about how to use a networked computer to enter vr (virtual reality).

My methodology is one which attempts to harness the pleasure experienced by users of CMC. Other critics have offered anthropological analyses (Bassett, 1997). Such critiques are useful, but in providing a 'view from outside' there has been a tendency towards scepticism, if not cynicism, about cybercultures, even in the most careful inquiries into the topic (Robins, 1995). In its tone, my project has more in common with research conducted by some psychologists who tend to be interested in *how* relationships develop, rather than in criticising the venue and mode of the exchanges, though it is not, in itself, based in the field of psychology (Turkle, 1995). This article is also an autobiographical search for meaning in virtual relationships, and I offer a relatively intimate perspective based on an awareness 'from the inside'. Yet this does not mean that I am uncritical of CMC; rather that my narrative accepts that vl (virtual life) is relevant, is here, now.[2]

What is cyberspace? Where is it?

Cyberspace is an expression first coined by William Gibson in his influential novel *Neuromancer* (Gibson, 1984). Gibson, famously, did not use a computer to produce his work, but composed on a mechanical typewriter. He was affected by the trail-blazing scientific and technological work on CMC which was taking place, and his imaginative vision in turn influenced those working on computer technology. Following Gibson, cyberspace has come to mean the kind of 'somewhere nowhere' where CMC occurs. Gibson referred to cyberspace as a kind of 'consensual hallucination'. At this time—late 1990s—vr is the nearest working model we have to this concept: an absorbing state of psychic and emotional communication.[3]

I am interested in two related questions: How do virtual friendships develop between computer users who 'say they are women'? and what are the implications of these friendships for the construction of femininity? Perhaps oddly, considering the communication function of the Net, very little work has been undertaken on affectional relationships in cyberspace (Kaplan and Farrell, 1994; Parks and Roberts, 1997). Even the suggestively-entitled *Nattering on the Net* written by the feminist Dale Spender does not engage with the friendships the new technology enables (Spender, 1995). In vr people are, by and large, pseudononymous and therefore of unknown 'real' gender: it is just not possible to talk about 'woman' as a simple biological term. This is scarcely a new idea, of course, as feminist thought has offered a number of challenges to the idea of women as located solely, or predominantly, within a biological discourse. Two of the most influential challenges are directly relevant to my argument. First, the analysis of 'gender' as a separate category from 'sex', an idea which gained popularity in the 1970s in Anglophone feminism, and which still remains an important classification within liberal feminism (Oakley, 1972; Rubin, 1975). And second, the notion of gender as a 'performative' category which gains its meaning from the repetitive performance of that gender, and not from any biological reality (Butler, 1990).

In vr these tendencies to de-naturalise gender are given an ambivalent twist. On the one hand, the distinction between biology (in this case the self who sits at the computer keyboard) and construct (the virtual self) is brought into sharp relief, and much of the writing of vr enthusiasts celebrates this disembodied and ungendered virtual self. According to some MOOers, vr allows a mutability which cannot occur irl (in real life):

> In my unity with my computer I am nolonger (sic) woman as opposed to man. I am an-other. I am fluid, dynamic, a hybrid. I

> have no essential nature, not because I can act out any social role at will, but because I am nolonger (sic) just human (Haskel, 1996).

On the other hand, 'gender' is one of the dominant discourses of vr. Characters are *always* gendered—it is part of the core programming of a character's desc (description)—though attributes such as race, or age, or sexual identity are optional. Yet one of the first questions people often ask in vr is 'what is your rl gender?' or 'are you really female?' Given that for many players the ability to choose their gender is one of vr's most attractive features such gender-focused comments might strike those of us irl as somewhat paradoxical—were it not for the fact that on most vr sites users have available to them a choice of ten genders, each with their own pronouns. These genders are female and male (as irl); spivak (gender ambiguous); neutral; splat (hard to translate—a kind of 'thing'); royal (we); egotistical (I); 2nd; either; and plural. Gender is not only chosen, but it is also variable: one's gender can be changed through the simple programming step of typing @gender >   < at any time. In vr, then, no-one can be gendered by default as everything one is is programmed into the computer: gender is a category which is both over determined and malleable, and female virtual friendship can only ever be between computer users who 'say they are women.'[4]

GIRL TALK

This section reproduces an edited version of conversations which occurred between three virtual friends—gash, Lenni, and myx—in 1996/97, either through emails or through meeting up on LambdaMOO.[5] Our discussions focus around four areas: how friendships are generated and sustained; how they differ from those irl; connections between friendship, sensuality, and sexuality in vr; and the function of CMC in blurring the boundaries between work and play. Throughout our chat, as you will see, ideas of gender function as an intriguing and somewhat wild factor. I have edited out the exacerbated formalities of logging on and off, of bidding each other hullo and goodbye, but have left in the casual and often phonetic spellings indicative of both emails and MOOchat. In vl conversations individual contributions 'leapfrog' over each other, and are constructed through short exchanges, interjections, and stroking comments. This is not dissimilar to rl talk, although the first hand inscription of text-based CMC gives it a specific quality.

> *myx exclaims, "gash!"*
> ***This is emba***You exclaim, "heres gash!"
> ***rrasing—i have*** ... iridescent clouds swirl as GashGirl materialises from the
> ***onl*** Spires. . .
> ***y just got it and can't use it yet!*** GashGirl apologises for being
> late . . . sorry . . . had to feed son b4 his exam.
> ***em***
> Gashgirl smiles in an attempt at appearing maternal
> *hugs gahs*
> I see no "gahs" here
> *hug gash*
> ***:is*** You hug GashGirl
> ***very*** *myx says, 'hi sweetie. . . well, even i do that occasionally (feed my son)*
> ***impressed by your mater****myx hugs gash*
> ***nalism***
> Lenni is very impressed by your maternalism[6]

Of the three of us, gash (Francesca de Rimini) is irl a cyber performance artist, Lenni (Sue Thomas) is a writer whose novels and articles explore aspects of vl, and myx (Ann Kaloski) is a feminist academic who writes and teaches about vr and other aspects of cyberspace. Gash and Lenni spend a lot of time in vl, and derive much of their creativity from friendships developed in cyberspace. In contrast, myx prefers rl, and does not seem to have the same kind of 'talent for virtuality' as her two friends. Though all three communicate most often with each other online, Sue has met both Francesca and Ann irl, but Ann and Francesca know each other only through cyberspace.

( )

Lenni: I've been thinking about the question of 'how to make friends and influence people online', and it seems to me there are certain protocols online which must be observed if a potential friendship is to be nourished. Much affection, *no*[7] direct questions for quite a while—esp about rl things, decorous and polite behaviour—not logging off too quickly (myx!!) ... [8]

myx: yes, I know, I know ...

Lenni: ... not suddenly teleporting out of a room where you are talking with your new friend, not suddenly teleporting in without asking first or being invited.... Indeed, although vl enables the most extraordinary openness, it also demands a quite exaggerated politeness at times.

Gash: I agree with you there—it's almost baroque at times. Is it, I wonder, a bit like how we become socialised as kids ... the rules just kinda grow ... one learns to be very sensitive to nuances—actions—emotes[9] and so on. But the rules don't seem oppressive to me .. they are maybe the only structure in an environment seemingly unwritten upon . . .

myx: and yet, of course, precisely and literally 'written.' I still become quite astounded at how relations can be developed through words, only words.

gash: Yes, I have been feeling really low—over a vl become rl bloke—and I'm getting all these great letters from women—it's so much easier to give support via this medium than irl—I can barely bring myself to pick up the fone and call good friends—which means that rl friendships languish as the online ones are given lots of attention. In fact, my housemate returned from sydney last nite and told me 2 of my good rl g/fs were really hurt that i hadn't told them about my latest crisis—that i had been mainly confiding in my online g/fs rather than my 'real' friends who 'really' know me and have met him irl. Made me start thinking about how sometimes it's safer to talk about painful stuff with people who know one less well ... without a sense of their history—for me the rl friends mite have been judgmental—there's gash breaking her own heart again—whereas with the vgirls[10] one is both more and less open—there's a safety zone there—maybe?

myx: I know what you mean. Vr friends seem to have something of the 'intimate stranger' in them ...

gash: It's been thru emails and some Lambda relations that I begin to feel better—it seems such a good medium for consoling peopl—getting sweet messages like 'buck up chuck' all the time.

myx: Somehow you can be physically fairly inert, and still type in a few words to ask for help. It seems to be different from the phone. Even voice-talking requires too much effort when you're really miserable, whereas typing can be done at your own pace. And I also like the way it's possible to be with people—to watch conversations scroll down your screen— without *having* to take part.

Lenni: That's called lurking

myx: Hmm, and I know lurking is 'a bad thing' in vr, but it is, in fact, only a form of listening—something women are supposed to be good at ......

Lenni: But whereas irl one can be part of a group and not talk, at least everyone is aware of your body and your facial expressions. You are still 'there'. But in vr it's quite easy to forget that someone is in a virtual room if they don't *do* anything: don't talk, or offer some other sign of their presence.

myx: Sometimes I get really involved—I *am* in cyberspace, and at other times I am drifting in and out.

Lenni: Yes, one of the aspects I do like about vr friendships is that you can regulate them in a different way to rl ones. When you're in vl, no-one has any idea of what you might be doing irl. Want to go and make a snack in the middle of a long confession? Do it, and then blame it on the lag![11] Getting really bored? Disconnect yourself—oops! Server went down ... and any of those excuses which can be too difficult to invent even on the phone—crowd of people just arrived, crying baby, minor earthquake —they can all be used to good effect in your vr friendships.

(Pause)

On the other hand, you can have such extraordinarily intense friendships online. I keep a box of tissues by the computer—I've cried more since I went into vr than I have done, ever.

Gash: For me, there's something so special about the women I've met/ come to care about / have fun with online—we share professional and creative interests—we start planning projects together—like this one, or tours, or events—so there's this mentoring stuff going on—but it doesn't seem like cheesy networking.

myx: Why, I wonder?

gash: I guess one thing is that the relationships seem to have time to grow; there's none of that frantic circulating and tedious chat over coffee ...

myx: trying to impress people ...

Lenni: the friendships are so ever-present, so accessible. It's a network you don't have to get dressed and go out to—it's in the corner of your room.

gash: There's also a qualitative difference in relationships. I've enjoyed interactions with a rl women friend of mine on Lambda. Depending on which character she is at any particular time, when we're talking online I imagine her as either this rough country boy, or a beautiful spunky man. It does add another dimension to our relationship, but it's hard to figure out what that is.

(Pause)

She writes great e.mails—is that like saying 'she gives good head', I wonder!

myx: Here we go again! Why is the language of MOO friendships so sexual?

gash: You're right. I've been thinking about how women form friendships through flirting with each other online; you know, even if you fleshmeet u never have to 'put out' as it were. But it's a different kind of flirting that goes on—makes the friendship really warm and sweet ...

myx: But it's more than that for many women ...

gash: Yes, I do know quite a few women who use lambdmoo as a site for sexual play—and these women so often seem not to care about the rl genders of their playmates, or even that they be human in their virtual guises—women i've met who seem to embrace the abstract within the virtual, often more so than men ...

myx listens

gash: ... and they use these contexts sometimes for growing friendships ... thru talking dirty, playing dirty, dismantling the rules which are heavy with the dust of patriarchy ... and so from such games a tenderness can evolve. Sometimes.

Lenni: must be careful not to romanticise all that happens here ... although i have made most of my friends through hanging out in sr.[12]

gash: It's been different for me.. I do lurk in sr a bit, but any people i've met and developed ongoing relationships with have paged[13] me cos they found my desc interesting, or i've paged them from my room because I found their depictions intriguing.

myx: ... it's one way virtual communities differ from rl ones ...

gash: ... you don't have to go to the virtual pub or cafe to meet people, you can hang out in your room waiting for that potentially interesting creature to log on, then page them and take it from there. You usually know in one or two conversations if there is common ground ...

Lenni: But I do find the flirtatiousness between women good-natured and friendly.

gash: ... and whereas flirting irl with friends can be weird cos there's always this underlying thing of ... well will we really *do* it someday— for me anyway. But with online friends one can flirt away without this question ever having to be considered unless one seriously wants to.

Lenni: Whereas flirting with blokes even in vr is much more sexual, more kind of goal driven—I hate making these generalisations, but that's how it seems to me.

myx: But how do we know if we're talking with someone who identifies as a woman or a man irl? Or is that the point? Are we talking less about friendships between women, and rather more about identifying an aspect of feminine friendship.

Lenni: It's the ways in which the feminine is generated that seems pertinent to me. I think vr is a place where the sex of the body doesn't matter. You can be friends with the person underneath, and men can 'be' feminine in a way that's much more difficult irl because there's always the male body to contend with. I could have friendships with rl men, but they *feel* like women, and that's all that counts.

myx: Hmm. I don't know about that! I agree that gender expression isn't directly analogous to the sexed body, but I don't see how the body can just be ignored.

Lenni: But you create your own body through words.

myx: Yes, but you are more than that invented body. The other flesh body *does* exist, however much one might try to ignore it online. And it exists in a way that can't just be morphed[14] into the background.

Lenni: Of course that is true in the sense of being one scientific fact. But when I'm online I *do* leave my body. Like one does in a dream. We know that dreams are affected by the physical body, but while one is dreaming there is a loosening of that physical-psychic relationship, and in that dislodging we experience new aspects of ourselves. I know we're gendered. But what is interesting to me is how far we can become de-gendered, or even ungendered in vr.

myx: You have a point! But I worry about 'ungendered'. Because we're not just talking about a rl body, but all the gendering one accumulates through life. You don't for instance, have any difficulty in recognising the effects of rl national culture on MOOtalk—US & UK users, for instance, deploy different terminology. Why, then, does the idea of rl gendered culture appal you? On a really pragmatic level, who is likely to have most access to the Web?: white, young men at Universities and in business! Who is likely to be able to afford the technology? OK, we don't know for sure—stats are hard to come by, but men, men, men are online.[15]

Lenni: But the UK figures for women using mobile phone has just exceeded that of men. Not just for safety, but talk—gossip—chat. Might not the same kind of pattern occur with CMC?

myx: Yes, I think it might. And the movement towards simple, affordable Web technology which can be linked to the TV will also enable women who spend a lot of time at home, as carers, or homeworkers, to go online. But we don't really know what the sex/gender makeup of CMC users is—there hasn't been any detailed research done that I'm aware of.

Perhaps we need to work towards nuancing the 'feminine' aspects in more detail: what does a 'feminine friendship' actually *mean.*

gash falls down laughing.

Lenni: you don't ask easy questions :-)

gash: I was lying in bed last night thinking about MOO flirting—and I was wondering if with all of our special new friendships online—it becomes a little like falling in love—that craving to connect everyday, to hear what's going on in their lives, the minutiae and the big things—that warm glow when the person affirms our existence, tells us we are cool or sweet or lovely or sassy—and all this without the pressure to be a sextoy/plaything /fuckable rl body. . .

Lenni: . . . it's that delight in gradually revealing our selves, our stories, to an interested other.

gash: Yes, for example, I have been having for the past few weeks this quite delicious email dialogue with a young woman with whom I do some arts admin work from time to time—so by day we see each other under the harsh floro lights and gray carpets of the office, and our interactions are cheerful and funny, but no more, then we start e.mailing about work related stuff—I'm outa town and need her to send me stuff—and then this other discourse begins to creep thru the mail—at first she's giving me advice on my virtual lover then the greetings become ever more affectionate—then before I know it we're flirting, and I think, this can't be—we're *friends* .. we work together—I don't 'fancy' her in that way, and the reverse I'm sure—and when we see each other irl we don't mention this undercurrent that's been running thru the mail—but it colours the rl interactions in some way—not a bad way—just produces a slight shift—it's like the virtual becomes a playground for special 'let's pretend' games which never need to be acted out irl, but it makes the rl friendship closer because we have been fearless enough to pursue other lines of affinity in the virtual world.

myx: This reminds me of childhood friendships—playing at being other people ... grown-ups, or glamorous bods, or fairies, or witches ...

Lenni: So ru saying that vl friendships are childish . . .

myx laughs

myx: Child-like, not child-ish. As we reach adulthood most of us hide, or maybe even lose, our ability to relate to others as different parts of ourselves. Vr is so enabling for this kind of palpable dreaming.

I log off and put my computer to sleep, letting its mechanical snoring synchronize with the bird's morning song to soothe me, too, back to sleep and into other dreams.

APPENDIX:
HOW TO ENTER VIRTUAL REALITY

A. USING THE WORLD WIDE WEB.

One of the simplest ways is via the LambdaMOO link accessible on **www.gotham-city.net/lambda.html** If this site is down (not accessible) type **LambdaMOO** into any search engine, and you will be given some alternative links.

B. USING TELNET.

LambdaMOO is a telnet site (telnet allows a user to log onto a remote computer and engage with that system more or less directly). If you are familiar with telnet, go directly to lambda.moo.mud.org port 8888.

Whichever way you log on, you will eventually be faced with the following message:

```
* * * * * * * * * * * * * * * * * * *
*  Welcome to LambdaMOO! *
* * * * * * * * * * * * * * * * * * *
```

This screen then gives some details about Lambda, and ends:

```
For assistance either now or later, type 'help.'
The lag is >   <; there are >   < connected.
```

1. You need to connect as a guest. Type in

co guest

If your words do not appear on the screen, don't worry—they are still programmed into the Lambda system, and you will be able to see the actions and words of other users. However, it is easier if you can see your own words, and for this you need an 'echo'. Systems differ, but if you look on the menu for 'local echo' and make sure this is 'on', you should be ok.

2. You'll then be given some information about Lambda, type

yes or **y**

3. You'll be logged in as a guest, and your name will either be 'Guest', or a variation on this such as 'Red_Guest'. Write down your name—you'll be glad of this later!

4. You are asked if you want to enter a 'noisy' or a 'quiet' environment.

(a) To plunge straight in and ask help of others who are logged on, type:

noisy

and you will be in The Coat Closet.

(b) To take things slowly, type:

quiet

and you'll find yourself in The Linen Closet.

Follow the instructions, see what happens . . .

After typing something, press the RETURN button.

Now you are in cyberspace in a virtual room. This is a textual environment where you can write your self into existence, and begin to communicate with other characters.

5. While you are getting used to this, you need to make sure you can read the words which will be scrolling down your screen. To fix the page and line length for most computers, type

@pagelength 20

@linelength 60

6. To leave/log off at any time type: **@quit**

7. What do you like to do when in a new place?

(i) look around—type **look here** or **l here** for a description of the room.

(ii) speak to people—type quotation marks followed by a greeting,
eg. **"hi!** or **"hallo**—and see what happens on your screen

(iii) do things—type a colon, followed by your emotion,
eg. **:smiles** or **:feels nervous** or **:blows a kiss**
or anything else you want. Watch the screen.

(iv) if you want to say something to one particular person,
type: dash name of person greeting
cg. **-Technicolor_Guest this is great!**

> You will find that you need to type accurately. MOO language is a form of programming which, for convenience, uses terms which originate in US-English. As with all programming, one misplaced bit of data (Guets instead of Guest) confuses the computer. This is a friendly environment, however, and you will be told 'I don't understand that.' Just try again!

Now it's time to write your own body.

8. WRITING YOUR BODY.

(i) Setting your gender. There are 10 genders: female, male, spivak, neuter, splat, plural, 2nd, royal, egotistical, either.

Set your gender now by using the formula

@gender ...

Watch the screen to see what pronouns describe you.

You can change your gender at any time by repeating this last step.

(ii) Describing yourself. Using up to 25 words, type in a description for your character. As with gender, this can be changed at any time.

@describe me as ...

(iii) Type **look me** and watch the screen

(iv) **look** at other characters in the same room as you (e.g. **look Green_Guest**)

9. Practice talking to others, and expressing emotions. (See point 7.)

If you want to speak to someone privately, type:

page name of person message

e.g. **page Green_Guest your desc is great**

Two aspects of virtual communication you might find confusing at first are:
the lag—this is the time between typing something and it appearing on your screen. Have patience!
split sentences—as you begin to talk more, you will find that you will sometimes be typing a phrase when someone butts in. You get used to it, and it does offer its own fun. Just continue to type, ignoring the interruptions; and if you get lost, press the RETURN button and re-type your message.

10. Getting help.

Type **help** and the programme will offer you some guidance.

Or ... read through this guide.

Or ... ask someone online—politely

Talk to other users, move around—make friends!

Notes

1. Atkinson (1995). This novel is set in York, England, my current rl home town, the protagonist is roughly the same age as me, and I identify with some of her life-experiences. Consequently, reading this novel is, for me, a particular kind of slippage between 'real life' and 'fantasy'—the heroine is like me and like my friends in her doppleganger life. See Pearce (1997: 252-56) for a discussion of the similarities between paper texts and virtual reality.

2. Vl (Virtual Life) and vr (virtual reality) are used more or less interchangeably by many people, including myself. However, some prefer vl as it does not, unlike vr, subsume the virtual to real (meat) life.

3. The vr I write about in this article is text-based; that is, it is not the image-based vr of popular imagination, portrayed in films such as *Lawnmower Man* and novels like Tad Williams' *Otherland* (1996). Such visual vr represenations are still the stuff of laboratories, art-shows, and imagination—but only just. Neither am I writing about the internet-like engagement of humans with machine. Instead, this article considers feminine friendships generated by users of cyberspace who communicate in character, in realtime (as in phone conversations). For a valuable overview of the background to virtuality, in the context of other developments in the internet and other cybertechnologies, see Reid (1994).

4. See Kaloski (1997) for a more sustained discussion about MOO gender.

5. There are a number of differences between email and MOO discussion, most notably that emails tend to be more regulated, and can be more considered (like postal letters, or perhaps, more accurately, like

postcards) than the real time, often frantic MOO conversations. For the purposes of this article I have, however, cohered our exchanges into one long dialogue. This has the advantage of not obscuring the issues with the busyness of a printed page from vl.

6. This is a section of a vl conversation between gash, Lenni, and myx which was saved by Sue Thomas (Lenni). I have here used different fonts to differentiate between the comments of gash, Lenni, myx, and the computer. This is a device for the paper page: the computer screen text is all in one font.

7. Asterisks are deployed in CMC to accentuate words and phrases in an environment lacking in aural indicators of conversation, and where programming restrictions exclude the usual typographical methods of underlining and italics. The use of asterisks is considered more polite than other forms of textual emphasis such as capitalisation, which is the vr equivalent of shouting.

8. Dots occupy a special place in CMC. As in academic work, they stand in for something which is missing, but whereas in essays they represent an already-written sentence which is not relevant to the current work, in textual conversations dots suggest a more tentative space. It is a place, I would suggest, on the borders of emotion and thought: either a matter that both/ all participants in a conversation understand really well, and do not need to set down, or, alternatively, something that one 'feels' but doesn't quite have the words for, yet.

9. 'Emotes' or 'emoticons' are also known as 'smileys' after the most used icon :-) . If that symbol does not make sense to you, turn this book 90° clockwise, and look again. These typographical symbols have developed as a way of enabling the narrow band-width communication of vr to express some subtlety. For instance, if you type 'that's so stupid', adding :-) would indicate a friendlier and more ironic comment than is possible by the words alone. Other common emotes are

:-(	frowning/ sad
;-)	winking
( )	hugging
:*	kissing
:-X	I'll say nothing
:-p	sticking out tongue

@--`-,---- a rose

10. The vgirls are an Australian cyberfeminist group.

11. The 'lag' is the time between text being typed and its appearance on the screen—either your own screen, or that of the person(s) you are communicating with. It is a little like the aural gap evident in television reports which utilise satelite links between the UK and US. The vr lag varies in time immensely, depending on how many people are on-line, and how busy they are. The LambdaMOO programme can only take so much data at any one time. Although the lag can be irritating, it does lend itself to amusing and sometimes quite creative conjunctions as different parts of conversations weave their own pattern.

12. Sensual Respites, one of the LambdaMOO rooms, number #72239.

13. A method of sending a private message from one person on Lambda to another.

14. Morphing is the word used to describe what occurs when a person in vr changes into one of her other characters. This is an act which can be performed easily and quickly.

15. Try the following sites for some valuable statistics: http://www.multimedia.calpoly.edu/cpp/women/women.html and http://www.womenspace.ca/

Ann Kaloski is a part-time lecturer at the Centre for Women's Studies, University of York, York, England, YO10 5DD. Contact her by letter post or by email: eakn1@york.ac.uk

Gash's homepage is http://www.cs.un.edu/~hfspc002/gash/index.html

Sue Thomas' homepage is http://trace.ntu.ac.uk/suethomas/index.htm

Editorial Conclusion

We have decided to close with a piece which though pitched differently to the rest of the book, in many ways illuminates the key issues and raises further questions. Jackie's chapter highlights the balance this book has tried to strike between the academic and the personal approaches to the topic of friendship. Her chapter describes what is perhaps a familiar process for many of the people we anticipate will read this book: the discovery of feminist work on women and the corresponding personal development which this work helps to engender. She writes specifically as an educated white middle-class woman who undergoes a transformation to identify herself as a lesbian feminist. We felt it was important to position Jackie's chapter in and as part of an academic book, in order to illustrate both the hierarchy that is often attributed to 'theory', and the exclusion from academic studies of feminist theorising of friendship. 'The Personal is Academic' draws upon many themes contained in the preceding chapters: women's friendship as a space of auto/biography, as a site of resistance amid struggle for priorities, as a mode of understanding women's lives in the past and providing the strength needed for political action in the present, and as a means of constructing one's personal understanding of female sexuality.

Jackie's piece emphasises the privilege of her background and the advantages which led her to discover women's studies, albeit once her privileged status appeared to have disappeared (i.e. with motherhood). Class has been briefly discussed in this book as one of the factors affecting friendship; like many other factors, however, it has perhaps inevitably taken second place to issues of sexuality. Questions of sexuality do not on the whole disrupt the narrative of this book; on the contrary, they can work as a linking factor. Nowhere is this clearer than in Jackie's chapter, where she discusses two women-only enclaves (a Women's Studies course, and a circle of friends from Greenham Common) where lesbianism is accepted as the norm. Her contribution is unique in this book in that it considers the transition from a conventional, less feminist lifestyle, to one that is dominated by personal politics and the recognition of 'other' desires and relationships.

With its narrative of change, Jackie's chapter provides us with a way of talking about differences in friendships, but like many of the chapters in this book, a slippage occurs between 'women', 'feminism' and 'women's studies'. There can be vast differences in the meaning of women's friendship for women or girls who are not necessarily feminists, and for women who are feminists, particularly academics who, in addition to their experiences as 'women', may have imbibed more theoretical understandings (demonstrated in the chapters by Jane Montague and Ali Andrew, and Juliet Betts and Shantu Watt). Jackie's chapter illuminates the complex relationships between not only women's studies and feminism, but also women's friendships and women's sexuality. In this volume, 'celebrating women's friendship' has frequently been used to mean celebrating both heterosexual and lesbian feminist friendships. Laura Potts and Vicki Bertram both question the meanings of friendship for lesbian women, and Jackie uses her conclusion to show the subtle lines of difference that such friendships entail. Her chapter also sounds an optimistic note: in her correspondence with us over the writing of this conclusion, she said: "the 'happy ending' is deliberate in posing an antithesis to the often negative or problematic connotations attached to feminist scholarship."

We are unapologetic about celebrating friendship, because it has been invaluable to feminism in Britain: despite areas of difference which remain to be negotiated, the optimism underlying Jackie's chapter remains the abiding tone of women's friendship in Britain today.

The Personal is Academic: a Different Pattern

Jackie Scott-Mandeville

There's no doubt about it: I was a late developer, conditioned by a 1950s childhood of stereotypical femininity and influenced by the opportunities opened up to youth in the 1960s which promoted ideals and illusions that permeated a generation. I took higher education as my right, not a new-won privilege. I sailed through college, riding the crest of waves of social change, participating in sit-ins, demonstrations, debates, shouting slogans with everyone else.[1] Besides, beguiled by the heady scent of kaftans, kohl and karma, 'love and peace, man,'[2] and given the availability of the Pill and the dubious delights of sexual permissiveness, I was too exhilarated to realise the subtle implications of the social revolution taking place, never plumbing the depths of what my experience might mean. I read *The Female Eunuch* along with *The A-Z of Sex*; *Sexual Politics* as well as socialist politics.[3] I, like many of my contemporary women friends, were mesmerised by the apparent equality with men, sharing their lives and aspiring to our own independence. But, predictably, my path veered back conventionally to job and marriage at the end of those dizzy, dancing days on a ferris-wheel of fantasy and freedom.[4] My life relegated itself to service without my being aware of the facts, only the ways in which I was fulfilling expectations. The fact that upon marriage my husband lost all interest in and desire for me, diminishing my role to one of housekeeper, somehow got confused, by default, into a self-deception that I was in fact independent, self-reliant with a modern partnership, tolerant of affairs as part of the equality programme. As a 'Girl About Town'[5] I led a frivolous but superficially satisfying life of South Bank and Covent Garden,[6] with ballet and Latin classes in between. Latin?

Because one of the few constructive offshoots of my hardly-won degree was a life-long interest in all things medieval and I wanted to go to Birkbeck to study part-time. (I had no idea at the time of Birkbeck's origins, its purposeful flexibility and accommodating of women's needs.)[7] But my academic ambitions were secondary to my husband's next move up the career ladder which meant leaving London and foregoing personal fulfilment.

The penny dropped with the coming of children. Suddenly (and it was sudden: my first son timed his unexpected arrival so as to prevent my husband leaving to marry someone else) I had one baby and then a second son appeared and my life sea-changed.[8]

The myth of my self-named independence evaporated with the smell of zinc and caster oil. The shock waves were insistent and regular. I could not believe the reality of my new state of life. I was now totally dependent with dependants upon me. I loved my babies but I found myself in a world which I thought had died as I grew up.[9] Surrounded by petty everyday detail, by women obsessed with childhood behaviour patterns and developmental stages, by clinics and nurseries, by housekeeping dilemmas, my mental life became a nightmare of confusion and contradiction, the latter because I enjoyed the pleasures of motherhood and found the daily repetitive routine peculiarly compelling. The full meaning of the euphemism 'coffee-morning' struck home as the feelings, anxieties, angers, frustrations, bitterness poured forth from confined mothers. Fractured, distracted states of mind remembered later were formative to later perception of the reality of feminism. If I had never been a mother, would feminism have affected me so much? Thoughts festered at night when my time was at last my own.

I turned to books and the first one I picked up was Betty Friedan's *The Feminine Mystique*. I couldn't believe it. Although written twenty years earlier she might have been a fly on the wall of my life and the lives of the women around me: the 'problem with no name'. By the time I read this book, Betty Friedan was down in the feminist annals as a pioneer of the second wave. But what did I know of all this? I found Elizabeth Janeway's *Man's World, Woman's Place* and once again, this woman was iterating my thoughts and feelings and frustrations. The shades began to fall from my eyes and mind. I devoured feminist books relating to maternity. Ann Dally's *Inventing Motherhood* made an indelible impression and opened doors to further back in maternal history. I found the Virago book *Maternity, Letters from Working Women* published originally in 1915 and realised with sudden revelationary insight that my experience was universal and had an historical perspective. Experience and new knowledge combined to alter my whole perception of life. I began to understand where I was, what I was, and I wanted to change things. Germaine Greer was no longer irrelevant.[10]

The pattern changed slowly. Depressingly bourgeois, I moved again with my husband's next career jump to a big house with home help and my own car. The boys went off to Montessori nursery school and with the timespaces allowed by their absence I pursued an increasing interest in the background to my existence. My scope widened and I found I was uncovering disjointedly, as, unknown to me then, many of my contemporaries were uncovering systematically, the hidden background of women's history. I spent housekeeping on visits to London, to Sisterwrite, Silver Moon and ferreting in the Fawcett Library, continually astonished at the range of amazing achievements women had already made. Josephine Butler and Emily Davies became my new heroines and I took a schoolgirl delight in transforming my previous, stereotyped vision of nineteenth-century women.[11] I began to pester my mother to fill in gaps of twentieth-century women's experience from her own life.[12] I talked and talked to other women, assimilating a wealth of women's knowledge which I could fit into my growing mental tapestry of women's lives over the last two centuries. The talking was not one-sided: friendships began, grew and became an essential part of my life.[13] My world was woman-centred by its very nature and the formation of friendships was part of the everyday oiling of social wheels. Friendships with mothers of my boys' friends; friendships begun in the middle of Waitrose, on a peace-march—especially at Greenham,[14] in woman's meetings, whether 'Housewives Register'[15] or the new consciousness-raising groups. I no longer lived in a vacuum but could relate my life to all these other women's lives through studying lives and letters, biography and autobiography, novels and experience and by experiencing it myself through friendship, and by so doing, make sense of what I felt and why I felt it.

There was another dimension to my existence. The top layer of conventional female reality was not only being steadily eroded as a second layer of new knowledge emerged but a third layer was intruding and affecting both the other layers: a metamorphosis was taking place and irrevocably reshaping and recrystallising my character. It began the year I was first pregnant during a 'temp' job compiling reports for a computer consultant to my husband's firm. The first day I met the consultant she had come up behind me as I sat before a computer and touched my shoulder. Our eyes met and immediate attraction, an electrical pulse between us led within two weeks to our becoming lovers. Nothing I had ever been taught, experienced, known, envisaged, anticipated, could have prepared me for what was a watershed in my emotional and sexual life.[16] The impossibility, yet the verity, of such a love, such a desire, such a revelation of experience meant the end of thirty years of naive, protected, male-oriented existence and a life of emotional and sexual frustration. The affair was not long-lived, burnt out as quickly as it had flamed, but I would never be the same woman—I was now a woman's woman. That first real love affair subconsciously influenced my developing thirst for feminist knowledge as the two desires seemed to develop alongside each other simultaneously. Yet my social experience, the disillusionment in women's equality, the frustrations of second-status, the mundane world of maternity, the sterility of marriage, the closing of doors of opportunities, were more affecting than my inner private world of desire. But as I found more threads to weave, the tapestry of my life began to be re-created in a different pattern. Via Greenham, women's groups and consciousness-raising I developed a different discipline. The delving into women's history reproduced itself in the various levels of the women's groups' activities and resulted in my teaching women's history as fast as I was learning it myself.[17] My own enthusiasm communicated itself to the students, women like myself, thirsty for knowledge and inspiration, reassured by identification with their foremothers. The period was ripe for exploration—the mid-1980s saw a plethora of women's historical publishing. On both sides of the Atlantic women were poring over their previous lives, researching, writing, planting women firmly on the map of history. Alongside my teaching and research I was meeting like-minded women—and not only like-*minded*. Liaisons occurred that were a mixture of satisfying confirmation of the primacy of women's sexuality and its belonging to women and disappointingly emotionally strained relationships. Consequent to a particularly disturbing affair with a much older, firmly closeted married woman, my energy and stability began to fail me. I found myself unable to tolerate the divisions set up by my married life (the comfortably-off company wife, the charity volunteer, the 'good mother') contrasting with an increasingly feminist lifestyle (running women's groups, teaching women's studies, supporting feminist networks, participating in women's peace campaigns) and an emerging lesbian identity.[18] I was ready to come out and took the inevitable step and divorced my husband.

With an apposite sense of irony I used my divorce settlement money to follow my interest in being with women, personally and academically. The excitement and tingling sense of anticipation mixed with a terrifying anxiety when I was accepted for a postgraduate degree in Women's Studies were feelings acknowledging the significance of the next change in my life. I was never confident that my academic prowess was up to much,[19] but the encouragement from the beginning from my tutors and sister students lifted me beyond the realms of humdrum expectation and the sky became the limit. Shedding the conventional top layer of my previous existence left me free to begin weaving the remaining life-threads into a web of substance. My friendships with the women on the course formed the groundbase from which the voyages into new and deeper realms of knowledge began. Everyone was a friend: it seemed to me that everyone was there for everyone else and the previous eight years' experience of building friendships with women came to fruition in the confidence I felt in developing new and vital relationships with such a wonderful variety of women. Yet we never crowded each other. There was time for everything, for study in a wonderful library for six hours a day if I wished (while the children were safely in school) and even the librarian[20] was the most marvellously helpful and enthusiastic woman who seemed to intuit one's floundering and turn it into constructive searching in no time at all. But studying alone was only half of the work: the other half was sharing it all, through the most stimulating of discussional seminars where nervousness evaporated with the encouraging smiles of all around me. Even when we all disagreed and argued over areas of contention the sisterhood strength usually won out and ironed personal antipathies along smoother lines. And the social round where I was not the only one exploring new horizons with the exhilaration and stimulation of the company of women, women in various stages of rebirth (from one, literally, coinciding her pregnancy with her course, to full-time scholars reinventing the world of female academia), was constantly inspiring. I was a latecomer to feminism and feminist ideology, thought and practice, learning much from my companions who, though mostly much younger than me, had transcended convention and were searching for a feminist structure to their lives, this made for a very secure, mutually supportive, environment.[21] During the earlier years in women's groups, even at Greenham, I was often at odds with, at the same time as being close to, women who did not seem to be taking feminism quite so seriously as I was. And, of course, the women I knew were not lesbians. Most of the women on the course weren't either—but many were. It was the first time I was accepted for exactly who I was, with no reservation. I am not the closet type and was uncomfortable not feeling free to be honest with the women around me. On this Women's Studies course, it was different—lesbian women were an essential part of the circle, just as much as the heterosexual women.

I do not know whether it was fate, a juxtaposition of stars, the fruition of my years of searching and researching, experiencing and exploring, a destiny determined, a combination of circumstances, which brought together my emotional, sexual and intellectual fulfilment all in one year. I met, fell in love with, and moved in with, my future lifelong lover in the middle of my MA course, and the personal and the academic came together in an exuberance of living and loving, seeking and finding.[22] The lesbian me also found fulfilment in finding out about lesbian history, another area of academic research coming into its own, just as I was. As I discovered the 'lesbian continuum' and the myths and social constructionism of compulsory heterosexuality through Mary Daly, Luce Irigaray and Adrienne Rich—to name a few—I also discovered the joys of a sexuality that I must have been born with. Textuality and sexuality were intermingled as I uncovered for myself women lovers of the past through their writings and through biographies newly published, and my present lover helped me write my own contribution to revitalising a woman from the past. My own identity recreated itself and reformed in a marvellously self-protecting world of women. As I wandered through the texts relating to women in the past, I realised that women's relationships with each other had been of primary significance—for most of my life (thirty-nine years of it) I had thought for women, men had come first and women second. This was plainly just not true. Sharing in seminars evidenced that others on the course were also finding this out, but I wanted to make sense of this discovery. Was it a recent phenomenon? Was it only material to those of recent generations with the freedom for friendships? My earlier study of first-wave feminists had indicated strongly how the mid-nineteenth-century women were very interdependent in their pursuit of feminist goals, whether it was the vote, higher education or repeal of anti-female legislation, but most of these women married, had families and their feminism was often only an essential part of their lives when young.[23] I now found that so many of the women I was studying never married and not only did they not form partnerships with men, their relationships with women were of great significance.[24] Did this also mean that lesbianism itself was a common practice before the sexologists and psychologists got hold of the principle of inversion and made it a taboo for the first half of the twentieth century? According to Lillian Faderman, yes; and her book

(*Surpassing the Love of Men*) was a significant influence. In fact the inspiration for my dissertation arose from her description of a profoundly important nineteenth-century women's friendship, that of Geraldine Jewsbury and Jane Carlyle. Not only did I have an opportunity to examine a particularly devoted friendship through well-documented sources: the ambivalence of their feelings, Geraldine's in particular, led to my asking questions about nineteenth-century concepts of sexuality which had nothing to do with the prevalent patriarchal views, but opened another window on to the whole field of women's interaction with each other. I did not realise until nearly the end of the year that I was embarking on something relatively unexplored and the excitement generated by my journey—into a territory not unknown but one hitherto lost, hidden, obscured—has been maintained ever since. Through endless 'was she, wasn't she' discussions with my lover, we eventually decided that the evidence pointed to Geraldine's infatuation with Jane Carlyle not being of a specifically lesbian nature—but not because Geraldine was definitively not a lesbian, but because the deeper realms of women's sexuality were not explored by most nineteenth-century women—their limited range of knowledge,[25] lack of freedom of expression, the corsets of conventional respectability, inhibited many from pursuing their inclinations to what, to the 1980s woman, may have been its logical result. This conclusion opened the way to a new path of exploration—the nature of women's friendships and how they varied according to their period. The connecting chain between the chapters of my MA dissertation and the paper I gave to the 'Celebrating Women's Friendship' conference in 1995 was increased link by link, with new reading in the years between, enhanced by new publications coming out every year from this emerging rich new vein of lesbian-feminist research which contributed to my search.[26] The links are still being formed.

The year at York was the most vibrant and vital I have ever known and the satisfaction of successfully gaining that degree to add self-respect to a heart already full of happiness vindicated my existence. I was in my fortieth year and left university to embark on the second half of my life as a new woman. During the year I had shed all vestiges of the old life and when I emerged whole and complete I had a new direction. No more division, no more abstract longing for something, not knowing what. I knew, I knew what I wanted to know, I had a whole world of learning and experience in front of me. And I could combine the desires for personal fulfilment and academic pursuit. Never mind that I could not become a full-time academic—I still had my children to support and bring up and my partner had hers too—but there was a world of women in books as well as life and if I wanted to, I could write my own.

Notes

1. My period at college spanned the years 1968 to 1971: the hero figures included Danny the Red (Daniel Cohn-Bendit, leader of the 1968 Paris 'revolution') and Tariq Ali (then President of the Oxford Union), Tony Benn and Barbara Castle, leading, progressive figures in the Labour government. The emphasis was far from feminism and concentrated on social politics.

2. I spent my vacations in California (where my parents lived): the magnets included Haight-Ashbury in San Francisco and the 'Hair' stage-show in Los Angeles. Flowers in the hair and 'love-in' parties prevailed.

3. Feminist polemic got immersed into the general movement towards sexual equality: to many of us young people, our interest in sexual knowledge and awareness outweighed our interest in our woman's situation.

4. The phrase is adapted from a popular folk cult song of the period by Judy Collins, 'Both Sides Now'.

5. A popular phrase which, with a magazine of that name, circulated among young career women in London in the early seventies.

6. When tickets to the opera and ballet could be had for as little as fifty pence and the National Film Theatre was new and vibrant.

7. Birkbeck College was one of the few at the time which offered part-time MA courses in medieval studies.

8. This paragraph, as may be imagined, hides a multitude of emotionally traumatic events and feelings which, as much as anything, had to do with the changes that emanated later.

9. My mother, amongst others, gave my generation to believe that they had changed the world for mothers after the war (the Second World War). Women like me had no idea that the world had not changed in the least for the particular category of mothers.

10. I hadn't taken Germaine Greer seriously when she was first expounding her revolutionary feminism. So much was ridiculed when I was at college, it was *infra dig* to espouse overtly feminist causes. At the time, the biological foundation of *The Female Eunuch* meant so little. Ten years later, with two babies and my whole life seemingly surrounded by biology, the significance of her work penetrated my brain profoundly and I have been a firm follower of hers ever since, despite some of the more outlandish of her ideas. Her books seem to coincide with my life phases—*Sex and Destiny* and *The Change* particularly.

11. Books such as *Strong-Minded Women* and *Significant Sisters* became well-thumbed and led, through their bibliographies, to ever-widening reading sources. Fiction, too, was re-read in a new light: Elizabeth Gaskell no longer for fireside leisure hours, but respected for avant-garde views. The connections between campaigning figures and their literary counterparts clarified into an overwhelming sense of feminist solidarity, albeit middle-class, which accounted, to me, for the success of the suffragette movement, built on fifty years of hard work and frustrating campaigning.

12. Apart from finding that my contemporaries' and my feminism was hardly new, I was re-orienting my mother's and my grandmother's lives in the light of what I was finding and understood their own feminism (even if they could not give it that name)—my grandmother's influenced by the suffragettes, the new thinking of the twenties (including birth control) and my mother's influenced by the war.

13. As I formed friendships I was increasingly aware, through reading of the nineteenth- and early twentieth-century networks, of the importance of friendship between women in the forwarding of feminist ideas.

14. I was fortunate enough to be close to Greenham in the early 1980s when the annual 'Ring Round the Base' was at its height. This drew women from all walks of life to the double vision of peace and women's space that Greenham represented. Those Sundays spent calf-deep in mud, linking arms and hands with women I'd never met but with whom I felt a kindred spirit, were indescribably illuminating.

15. The National Housewives Register was set up by a 'housewife' in 1961 through a letter to the *Guardian* which created such a response that the register came into being as a forum for women to get together in local groups to escape the humdrum of maternal cares and talk about things other than nappies and breastfeeding! I believe it is still going, with its name changed to 'National Women's Register.'

16. Perhaps one of the reasons I was able to believe in such sexuality is that my sister came out years before, when she was nineteen, and the word lesbian was familiar to me, even if I found that it was far from familiar to, and aroused considerable hostility from, many of the women in my immediate social circle. This changed when I moved into specifically feminist/lesbian circles with Greenham and peace-group women and women's groups.

17. I was asked to teach a WEA (Workers' Educational Association) women's studies course and the first one I did proved successful enough that I was asked to teach further courses and eventually went on to become a voluntary women's officer with the WEA.

18. The situation of the 'closet dyke' is one that intrigues yet repels me. My experience taught me that there are so many women leading double lives: on the one hand, enjoying sexual liaisons with other women in the

privacy of their own homes, using the accepted respectability of women's friendships to pursue affairs in secret; on the other, continuing to collude with the patriarchal system, remaining married and financially supported by a husband. I could not tolerate this myself and the contradictions of the hypocritical situation I found myself in contributed significantly to making the decision to divorce.

19. My first degree was not of a high grade but the optimism communicated to me by the convenors of the Women's Studies course, their faith in me and my enthusiasm right from the start at the interview prevailed.

20. Elizabeth Heaps was amazing and taught me the early rudiments of using information technology in research as well as being the most helpful librarian I have ever met and a wonderful person in her own right.

21. Mutual support even meant my closest friends on the course willingly childsitting so that I could spend time alone with my new lover. I hope I was able to give back as much as I was given: the unconditional giving by women to each other was one of the greatest and most pleasurable experiences I have met with; intimacy without commitment, friendship without demands, a family network which created bonds, which even if they only lasted the year, were invaluable to everyone's future expectations.

22. Funnily enough, I met her, not on the course, but through my previous circle of lesbian friends, a circle I had been new to. When I returned, after only a term on the course, I was already a far more confident woman and they recognised a very clear development from the 'uncertain woman' to one who knew very definitely where she was going.

23. My mentoral inspiration at this time came from my tutor, Jane Rendall, under whose gentle and unassuming demeanour lay a formidable intelligence and an impressive array of feminist knowledge and awareness. She was working on the relationship between Barbara Leigh-Smith-Bodichon and Bessie Rayner Parkes, work which became a chapter in the book *Sexuality and Subordination*, and which was entirely relevant to my own work on nineteenth-century women's friendships.

24. Most of my reading prior to the course had been recent mainstream women's history, written by women who did not necessarily have a feminist and certainly not a lesbian bias. It was not until the course gave me opportunities and directions to delve deeper that I found sources that opened up a new field of understanding.

25. By this I mean, the lack of access most women had to knowledge of the scale of women's experience; the limited range of education available to most women; and the fact that what knowledge there was, was dominated by patriarchal views.

26. One interesting aspect of new publications is that feminist historians are no longer afraid to discuss the lesbian sexuality of their subjects, even if their explorations are tentative. The biography of Daphne du Maurier by Margaret Forster is a case in point (and to a lesser extent, Lyndall Gordon's biography of Charlotte Brontë). Two publications, *Portraits to the Wall* (by Rose Collis) and *Daring to Dissent* (also with contributions from Rose Collis) face the issue head on and discuss with refreshing lack of trepidation some fascinating lesbian relationships. These works and the fact of their publication provide encouraging signs of public acceptability of lesbian-specific texts.

Jackie Scott-Mandeville was raised during the 1950s and 1960s in the Home Counties. Jackie reacted against the stereotypical confines of marriage and domesticity in the 1970s, turning towards feminism and the women's campaigns of the 1980s. The consequences were divorce, return to higher education and sexual liberation from men. After teaching, and gaining a degree in, Women's Studies, she and her lover lived in Oxford for ten years bringing up their four children. They now have a home in the Scottish Highlands where the cultural diversity and relaxed environment should provide the time and stimulation for Jackie to write those books she always intended to write!

Bibliography

A.J.R., ed. 1913. *The Suffrage Annual and Women's Who's Who*. London: Stanley Paul and Co.

Aaron, J., and S. Walby, eds. 1991. *Out of the Margins: Women's Studies in the Nineties*. London: The Falmer Press.

Abel, E. 1981. E/Merging Identities: The Dynamics of Female Friendship in Contemporary Fiction by Women. *Signs: Journal of Women and Culture in Society* 6, no. 3: 413-435.

Abu-Lughod, L. 1985. A Community of Secrets: The Separate World of Bedouin Women. *Signs: Journal of Women in Culture and Society* 10, no. 4: 637-57.

Allan, G. 1989. *Friendship: Developing a Sociological Perspective*. Hemel Hempstead: Harvester Wheatsheaf.

Anderson, K. *et al.* 1988. *Family Matters: Sociology and Contemporary Canadian Families*. Toronto: Nelson Canada.

Andrew, A. and J. Montague. 1994. From Conversation to 'Living Biography': Issues of Principle and Practice. Presentation given at the British Sociological Association Study Group on Auto/Biography Annual Conference, Manchester, December.

Arcana, J. 1979. *Our Mother's Daughters*. Berkeley: Shameless Hussy Press.

Atkinson, K. 1995. *Behind the Scenes at the Museum*. London: Transworld Publishers Ltd., Black Swan Books.

Baldick, C. 1990. *Oxford Concise Dictionary of Literary Terms*. Oxford: Oxford University Press.

Barrett, M., and M. McIntosh. 1982. *The Anti-Social Family* London: Verso.

Barrow, L., and I. Bullock. 1996. *Democratic Ideas and the British Labour Movement*. Cambridge: Cambridge University Press.

Bassett, C. 1997. Virtually Gendered: Life in an On-line World. In *The Subcultures Reader*, ed. K. Gelder and S. Thornton. London: Routledge.

Baxendale, J., and C. Pawling. 1996. *Narrating the Thirties: A Decade in the Making, 1930 to the Present*. Basingstoke: Macmillan.

Beattie, A. 1993. The Changing Boundaries of Health. In *Health and Wellbeing: A Reader*, eds. A. Beattie et al. London: Macmillan.

Beattie, A. et al., eds. 1993. *Health and Wellbeing: A Reader*. London: Macmillan.

Bedi, S. 1993. *The Fire Sacrifice*. London: Heinemann.

Belenky, M., B. Clinchy, N. Goldberger, and J. Tarule. 1986. *Women's Way of Knowing*. New York: Basic Books.

Bell, A. O., ed. 1977. *The Diary of Virginia Woolf*. London: Hogarth Press.

Bell, C. and H. Roberts, eds. 1984. *Social Researching: Politics, Problems, Practice*. London: Routledge and Kegan Paul.

Benhabib, S. 1987. The Generalized and the Concrete Other: The Kohlberg-Gilligan Controversy and Feminist Theory. In *Feminism as Critique: Essays on the Politics of Gender*, eds. S. Benhabib and D. Cornwell. Cambridge: Polity Press.

Benhabib, S. and D. Cornwell, eds. 1987. *Feminism as Critique: Essays on the Politics of Gender*. Cambridge: Polity Press.

Benjamin, J. 1988. *The Bonds of Love: Psychoanalysis, Feminism, and the Problem of Domination*. New York: Pantheon Books.

Bernikow, L., ed. 1979 (first published New York: Vintage, 1974). *The World Split Open: Women Poets 1552-1950*. London: The Women's Press.

Black, F. G. 1940. *The Epistolary Novel in the Eighteenth Century: A Descriptive and Bibliographical Study*. Oregon: Oregon University Press.

Blau DuPlessis, R. 1994. "Corpses of Poesy": Some Modern Poets and Some Gender Ideologies of Lyric. In *Feminist Measures: Soundings in Poetry and Theory*, eds. L. Keller and C. Miller. University of Michigan Press.

Blieszner, R. and R. Adams. 1992. *Adult Friendship*. Newbury Park: Sage.

Borland, K. 1991. "That's Not What I Said": Interpretive Conflict in Oral Narrative Research. In *Women's Words: The Feminist Practice of Oral History*, eds. S.B. Gluck and D. Patai. London: Routledge.

Bornat, J. 1994. Is Oral History Auto/biography? *Auto/Biography*, 3, nos. 1/2: 17-30.

Brain, R. 1977. *Friends and Lovers*. St Albans: Paladin.

Brittain, V. 1928. *Women's Work in Modern England*. London: Noel Douglas.

Brontë, C. 1966 (first published 1847). *Jane Eyre*. Harmondsworth: Penguin.

Broughton, J. 1983. Women's Rationality and Men's Virtues: A Critique of Gender Dualism on Gilligan's Theory of Moral Development. *Social Research* 50, no 3: 597-624.

Bullock, I., and R. Pankhurst, eds. 1992. *Sylvia Pankhurst: From Artist to Anti-Fascist*. London: Macmillan.

Burnett, J. 1976. *Useful Toil: Autobiographies of Working People from the 1820s to the 1920s*. London: Allen Lane.

Bush, A., and R. Swingler, eds. 1935. *The Left Song Book*. London: Gollancz/Left Book Club.

Butler, J. 1990. *Gender Trouble*. New York and London: Routledge.

Butler, M. 1997 (first published 1975). *Maria Edgeworth: A Literary Biography*. Oxford: Clarendon Press.

Cartledge, S. and J. Ryan, eds. 1983. *Sex and Love*. London: The Women's Press.

Chodorow, N. 1978. *The Reproduction of Mothering: Psychoanalysis and the Sociology of Gender*. Berkeley, CA: University of California Press.

Clarke, J., C. Crichter, and R. Johnson, eds. 1979. *Working-Class Culture: Studies in History and Theory*. London: Hutchinson.

Clifford, J. 1983. On Ethnographic Authority. *Representations* 1, no. 2: 128-135.

Coates, J. 1996. *Women Talk: Conversation Between Women Friends*. Oxford: Blackwell.

Cohen, A. 1994. *Self Consciousness: An Alternative Anthropology of Identity*. London: Routledge.

Collis, R. 1994. *Portraits to the Wall: Historic Lesbian Lives Unveiled*. London: Cassell.

Colvin, C., ed. 1977. *Maria Edgeworth: Letters from England, 1813-1844*. Oxford: Clarendon Press.

Cook, J., and J. Clarke. 1989. Racism and the Right. In *Reactions to the Right*, ed. B. Hindess. London: Routledge.

Cook, J., and S. Watt. 1992. Racism, Women and Poverty. In *Women and Poverty in Britain in the 1990s*, eds. C. Glendinning and J. Millar. Brighton: Harvester Wheatsheaf.

Corbett, M. J. 1992. *Representing Femininity: Middle-Class Subjectivity in Victorian and Edwardian Women's Autobiographies*. Oxford: Oxford University Press.

Cosslett, T. 1988. *From Woman to Woman: Female Friendships in Victorian Fiction*. Atlantic Highlands, New Jersey: Humanities Press International.

Cotterill, P. 1992. Interviewing Women: Issues of Friendship, Vulnerability and Power. *Women's Studies International Forum* 15, nos 5/6: 593-606.

Cotterill, P., and G. Letherby. 1993. Weaving Stories: Personal Auto/Biographies in Feminist Research. *Sociology* 27, no. 1: 67-79.

Coward, R. 1992. *Our Treacherous Hearts: Why Women Let Men Get Their Way*. London: Faber and Faber.

Cowman, K. 1997. The Stonethrowing Has Been Forced Upon Us: The Function of Militancy Within the Liverpool WSPU, 1906-14. *Transactions of the Historical Society of Lancashire and Cheshire* 145: 171 - 92.

Curran, J., and V. Porter, eds. 1983. *British Cinema History*. London: Weidenfeld and Nicholson.

Dally, A. 1982. *Inventing Motherhood: The Consequences of an Ideal*. London: Burnett Books.

Daly, M. 1978. *Gyn/Ecology*. Boston, MA: Beacon Press.

Daly, M. 1984. *Pure Lust: Elemental Feminist Philosophy*. Boston, MA: Beacon

Press.

Daly, M. 1988. *Webster's First New Intergalactic Wickkedary of the English Language*. London: The Women's Press.

Danet, Brenda 1994. "Smoking Dope" at a Virtual Party: Writing, Play and Performance on Internet Relay Chat. msdanet@pluto.msc.huji.ac.il

Davies, M. L., ed. 1977 (first published 1931). *Life As We Have Known It*. London: Hogarth.

Davies, M. L. 1978 (first publised 1915). *Maternity: Letters from Working Women*. London: Virago Press.

Delafield, E. M. 1984 (first published 1930). *The Diary of a Provincial Lady*. London: Virago Press.

Denzin, N. 1989. *Interpretive Biography*. Sage International Qualitative Methods Series 17, London: Sage.

Diehl, J. Feit. 1993. *Elizabeth Bishop and Marianne Moore: The Psychoynamics of Creativity*. Princeton, NJ: Princeton University Press.

Donoghue, E. 1993. *Passions Between Women: British Lesbian Culture 1668-1801*. New York: Harper Collins.

Du Maurier, D. 1975 (first published 1938). *Rebecca*. London: Pan.

Duck, S. 1988. *Relating to Others*. Milton Keynes: Open University Press.

Duck, S. 1991. *Friends for Life: The Psychology of Personal Relationships*. Hemel Hempstead: Harvester Wheatsheaf.

Duck, S., D. J. Rutt, M. Hoy Hurst, and H. Strejc. 1991. Some Evident Truths About Conversation in Everyday Relationships: All Communications Are Not Created Equal. *Human Communication Research* 18: 228-67.

Dyhouse, C. 1989. *Feminisms and the Family in England 1880-1939*. Oxford: Blackwell.

Dyos, H. J., and M. Wolff, eds. 1973. *The Victorian City: Images and Realities*. London: Routledge and Kegan Paul.

Edgeworth, M. 1800 (first published 1795). *The Parents' Assistant: or, Stories for Children*. Cork: George Cherry.

Edgeworth, M. 1801. *Moral Tales for Young People*. 5 vols. London: J. Johnson.

Edgeworth, M. 1909 (7th ed., first published 1809). Stories of Harry and Lucy. In *Early Lessons*. London: George Routledge and Sons.

Edgeworth, M. 1993 (first published 1795). *Letters for Literary Ladies to which is added an Essay on the Noble Science of Self-Justification*. With an Introduction by Claire Connolly. London: Guernsey Press, J. M. Dent.

Edgeworth, M. and R. L. Edgeworth. 1974 (first published 1798). *Practical Education*. 2 Vols. With an Introduction by Gina Lurie. London: Garland Publishing.

Eichler, M. 1983. *Families in Canada Today: Recent Changes and Their Policy Consequences*. Toronto: Gage Publishing.

Elias, E. 1978. *On Sundays We Wore White*. London: W. H. Allen.

Elshtain, J. B. 1982. Feminism, Family and Community. *Dissent* 29: 442-49.

Erkkila, B. 1992. *The Wicked Sisters: Women Poets, Literary History, and Discord*. Oxford: Oxford University Press.

Evans, M. 1993. Reading Lives: How the Personal Might Be Social. *Sociology* 27, no. 1: 5-13.

Faderman, L. 1981. *Surpassing the Love of Men: Romantic Friendship and Love Between Women from the Renaissance to the Present*. New York: William Morrow.

Faderman, L. 1992. *Odd Girls and Twilight Lovers: A History of Lesbian Life in Twentieth-Century America*. New York: Penguin Books.

Favret, M. A. 1993. *Romantic Correspondence: Women, Politics and the Fiction of Letters*. Cambridge: Cambridge University Press.

Fehr, B. 1996. *Friendship Processes*. Newbury Park: Sage.

Finch, J. 1984. "It's Great to have Someone to Talk to": The Ethics and Politics of Interviewing Women. In *Social Researching: Politics, Problems, Practice*, eds. C. Bell, C. and H. Roberts. London: Routledge and Kegan Paul.

Finch, J. 1989. *Family Obligations and Social Change*. Oxford: Polity Press.

Finch, J., and J. Mason. 1993. *Negotiating Family Responsibility*. London: Tavistock/ Routledge.

Fischer, C. 1982. What Do We Mean By Friend? An Inductive Study. *Social Network* 3: 287-306.

Flax, J. 1987. *The Conflict Between Nurturance and Autonomy in Mother-Daughter Relationships and Within Feminism*. Berkeley, CA: University of California Press.

Fletcher, R. 1996. A Star Chamber of the Twentieth Century: Suffragettes, Liberals and the 'Rush the Commons' case. *Journal of British Studies* 35 (October): 504 - 30.

Forrest, L., and J. Giles. (1999) Feminist Ethics and Issues in the production and use of Life History Research. In *Women's Lives Into Print: the Theory and Practice of Feminist Auto/biography*, ed. P. Polkey. Basingstoke: Macmillan.

Forster, M. 1993. *Daphne du Maurier*. London: Chatto and Windus.

Fraser, N., and L. Gordon. 1992. Contract Versus Charity: Why is There No Social Citizenship in the United States? *Socialist Review* 22, no. 3: 45-68.

France, L., ed. 1994. *Sixty Women Poets*. Newcastle: Bloodaxe Books.

Freeman, A., and J. Cook. 1992. Pretending Everything is OK: Women and Stress. Workshop given to British Psychological Society Women and Psychology Conference, University of Lancaster, July.

Freeman, M., ed. 1995. *Always, Rachel: The Letters of Rachel Carson and*

Dorothy Freeman 1952-1964. Boston: Beacon Press.

Fremlin, C. 1940. *The Seven Chars of Chelsea*. London: Methuen.

Friday, N. 1977. *My Mother, My Self: The Daughter's Search for Identity*. New York: Dell.

Friedan, B. 1963. *The Feminine Mystique*. London: Gollancz.

Friedman, M. 1993. *What Are Friends For? Feminist Perspectives on Personal Relationships and Moral Theory*. Ithaca, NY: Cornell University Press.

Gamarnikow, E. et al., eds. 1983. *The Public and The Private*. London: Heinemann.

Gardiner, J. Kegan. 1981. The Us(es) of I/dentity: A Response to Abel on E/Merging Identities. *Signs* 6, no. 3: 436-442.

Garner, L. 1984. *Stepping Stones to Women's Liberty*. London: Heineman.

Garner, L. 1990. *A Brave and Beautiful Spirit: Dora Marsden, 1882-1960*. Aldershot: Avebury/Gower.

Garner, L. 1992. Suffragism and Socialism: Sylvia Pankhurst 1903-14. In *Sylvia Pankhurst: From Artist to Anti-Fascist*, eds. I. Bullock and R. Pankhurst. London: Macmillan.

Gibbs, L., ed. 1994. *Daring to Dissent: Lesbian Culture From Margin to Mainstream*. London: Cassell.

Gibson, W. 1984. *Neuromancer*. London: Victor Gollancz Ltd.

Giddens, A. 1992. *The Transformation of Intimacy: Sexuality, Love and Eroticism in Modern Societies*. Stanford: Stanford University Press.

Giles, M. J. 1989. *'Something that bit better': Working-class women, domesticity and 'respectability', 1919-1939*. Ph. D. thesis. University of York, England.

Giles, J. 1995. *Women, Identity and Private Life in Britain 1900-50*. Basingstoke: Macmillan.

Gilligan, C. 1982. *In A Different Voice: Psychological Theory and Women's Development*. Cambridge, MA: Harvard University Press.

Glendinning, C., and J. Millar, eds. 1992. *Women and Poverty in Britain in the 1990s*. Brighton: Harvester Wheatsheaf.

Gluck, S.B., and D. Patai, eds. 1991. *Women's Words: the Feminist Practice of Oral History*. London: Routledge.

Goldsmith E., ed. 1989. *Writing the Female Voice: Essays in Epistolary Literature*. Boston: North-Eastern University Press.

Gordon, E. 1991. *Women and the Labour Movement in Scotland 1850 - 1914*. Oxford: Clarendon Press.

Gordon, L. 1994. *Charlotte Brontë: a Passionate Life*. London: Chatto and Windus.

Gouldner, H. and M. S. Strong. 1987. *Speaking of Friendship: Middle-class women and their friends*. New York: Greenwood Press.

Greer, G. 1970. *The Female Eunuch*. London: McGibbon and Kee.

Greer, G. 1984. *Sex and Destiny: the politics of human fertility*. London: Pan.

Greer, G. 1993. *The Change: Women, ageing and the menopause*. London: Penguin Books.

Grima, B. 1993. *The Performance of Emotion Among Paxtun Women*. Oxford: Oxford University Press.

Groves, D., and J. Finch. 1983. Natural Selection: Perspectives on Entitlement to the Invalid Care Allowance. In *A Labour of Love: Women, Work and Caring*, eds. D. Groves and J. Finch. London: Routledge and Kegan Paul.

Groves, D., and J. Finch, eds. 1983. *A Labour of Love: Women, Work and Caring*. London: Routledge and Kegan Paul.

Hall, S., and T. Jefferson, eds. 1975. *Resistance Through Rituals: Youth Subcultures in Post-war Britain*. London: Hutchinson.

Hallett, C., ed. 1989. *Women and Social Services Departments*. Brighton: Harvester Wheatsheaf.

Hamilton, R. 1990. A Politics of Intimate Life: A Funny Thing Happened On The Way Through The Eighties. *Atlantis* 15, no. 2: 82-9.

Hanff K. J. 1988. *The Properties of Breath*. Newcastle: Bloodaxe Books.

Hanscombe, G., and S. Namjoshi. 1986. *Flesh and Paper*. Seaton, Devon: Jezebel Tapes and Books.

Hanscombe, G., and S. Namjoshi. 1991. "Who Wrongs You, Sappho?"—Developing Lesbian Sensibility in the Writing of Lyric Poetry. In *Out of the Margins: Women's Studies in the Nineties*, eds. J. Aaron and S. Walby. London: Falmer Press.

Haraway, D. 1990. A Manifesto for Cyborgs: Science, Technology and Socialist Feminism in the 1980s. In *Feminism and Postmodernism*, ed. L. Nicholson. London: Routledge.

Harding, K., and C. Gibbs. 1980. *Tough Annie: From Suffragette to Stepney Councillor*. London: Stepney Books.

Haskel, L. 1996. Cyberdykes: Tales from the Internet. In *Assaults on Convention: Essays on Lesbian Transgression*, eds. N. Godwin, B. Hollows, and S. Nye. London: Cassell.

Hawkes, E. 1987. Woolf's Magical Garden of Women. In *New Feminist Essays on Virginia Woolf*, ed. J. Marais. London: Macmillan.

Hazekamp, J., W. Meeus, and Y. te Poel, eds. 1987. *European Contributions to Youth Research*. Amsterdam: Free University Press.

Heller, Z. 1990. Ruling Passions on Approved Lines. *The Independent on Sunday* 18 November: 36.

Henfrey, J. 1994. *Coming Home and Other Stories*. Leeds: Peepal Tree.

Hesketh, P. 1992 (first published 1966). *My Aunt Edith*. Preston: Lancashire County Books.

Hindess, B., ed. 1989. *Reactions to the Right*. London: Routledge.

Hite, S. 1994. *The Hite Report on the Family: Growing Up Under Patriarchy*. London: Bloomington.

HMSO. 1931. *Census of England and Wales for 1931: General Report*. London: HMSO.

Holton, S. S. 1996. *Suffrage Days: Stories from the Women's Suffrage Movement*. London: Routledge.

Homans, M. 1981. *Women Writers and Poetic Identity*. Princeton, New Jersey: Princeton University Press.

Hood, S. 1983. John Grierson and the Documentary Film Movement. In *British Cinema History*, eds. J. Curran and V. Porter. London: Weidenfeld and Nicholson.

hooks, b. 1984. *Feminist Theory: From Margin to Centre*. Boston MA.: South End Press.

hooks, b. 1989. *Talking Back: Thinking Feminist, Thinking Black*. Boston, MA: South End Press.

hooks, b. 1991. *Yearning: Race, Gender and Cultural Politics*. London: Turnaround.

Hughes, M.V. 1979 (first published 1940). *A London Family Between the Wars*. Oxford: Oxford University Press.

Humm, M. 1989. *The Dictionary of Feminist Theory*. 2nd ed. New York: Prentice Hall.

Hunt, M. 1994. *Fierce Tenderness: a Feminist Theology of Friendship*. New York: Crossroads Publishing.

Irigaray, L. 1980. When Our Lips Speak Together. *Signs: Journal of Women in Culture and Society* 6, no. 1: 69-79.

Irigaray, L. 1981. And the One Doesn't Stir Without the Other. *Signs: Journal of Women in Culture and Society* 7, no. 1: 60-67.

Irigaray, L. 1993. *Je, Tu, Nous*. London: Routledge.

Janeway, E. 1971. *Man's World, Woman's Place: A Study in Social Mythology*. Harmondsworth: Penguin.

Jeffreys, S. 1984. Does It Matter If They Did It? *Trouble and Strife* 3: 25-29.

Jeffreys, S. 1985. *The Spinster and Her Enemies: Feminism and Sexuality 1880-1930*. London: Pandora.

Jephcott, P. 1942. *Girls Growing Up*. London: Faber and Faber.

Jerome, D. 1984. Good Company: The Sociological Implications of Friendship. *Sociological Review* 32, no. 4: 696-718.

Kaloski, A. 1997. Bisexuals Making out with Cyborgs: Politics, Pleasure, Con/fusion. *Journal of Gay, Lesbian, and Bisexual Identity* 2, no. 1: 47-64. Extracted in *Bisexuality: A Critical Reader*. 1999. Ed. Merl Storr. London: Routledge.

Kaplan, N., and E. Farrell. 1994. Weavers of Webs: A Portrait of Young

Women on the Net. *The Arachnet Electronic Journal on Virtual Culture* 2, no. 3.

Kay, J. 1993. *Other Lovers*. Newcastle: Bloodaxe Books.

Keating, P. J. 1976. *Into Unknown England 1866-1913: Selections from the Social Explorers*. London: Fontana.

Krieger, S. 1982. Lesbian Identity and Community: Recent Social Science Literature. *Signs: Journal of Women in Culture and Society* 8, no. 1: 91-108.

Krieger, S. 1996. *The Family Silver: Essays on Relationships among Women*. Berkeley, CA: University of California Press.

Lasch, C., and W. Taylor. 1963. "Two Kindred Spirits": Sorority and Family in New England: 1839-1846. *New England Quarterly* 36: 25-41.

Liddington, J., and J. Norris. 1978. *One Hand Tied Behind Us: The Rise of the Women's Suffrage Movement*. London: Virago Press.

Light, A. 1991. *Forever England: Femininity, Literature and Conservatism Between the Wars*. London: Routledge.

Lochhead, L 1984. *Dreaming Frankenstein*. Edinburgh: Polygon.

Lorde, A. 1984. *Sister Outsider, Freedom*. CA: Crossing Press.

Luxton, M., ed. (1997) *Feminism and Families: Critical Policies and Changing Practices*. Halifax: Fernwood Press.

Lytton, C. 1914. *Prisons and Prisoners: Some Personal Experiences by Constance Lytton and Jane Warton, Spinster*. London: Heinemann.

McBride, T. 1976. *The Domestic Revolution: The Modernisation of Household Service in England and France 1820-1920*. London: Croom Helm.

McDowell, L., and R. Pringle, R., eds. 1992. *Defining Women*. Cambridge: Polity Press.

McPherson, D. 1991. *Order out of Chaos: The Autobiographical Works of Maya Angelou*. London: Virago Press.

MacDonald, E. E. 1977. *The Education of the Heart: The Correspondence of Rachel Mordecai and Maria Edgeworth*. Chapel Hill: The University of North Carolina Press.

Maguire, S. 1991. *Spilt Milk*. London: Secker and Warburg.

Maline, D., and S. Maslin-Prothero, eds. 1997. *Speaking Our Place(s): Women's Perspectives in Higher Education*. London: Taylor and Francis.

Mann, C. 1994. "How Did I Get To Here?" Educational Life Histories of Adolescent Girls doing A-levels. *Auto/biography* 3, nos. 1/2: 59-70.

Marais, J., ed. 1987. *New Feminist Essays on Virginia Woolf*. London: Macmillan.

Maynard, M., and J. Purvis, eds. 1994. *Researching Women's Lives from a Feminist Perspective*. London: Taylor and Francis.

Mendus, S., and J. Rendall, eds. 1989. *Sexuality and Subordination*. London:

Routledge.

Michie, H, 1989. Not One of the Family: The Repression of the Other Woman in Feminist Theory. In *Discontented Discourses: Feminism / Textual Intervention / Psychoanalysis*, eds. M. S. Barr and R. Feldstein. Champaign: University of Illinois Press. Extracted in *Feminisms: An Anthology of Literary Theory and Criticism*. 1991. Eds. R. R. Warhol and D. P. Herndl. New Brunswick: Rutgers University Press.

Michie, H. 1992. *Sororophobia: Differences Among Women in Literature and Culture*. Oxford University Press.

Milardo, R. M. ed. 1988. *Families and Social Networks*. Beverley Hills, CA: Sage.

Miller, N., and D. Morgan. 1993. Called to Account: The CV as an Autobiographical Practice. *Sociology* 27, no. 1: 133-143.

Millet, K. 1977. *Sexual Politics*. London: Virago Press.

Milner, M. 1986. *An Experiment in Leisure*. London: Virago.

Mitchell, D. 1977. *Queen Christabel*. London: MacDonald and Jane's.

Mitchell, H. 1977. *The Hard Way Up*. London: Virago.

Mitchison, N. 1979. *You May Well Ask*. London: Gollancz.

Modleski, T. 1984. *Loving With a Vengeance: Mass-Produced Fantasies for Women*. New York: Routledge.

Modleski, T. 1991. *Feminism Without Women*. London: Routledge.

Mohin, L., ed. 1986. *Beautiful Barbarians: Lesbian Feminist Poetry*. London: Onlywomen Press.

Montefiore, J. 1987. *Feminism and Poetry: Language, Experience, Identity in Women's Writing*. London: Pandora.

Morgan, S. 1988. *My Place*. Sydney: Fremantle Art Place.

Morrison, T. 1993. *Playing in the Dark: Whiteness and the Literary Imagination*. New York: Vintage Books.

Morton, H.V. 1933. What I Saw In The Slums. Labour Pamphlet VII.

Mulford, W., ed. 1990. *The Virago Book of Love Poetry*. London: Virago Press.

Nicholson, L., ed. 1990. *Feminism and Postmodernism*. London: Routledge.

Oakley, A. 1972. *Sex, Gender and Society*. London: Maurice Temple Smith.

O'Connor, N., and J. Ryan. 1993. *Wild Desires and Mistaken Identities: Lesbianism and Psychoanalysis*. London: Virago Press.

O'Connor, P. 1992. *Friendships Between Women: A Critical Review*. Hemel Hempstead: Harvester Wheatsheaf.

Office for National Statistics. 1997. *Social Trends* 27. London: The Stationary Office.

Oliker, S.J. 1989. *Best Friends and Marriage: Exchange Among Women*. Berkeley, CA: University of California Press.

Orbach, S., and L. Eichenbaum. 1987. *Bitter Sweet: Love, Envy and*

Competition in Women's Friendships. London: Arrow Books.

Orbach, S., and L. Eichenbaum. 1994. *Between Women: Love, Envy and Competition in Women's Friendships*. London: Arrow Books.

Orwell, G. 1987 (first published 1937). *The Road to Wigan Pier*. Harmondsworth: Penguin.

Ostriker, A, 1987. *Stealing the Language: The Emergence of Women's Poetry in America*. London: The Women's Press.

Owen, E. 1993. *Between Me and My Sister*. (unpublished).

Padel, R. 1996. *Fusewire*. London: Chatto and Windus.

Parks, M. R., and L. Roberts. 1997. "Making MOOsic": The Development of Personal Relationships On-Line and a Comparison to Their Off-Line Counterparts. Paper presented at the Annual Conference of the Western Speech Communication Association, Monterey, California.

Pearce, L. 1997. *Feminism and the Politics of Reading*. London: Arnold.

Pelling, H. 1965. *The Origins of the Labour Party*. Oxford: Oxford University Press.

Perry, R.. 1980. *Women, Letters and the Novel*. New York: AMS Press.

Personal Narratives Group., eds. 1989. *Interpreting Women's Lives: Feminist Theory and Personal Narratives*. Indiana: Indiana University Press.

Pestalozzi, J. H. 1801. *How Gertrude Teaches her Children*, n. p.

Pestalozzi, J. H. 1803. *The Mother's Book, or, A Guide for Mothers in Teaching their Children to Observe and Talk*, n. p.

Pethick Lawrence, E. 1938. *My Part in a Changing World*. London: Victor Gollancz.

Phillips, A. 1991. *Engendering Democracy*. Cambridge: Polity Press.

The Pilgrim Trust. 1938. *Men Without Work* Cambridge: Cambridge University Press.

Plath, S. 1981. *Collected Poems*. London: Faber.

Polkey, P., ed. 1999. *Women's Lives Into Print: the Theory and Practice of Feminist Auto/biography*. Basingstoke: Macmillan.

Potts, L. 1993. Best Friend Bereavement. *Everywoman* (Dec/Jan).

Prentice, A., P. Bourne, G. Brandt, B. Light, W. Mitchinson, and N. Black. 1988. *Canadian Women: A History*. Toronto: Harcourt Brace Jovanovich.

Priestley, J. B. 1984 (first published 1934). *English Journey*. Harmondsworth: Penguin.

Raeburn, A. 1973. *The Militant Suffragettes*. London: Michael Joseph.

Raitt, S. 1993. *Vita & Virginia: The Work and Friendship of Vita Sackville-West and Virginia Woolf*. Oxford: Clarendon Press.

Raymond, J. 1986. *A Passion For Friends: Toward A Philosophy of Female Affection*. Boston: Beacon Press.

Reid, E. M. 1994. Cultural Formations in Text-Based Virtual Realities.

http://people.we.mediaone.net/elizrs/work.html Last accessed 6 November 1999.

Reiter, R., ed. 1975. *Towards an Anthropology of Women*. New York: Monthly Review Press.

Rich, A. 1977. *Of Woman Born: Motherhood as Experience and Institution*. London: Virago Press.

Rich, A. 1980. Compulsory Heterosexuality and Lesbian Existence. *Signs: A Journal of Women in Culture and Society* 5, no. 4: 631-60.

Rich, A. 1981. *Compulsory Heterosexuality and Lesbian Existence*. London: Onlywomen Press Pamphlet.

Rich, A. 1989. *Time's Power: Poems 1985-1988*. New York and London: W. W. Norton and Company.

Richardson, M. 1953. *Laugh a Defiance*. London: Weidenfeld and Nicolson.

Roberts, H., ed. 1981. *Doing Feminist Research*. London: Routledge and Kegan Paul.

Roberts, M. 1986. *The Mirror of the Mother*. London: Methuen.

Robins, K. 1995. Cyberspace and the world we live in. In *Cyberspace/ Cyberbodies/Cyberpunk: Cultures of Technological Embodiment*, ed. M. Featherstone and R. Burrows. London: Sage.

Rosen, A. 1974. *Rise Up, Women! The Militant Campaign of the Women's Social and Political Union, 1903-1914*. London: Routledge and Kegan Paul.

Rosenzweig, L. 1993. *The Anchor of My Life: Middle-Class American Mothers and Daughters 1880-1920*. New York: New York University Press.

Rothblum, E., and K. Brehony. 1993. *Boston Marriages: Romantic But Asexual Relationships Among Contemporary Lesbians*. Amherst: University of Massachusetts Press.

Rowntree, B. S. 1901. *Poverty: A Study of Town Life*. London: Macmillan.

Rowntree, B. S. 1941. *Poverty and Progress: A Second Social Survey of York*. London: Longman.

Rubin, G. 1975. The Traffic in Women: Notes on the Political Economy of Sex. In *Towards an Anthropology of Women*, ed. R. Reiter. New York: Monthly Review Press.

Rubin, L. 1985. *Just Friends: The Role of Friendship in Our Lives*. New York: Harper and Row.

Sarah, E. 1983. Christabel Pankhurst: Reclaiming her Power. In *Feminist Theorists: Three Centuries of Women's Intellectual Traditions*, ed. D. Spender. London: Women's Press.

Sedgwick, E. K. 1985. *Between Men: English Literature and Male Homosocial Desire*. New York: Columbia University Press. Extracted in *Feminisms: an Anthology of Literary Theory and Criticism*. 1991. Eds. R. R. Warhol and D.

Price Herndl. New Brunswick: Rutgers University Press.

Sedgwick, E.K. 1991. *Epistemology of the Closet*. London: Harvester Wheatsheaf.

Segal, L. 1994. *Straight Sex: The Politics of Pleasure*. London: Virago Press.

Sherman, C. W. 1995. *Sisterfire: Black Womanist Fiction and Poetry*. London: The Women's Press. (First published New York: HarperCollins, 1994).

Shiva, V. 1989. *Staying Alive: Women, Ecology and Survival in India*. New Delhi: Kali for Women; London: Zed Press.

Side, K. 1996. Cartographies of Care: Mapping Out Family and Friendship Relations. Presentation given at the 9th International Women's Studies Network (U.K.) Conference, Mid-Glamorgan, Wales, July.

Side, K. 1997. In The Shadow of the Family: Women's Friendships with Women. In *Feminism and Families: Critical Policies and Changing Practices*, ed. M. Luxton. Halifax: Fernwood Press.

Side, K. 1999. Government Restraint and Limits to Economic Reciprocity in Women's Friendships. *Atlantis: A Women's Studies Journal* 23, no. 2: 5-15.

Skevington, S., and D. Baker, eds. 1989. *The Social Identity of Women*. London: Sage.

Sleight, J. 1988. *One-Way Ticket to Epsom: A Journalist's Enquiry into the Heroic Story of Emily Wilding Davison*. Morpeth: Bridge Studios.

Smith-Rosenberg, C. 1975. The Female World of Love and Ritual: Relations Between Women in Nineteenth-Century America. *Signs: Journal of Women in Culture and Society* 1: 1-30.

Smyth, E., and C. Hamilton. 1911. *The March of the Women: Dedicated to the Women's Social and Political Union*. London: Women's Press.

Souhami, D. 1991. *Gertrude and Alice*. London: Pandora Press.

Spender, D., ed. 1983. *Feminist Theorists: Three Centuries of Women's Intellectual Traditions*. London: Women's Press.

Spender, D. 1995. *Nattering on the Net: Women, Power and Cyberspace*. North Melbourne: Spiniflex Press.

Stacey, J. 1988. Can There Be A Feminist Ethnography? *Women's Studies International Forum* 11, no. 1: 21-7.

Stack, C. 1975. *All Our Kin: Strategies For Survival in a Black Community*. New York: Harper and Row.

Stanley, L. 1992a. *The Auto/biographical I: The Theory and Practice of Feminist Auto/biography*. Manchester: Manchester University Press.

Stanley, L. 1992b. Romantic Friendship? Some Issues in Researching Lesbian History and Biography. *Women's History Review* 1, no. 2: 193-216.

Stanley, L. 1993. On Auto/Biographies in Sociology. *Sociology* 27, no. 1: 41-52.

Stanley, L. 1994. Introduction: Lives and Works and Auto/biographical Occasions. *Auto/Biography* 3, nos. 1/ 2: i-ii.

Stanley, L., with A. Morley. 1988. *The Life and Death of Emily Wilding Davison*. London: The Women's Press.

Stevenson, J., and C. Cook. 1979. *The Slump: Society and Politics During the Depression*. London: Quartet.

Stiver Lie, S., and V. O'Leary, eds. 1990. *Storming the Tower: Women in the Academic World*. London: Kogan Page.

Symes, R. A. 1995. *Educating Women: The Preceptress and her Pen, 1780-1820*. Ph.D. thesis, University of York, England.

Tan, A. 1993. *The Joy Luck Club*. London: Minerva.

Tannen, D. 1990. *You Just Don't Understand: Men and Women In Conversation*. New York: Ballantine Books.

Taylor, P. 1979. Daughters and Mothers—Maids and Mistresses: Domestic Service Between the Wars. In *Working-Class Culture: Studies in History and Theory*, eds. J. Clarke, C. Crichter and R. Johnson. London, Hutchinson.

Temple, B. 1994. The Message and the Medium: Oral and Written Accounts of Lives. *Auto/biography* 3, nos. 1/2: 31-42.

Thompson, L. 1971. *The Enthusiasts: A Biography of John and Katharine Bruce Glasier*. London: Gollancz.

Thompson, M. 1981. Comments on Rich's "Compulsory Heterosexuality and Lesbian Existence". *Signs: A Journal of Women in Culture and Society* 6, no.4: 790-94.

Thompson, S. 1997. Who Goes There, Friend or Foe? Black Women and White Women in Academia. In *Speaking Our Place(s): Women's Perspectives in Higher Education*, eds. D. Maline and S. Maslin-Prothero. London: Taylor and Francis.

Thompson, T., ed. 1987. *Dear Girl: The Diaries and Letters of Two Working Women, 1897-1917*. London: The Women's Press.

Todd, J. 1980. *Women's Friendships in Literature*. New York: Columbia University Press.

Trevor, J. 1897. *My Quest for God*. Manchester: n.p.

Turkle, S. 1995. *Life on the Screen: Identity in the Age of the Internet*. London: Weidenfield and Nicholson.

Uhl, S. 1991. Forbidden Friends: Cultural Veils of Female Friendship in Andalusia. *American Ethnologist* 18: 90-105.

Vicinus, M. 1985. *Independent Women: Work and Community for Single Women 1850-1920*. London: Virago Press.

Walker, A., and P. Parmar. 1993. *Warrior Marks: Female Genital Mutliation and the Sexual Blinding of Women*. London: Jonathan Cape.

Walkowitz, J. 1992. *City of Dreadful Delight: Narratives of Sexual Danger in Late Victorian London*. London: Virago Press.

Warhol, R. R., and D. P. Herndl, eds. 1991. *Feminisms: An Anthology of Literary Theory and Criticism*. New Brunswick: Rutgers University Press.

Watt, S., and J. Cook. 1989. Another Expectation Unfulfilled: Black Women and Social Services Departments. In *Women and Social Services Departments*, ed. C. Hallett. Brighton: Harvester Wheatsheaf.

Watt, S., and J. Cook. 1991a. Racism: Whose Liberation? Implications for Women's Studies. In *Out of the Margins: Women's Studies in the Nineties*, eds. J. Aaron and S. Walby. London: The Falmer Press.

Watt, S., and J. Cook. 1991b. Where Do We Begin?. *Educational Change and Development* II, no. 2: 12-19.

Weedon, C. 1996. *Feminist Practice and Post-Structural Theory*. Oxford: Basil Blackwell.

Weinstock, J., and E. Rothblum, eds. 1996. *Lesbian Friendships: For Ourselves and Each Other*. New York: New York University Press.

Wilkinson, S., and C. Kitzinger, eds. 1993. *Heterosexuality: A Feminism and Psychology Reader*. London: Sage.

Williams, T. 1996. *Otherland: City of the Golden Shadow (Book 1)*. Harmondsworth: Penguin. See also Williams' homepage on http://www.tadwilliams.com/about.html

Woolf, V. 1977, first published 1929. *A Room of One's Own*. London: Granada Publishing Limited.

Yeo, S. 1977. A New Life: The Religion of Socialism in Britain. *History Workshop Journal* 4 (Autumn): 5-56.

Yorke, L. 1994. Primary Intensities: Lesbian Poetry and the Reading of Difference. In *Daring to Dissent*, ed. L. Gibbs. London: Cassell.

Young, I.M. 1990. The Ideal of Community and the Politics of Difference. In *Feminism and Postmodernism*, ed. L. Nicholson. London: Routledge.

Zagarell, S. 1988. Narrative of Community: The Identification of a Genre. *Signs: Journal of Women in Culture and Society* 13: 498-527.

Index

academia *2-4, 19, 21-37, 39-55, 237*
admiration *99, 141-3, 175*
advice works *112-3*
affection *5, 19, 221*
affirmation *15, 199*
agency *7-9, 196*
ambivalence *201*
America *2, 12, 63, 97, 110*
Angelou, Maya *27*
antagonism *190*
anti-racism *3, 44-50*
Arthurs, Doris *173-8*
attachment *60, 62, 66, 200, 207*
audience *29-34, 189*
auto/biography *3, 8, 16, 19, 21-37, 216-7, 237*
autonomy *10, 15, 16, 69, 91, 130, 150, 196*

Benjamin, Jessica *60-1, 65*
bereavement *80, 85-86*
'best friends' *2, 80-2, 181, 182*
Black women *39-42, 46-52, 54*
blame *43*
bonding *92*
Boston marriages *59*
boundaries *13-5, 41, 110, 200*
brotherhood *84, 127-8*

Canada *67, 73*
care, provision of *73, 83, 173*
celibacy *172-3*
challenges *5, 10, 50, 54*
children *100, 103-6, 109, 117, 240*
Chodorow, Nancy *59-61, 65, 190, 193, 199-202*
Christianity *12, 98, 127, 192*
class *3, 12-4, 18, 23, 29-30, 123, 128, 131, 141, 145, 155-181, 195*
  middle *41, 98, 100, 111, 114, 163, 166-76*
  upper *163*
  working *29, 163, 165-8, 176*
claustrophobia *195*
colleagues *8, 22, 33, 34, 40, 122*
commitment *5, 10, 15, 50-1, 54, 72, 87, 99, 150, 160*
commonalities *5, 11-12, 16, 23, 25, 41, 44, 54, 71, 87, 151*
communication *72, 196, 217-8*
communities *4, 10, 21, 69, 215*
companions *79*
competitiveness *83, 90, 190, 207*
comradeship *84, 121-50*
confusion *14, 185*
connectedness *5, 54, 60-1, 93*
correspondence *108, 111-8*
CV, the *23-4*
cyberspace *2, 4, 13, 15, 17, 215-35*

Daly, Mary *63, 79, 80, 84, 94-5, 246*
daughters *see* mothers-daughters
Davison, Emily Wilding *125, 129, 130, 139*
death *80, 86*

deference *136, 141-2, 156, 160, 165, 167, 172, 175, 178*
definitions *6, 44, 58, 81, 184*
Delafield, *(Diary of a Provincial Lady)* *170*
dependence *69, 177*
Dickinson, Emily *181, 185, 201, 202, 208*
difference *7, 11-3, 23, 25, 39, 41, 42, 54, 62-3, 71, 89-90, 92-3, 98, 101, 139, 185-7, 195, 200, 207*
  celebrating *42, 92*
diversity *92*
domestic service *155-79*
Du Maurier, Daphne *168, 175-7*

education *3, 12, 42, 45-6, 98, 101-18*
email *219-27*
emotes *221*
employment *8, 14*
envy *196*
equality *8, 23, 33, 69, 72, 94, 141, 151*
essentialism *62, 63, 66-7*
ethics *30, 35-6*
ethnicity *23, 30*
eulogies *136, 142-3*
exchange *5, 15, 31, 107*
expectations *83, 87*
experience *18-20, 29, 42, 47, 82*

Faderman, Lillian *59, 64, 186-7, 246*
family *9-11, 13, 14, 16, 21, 35, 57-8, 64, 68, 71-3, 83-9, 93, 109-11, 117, 156, 175, 178, 181, 203-4, 210*
  extended *4, 63*
  nuclear *11, 68, 72, 187, 204*
femininity *218, 225-7*
flirting *224-8*
Fremlin, Celia *161-77*
Freud *59, 61, 67, 167, 170-1, 177, 203*
friendship
  celebrating *4, 19, 42, 84, 189, 238*
  feminine *225-7*
  marginalisation of *178, 187, 204*
  trivialisation of *1*
  as voluntary *71-2, 83*
  webs of *137, 152*

gender *218-20, 226*
Giddens, Anthony *71-2*
Gilligan, Carol *60, 65*
Greenham Common *15, 242*
growth *44, 55*
guilt *10, 43*
Gyn/affection *62, 85, 87*

Hacker, Marilyn *208-11*
Haraway, Donna *88, 93*
heterosexuality *10, 16, 41, 60-8, 80-1, 91, 94, 168, 172, 178, 189-90, 208*
hierarchy 23, *160*
Higher Education *8, 21, 26, 41, 45, 47*
Hite, Shere *71-2*
honesty *9, 39, 101, 105, 221*
hooks, bell *16, 41, 89, 93*

idealism *87*
identity *13-5, 23, 28, 33, 87, 89,*

93, 118, 144, 185, 187, 198, 207
ideology *190*
independence *168*
Independent Labour Party *121-9, 145, 148*
individualism *10, 66, 68, 81-2, 89, 92, 189*
inequality *33, 44, 63*
insiders and outsiders *13, 46, 48, 53*
interdependence *16, 69*
interdisciplinarity *1, 20, 57*
intimacy *61, 63, 71, 83, 110, 170, 178, 187-91, 201, 207-8, 212*
invisibility *186*
Ireland *12, 97-119*
Irigaray, Luce *79, 211-2, 214, 246*

Jeffreys, Sheila *64, 66, 172*
Jewishness *12, 97-100*

Kay, Jackie *197-8, 201*
Ker, Dr Alice *132-135*
knowledge *17, 29, 61*

labour politics *121-136, 144*
LambdaMOO *215-32*
language *181, 183, 198, 210*
lesbian continuum *61*
lesbianism *2, 15-6, 62-7, 79-91, 168, 190, 204, 206, 245-7*
letters *2, 7, 9, 17-8, 97-119, 222*
liberal ideology *10, 47, 68, 92*
'living biographies' *27*
Lochhead, Liz *193-7, 199, 201*
Lorde, Audre *46, 89, 93, 189*
love *71, 81, 89, 176, 188-91, 227*
lovers *80, 84, 187, 210, 218*
loyalty *5, 10, 40, 83-4, 89, 131, 138-9, 156, 167, 172, 175, 178*

maids *3, 14, 18, 155-79*
marriage *4, 59, 68, 84, 98, 104, 166-8, 177-8, 184, 239*
methodology *5, 17, 19, 70, 144, 217*
Michie, Helena *14, 202-3, 214*
mirroring *185, 193, 195-6*
mistresses *3, 13-4, 18, 155-79*
Moss, Thylias *205-7*
motherhood *2, 9, 14, 60, 80, 98, 104, 171, 192, 196, 204, 208, 212, 220, 240*
mothers-daughters *11, 14, 65, 91, 199-212*
multiculturalism *42*
mutuality *5, 9, 13, 69, 83, 94, 99, 208*
mythology *1, 4, 95, 189*

non-competitiveness *43*
novels *17-8, 112-3, 168*
nurturance *91, 176, 192, 200*

O'Connor, Pat *1, 21, 23, 25, 33, 57, 70, 81, 83-4, 86-9*
obligation *9, 10, 15, 72*
openness *9, 39, 54, 101*
oppression *10, 39, 41-4, 47, 49, 58, 62-3*
oral history *18-9, 37, 173-6*
Orbach, S. and L. Eichenbaum *84, 89-93, 199-200, 207*
other *13-6, 93, 191, 201-2, 207, 211*
outsiders *13, 46, 48*

Pankhursts, the *123, 126, 139-143, 149, 151*
partnerships *10, 40, 80, 81, 84, 94*
patriarchy *10, 43, 58, 62-3, 89, 94, 195*
pedagogy *3, 98, 102, 104-5, 107, 112-5*
personal, the *9, 17-9, 82, 85, 237*
Plath, Sylvia *196, 198*
play *220, 225*
poetry *5, 18-9, 181-212*
politeness *221*
political, the *1, 8, 12, 16, 40, 69, 70, 122, 131*
popular culture *2, 4*
power *8, 10, 33, 39, 42, 46, 54, 69, 70, 72, 190*
private, the *1, 6, 7, 12, 21-37, 39, 43, 84, 85, 171*
privilege *41, 67, 237*
psychoanalysis *59, 195, 204*
psychosexual analysis *10, 58-9, 61-2, 64, 66, 82*
public, the *4, 6-7, 9, 12, 22-9, 31, 34, 39, 43, 83-86*
public/private *6-7, 21, 26, 28, 31, 34, 48, 147*

racism *3, 8, 39-54, 89*
radical feminism *10, 58, 61-7*
Raymond, Janice *62-70, 83, 85, 87, 94*
real life (rl) *218-28*
Rebecca (Daphne Du Maurier) *168, 170-3, 177*
reciprocity *5, 31, 69, 83, 176*
research *32, 35*
respect *105, 143*
responsibility *32*
Rich, Adrienne *61-6, 186, 189, 246*
Rigby, Edith *145-9*
risk *32, 42-3, 50*
ritual *84*
Roberts, Michele *191-3, 201, 208*
roles *33, 35*
romance *68, 81, 173, 177, 189*
romantic friendships *3, 59, 63, 67-8, 186*

sameness *7, 10-2, 15-6, 90, 92, 93, 139, 187, 195, 201*
self *13-4, 16, 28-35, 48, 61, 85, 88-91, 191, 192, 198-202, 207, 215*
self-affirmation *25*
selflessness *136-7, 142-3, 149-50, 208*
self-validation *5, 15, 33*
sentimentalism *10, 72, 87, 152*
separation *60*
servants *13-4, 155-77*
sexism *41-2, 46-7, 51-2*
sexology *67-68*
sexuality *1, 5, 11, 16, 68, 167-9, 172-3, 181, 187, 219, 224, 246*
shared experiences *5, 16, 25, 30, 32, 43, 87, 136-7, 150, 186*
similarities *23, 25, 41, 44, 71, 87, 114*
sisterhood *1, 4, 14, 19, 52, 54, 81, 86-9, 94, 139, 190, 202, 204, 245*
sisters *10, 14, 80-1, 88, 90, 175, 181, 184, 197-8*
Smith-Rosenberg, Carroll *58, 62-4, 186*
social policy *73*

social work *41, 45, 49, 52*
socialism *14, 88, 123-31, 164*
sociology *1, 19, 25-6, 29, 32, 49, 59*
solidarity *7, 150*
Stanley, Liz *25-6, 79, 122, 125, 129, 139, 142, 148*
status *33, 67, 156, 186*
struggle *39-40*
suffragettes *12, 121-53*
support *7, 9-10, 137-8, 146, 222*
symmetry *70*

talk *5, 7, 17, 23-5, 43, 61, 85, 219, 221-3, 227*
teaching *19, 27, 29, 47*
tension *11, 16, 87, 202*
texts *17-9, 37, 156, 158, 177, 186, 216*
theory *9-11, 19-20, 29, 44, 52, 57, 82*
tokenism *51*
tolerance *42*
trust *5, 9, 28, 30, 40, 54, 69, 83*

unity *13, 93, 141*

validation *10, 15, 28, 33, 85-6, 144*
virtual reality *7, 17, 215-32*

'we' *25, 32-3, 87, 91, 94*
white men *47, 50*
white women *8, 39-54*
Women's Social and Political Union *121-53*
Women's Studies *4, 15, 26, 28-9, 42, 44, 49-54, 244-5*
Woolf, Virginia *17, 94, 155, 159-60, 173, 176, 182-183, 186, 193, 197, 212*
work *1, 4, 5, 14, 21-37, 41, 44-8, 86, 106, 156, 164, 176, 220, 223, 227*
workplace, the *8, 13, 21, 33, 46, 167*
writing *98, 222, 226, 232*

About Raw Nerve Books

Raw Nerve Books is dedicated to publishing innovative and controversial works in the fields of gender and women's studies.

Our aim is to produce books which inspire new discussions in areas vital to feminism and which might, indeed, hit a 'raw nerve' with many readers. In order to facilitate the circulation of ideas we publish work rapidly and inexpensively. We discriminate in favour of work produced in forms that are increasingly being ignored in existing publishers' catalogues, such as short monographs, edited collections, or 'experimental' pieces.

Existing titles include:

White?Women: Critical Perspectives on Race and Gender
This is the first interdisciplinary collection to examine women and whiteness in Britain. Contains new research, as well as being accessible to undergraduates studying history, literature, cultural studies, sociology, and women's/gender studies. ISBN 0-9536585-0-3. £7.99. Ten colour, and three black and white illustrations.

Raw Nerve Books
Centre for Women's Studies, University of York
York YO10 5DD, UK
rawnerve@yellowpolka.demon.co.uk